ALL STAR SALES TEAMS

8 Steps to Spectacular Success Using
Goals, Values, Vision, and Rewards

DAN KLEINMAN

CAREER
PRESS

Franklin Lakes, NJ

ALL STAR SALES TEAMS
EDITED BY KATHRYN HENCHES
TYPESET BY EILEEN DOW MUNSON
Cover design by The Design Works Group
Printed in the U.S.A. by Book-mart Press

To order this title, please call toll-free 1-800-CAREER-1 (NJ and Canada: 201-848-0310) to order using VISA or MasterCard, or for further information on books from Career Press.

The Career Press, Inc., 3 Tice Road, PO Box 687,
Franklin Lakes, NJ 07417
www.careerpress.com

Library of Congress Cataloging-in-Publication Data
Kleinman, Dan.
    All star sales teams : 8 steps to spectacular success using goals, values, vision, and rewards / by Dan Kleinman.
        p. cm.
    Includes index.
    ISBN 978-1-56414-991-6
        1. Selling—Handbooks, manuals, etc. I. Title.

HF5438.25K5853 2008
658.85--dc22

2007046697

To Judy and Erin
for their patience in everything,
and
to Michael Snell
for his patience with this.

Contents

Introduction

For the president of one of the nation's leading specialty food manu-
facturers it is déjà vu all over again. Whether the economy is up or
down, or at a predictable point in the life cycle of his sales staff, many
of his best people will be lured away to other companies. Expenses
climb as it takes more money to either keep his current staff in place or
recruit new talent. Then there are his marginal players, who continue
to stay marginally in the game. Why can't he get *them* to leave? He feels
a hostage of the 80/20 rule. Twenty percent of the s taff makes 80 percent of the difference, and that 20 percent pushes the increasing cost of
his entire payroll. His expenditures grow faster than the productivity
being generated.

As this president mentioned to me, his concerns are echoed by his
peers. He exchanges ideas regularly with a group of executives from various industries, but with companies of similar size and maturity. "Cost of
doing business," they all lament.

They are wrong. And in the weeks following our discussion, this president proved that by creating an unbreakable relationship between productivity, rewards, retention, and development, he raised the bar and he
banished mediocrity. He established a cyclical climate in which increasing
revenues funded a reward system that focused on both retaining his key

players and developing his overall staff's potential. Those rewards, and that focus, produced more revenue and continue to keep the cycle going.

Last year, there were more than 14 million people directly engaged in the act of selling products and services in the United States. They were paid in excess of $260 billion. How many other company CEOs and heads of sales feel they aren't maximizing the costs associated with their selling efforts? How many feel they are not really in control of linking what they spend with what is produced?

After 30 years of designing sales reward plans for companies large and small, across a wide variety of industries, I have found that productivity and retention disappointments are rarely the results of a company's compensation structure. While some managers are always looking for the silver bullet (that one plan that will cure all ills), most come to realize that pay is part of a larger, but less costly, productivity and total-reward strategy.

Smart leaders do it differently, using the strengths of their organizations to become employers of choice. They prepare their sales teams to help structure a powerful reward system. They pay people appropriately, but always within the context of clearly expressed and compelling company values and goals.

Good salespeople expect a reward system to align with the realities of their environment, to focus on key deliverables, and to generate enthusiasm. Sales stars expect more. They expect vision, inclusion, and competence to frame continued success; they expect personal, professional, and organizational growth. Sales stars expect a lot, and they give a lot in return.

At times, customers or clients can get a better deal with another supplier or service provider, but keep coming back to the salesperson with whom they have a good relationship. Salespeople who command such loyalty listen carefully and respond decisively, and always act in their customer's and their company's best interests, earning trust and respect. If, due to a promotion or transfer, sales stars move on, clients and customers want to know how to continue to do business with them.

All Star Sales Teams is about sales stars—keeping them and growing them to form the organization's most productive nucleus. Growing a great sales team isn't just about meaningful rewards; it's about cultivating a productive team environment.

Sales stars gravitate toward strong managers who create a work environment that encourages people to thrive. Strong managers are ethical, balanced, and consistent. They care about the well-being of their staff, their community, their investors, and their customers. And they stay one step ahead, always planning, seldom surprised. They understand and control the sales process—including rewards.

This book identifies eight critical actions a company has to take before it can succeed in creating a productive environment where the right forms of reward produce the right kinds of behaviors. Each chapter addresses one of these critical actions:

1. Planning for change. Ensuring that whatever changes are made reinforce your organization's vision, strategy, and operating style.

2. Tailoring a compensation plan whose approach and result measures are aligned with your direction and priorities.

3. Identifying who you are as a company and letting that drive what marketplace information you need to establish sales rewards.

4. Linking realistic rewards, results, and staff expectations.

5. Maximizing the strengths of your sales management and neutralizing any weaknesses.

6. Engaging your sales staff in a participatory but balanced process of defining their reward structure.

7. Establishing a climate where involving departments other than sales in reward design is seen as both a valued responsibility and an expression of recognition.

8. Streamlining the rewards design process.

Without addressing these stages of sales reward development, finding and keeping the staff a company wants, and having the productivity it needs, will be a constant and futile effort. *All Star Sales Teams* equips a company to successfully integrate these sustainable actions into its organizational fabric and truly turn its sales force into a group of all stars.

Clarify Your Sales Objectives: *Planning for Change*

Planning Pitfalls

Considering that we had just met, Jed was a little too glad to see me. I wondered if this CEO expected me to provide a silver bullet to eliminate whatever problem was troubling him. He didn't keep me in suspense. As we sipped our obligatory cups of coffee, he explained that the firm's last two quarterly financials confirmed that business was okay, but not what shareholders, investors, and analysts had expected.

He stood up and began to pace. Maybe his key product's life cycle had reached its tipping point; maybe it was the way his company had been approaching the market; maybe it was the sales staff. He stopped and rolled his eyes. The sales staff was driving him nuts. A few superstars surrounded by mediocrity. There were too many maybes. He could feel his organization going on defense while his competition was on offense.

I offered a cautious question. "When we set up this meeting, you said you were about to launch a new initiative?"

"I'd heard you're the guy we needed to put together a pay package that gets our sales staff producing better results—results that would be based on our new initiative. Well, things have changed since I first called you."

Jed explained that he and his inner circle of seven had met for an off-site day of planning. When they gathered, he outlined the critical nature of the meeting. He told them the company's future hinged on their ability to plot a course out of the morass. In spite of some initial acting out around vested interests, the overall result was positive. At the end of a long day there were handshakes and backslaps as they left the meeting room. They had a plan, a strategy, for improving sales.

But as it turned out they had not just a strategy, but eight different strategies. Each person at the meeting left with a different take on decisions they had made, and each one had told their subordinates their own version of the agreed upon plan.

Jed said, "We were all at the same meeting, yet afterward, there was no consensus about what went on. We were poised to go in several different directions at once. Some of those directions were diametrically opposed to others. We were on multiple collision courses. So I told my managers that until we agree as to the next moves, there will be no next moves."

He looked out the window. "I just didn't anticipate the confusion. Not with this group." Jed turned back to me. "Steve said your approach to pay design takes all this potential chaos into account—that it's nothing you're not used to."

Our mutual acquaintance was right. There was a process we could follow to get everyone back on the same page and moving toward productive change. But first Jed would have to decide how he wanted to bring about change—through participative management or executive fiat. Based on the operating style of his company, his key players' readiness to work collaboratively on a common goal, and their histories of management interaction, what approach had the best chance of sticking, of producing meaningful change?

While it is always more inclusive and binding to gain acceptance of change through collaborative reasoning, it is not always an option. There are times when a leader must press forward. Fiat works if the CEO is trusted, is consistent and predictable in his application, and demands actions that promote and reinforce an agreed upon vision. Yet, even unilateral decisions need a context within which to judge their potential effectiveness. Jed decided to try planning through the meeting scenario one more time. But this time we were going to create a structure and method around the group process designed for success.

Putting Everyone on the Same Page

Before tackling the meeting itself, the participants' initial expectations have to be managed and a point of view has to be established among all the members. Depending on the capabilities of the management planning team (and we will address that issue a little later in this chapter) I have found the most productive approach to clarifying the group's objective is for the leader to put a clear and emphatic stake in the ground and surround it with a stimulating question or idea.

For example:

We have to increase sales revenues by 12 percent and unit sales by 7 percent by the end of the fiscal year just to meet target. As you all can see from our weeklies, we are not on track to meet those goals. Besides, meeting target isn't good enough for me. We need to exceed it. When we get together next Tuesday I want to reach agreement on how we are going to bring sales revenues up by 15 percent and unit sales up by 8 percent during the next three quarters. I want to do it without changing our pricing model. There's plenty still on the table to investigate: costs, our delivery and follow up, and our product line. Here's one thought to consider: What if we reduced our sales staff by 10 percent and dramatically increased the earnings opportunity for those who remain? As always, every option supported by analytics and sound reasoning will be thoroughly explored. Don't come empty handed. We are talking about our survival. Background and some perspective providing materials will be sent to each of you in the next two days. See you on Tuesday.

What are the messages?

☆ This is a critical agenda; survival is at stake (at least in the leader's eyes).

☆ An objective has been set beyond the known target.

☆ One tool has been taken off the table: pricing.

☆ Everything else is up for grabs provided that each proposed option is well thought out.

☆ Everyone is expected to contribute.

☆ A teaser is given that is designed to stir the pot: slashing sales staff.

The participants know the breadth of the agenda and their role. The teaser has added an element of uncertainty. Within the context of what each member knows about the leader and their teammates, individual decisions are going to be made regarding whether or how to approach the idea of sales staff reduction in the public forum of the meeting. If it is a team with a healthy and productive history the idea will not distract or confine them. It will stimulate creative thinking. It will initiate change. Minds are now focused on the upcoming meeting. Resources are being marshaled.

Rubber Chickens

Experience has taught me that in designing change, be it in sales, operations, or pay, the cavalier use of third party expertise can muddy the waters with tons of minutia wrapped in thick layers of jargon. In my days as a line manager, occasionally charged with hiring outside resources, I initially thought this self-created murkiness was a predictable predilection of the novice consultant or in-house technocrat. Not so. As the bigger firms trooped their gangs of thieves into my office, it was the practice leader, the senior player, who perpetuated the crime. My impatience was always tempered by the realization that most experts can't help themselves. They see nuances and permutations that the lay observer can't, won't, or doesn't need to comprehend. Rather than assess whether communicating all this detail is really relevant, they forge ahead with their brilliant monologues. And with each numbing sentence they lose more and more of their audience. It seems to be a form of self-justification. This felony is compounded when you consider the number of product, sales, marketing, financial, IT, and management experts sitting around any planning table.

When we eliminate the extraneous and distracting, and focus on salient ideas that are relatively easy to communicate and that promote meaningful change, we are left with what I call Rubber Chickens. Why the term, Rubber Chickens? Consider the following:

The presentation drones on. The pain generated from the serrated edges of the bottle cap you are pressing into your palm is all that is keeping you from passing out and pitching forward in your seat. You are not alone. The meeting room is filled with souls drifting in and out of consciousness. If you left now and someone in the corridor offered you a treasure chest of riches to repeat any part of what you supposedly just heard, you would be at a loss. A week from now reference to this presentation will draw a quizzical stare. A month from now it won't even be a memory.

It doesn't register at first. The speaker has stopped talking. You look up to see the man at the podium rigid and twitching. With great effort he reaches into his suit pocket and extracts a rubber chicken. Suddenly he relaxes, smiles, and places the chicken on the table beside him. The audience looks at each other quizzically. The speaker continues talking, but this time with a more attentive audience. Five minutes pass then another fit and another rubber chicken. The audience is paying even closer attention. Why the chickens? What triggers each event? Six chickens later the now totally focused audience leaves the auditorium taking with them an experience they won't soon forget.

Significant points of universal application should be as easy to remember as the incident with the rubber chicken. Rubber Chickens are universal rules or truths. Every organization adapts them to fit its culture and goals. To learn from them, every organization must keep them in mind long after they first appear.

The initial Rubber Chicken I offered Jed was this:

 Whenever you have a meeting, structure it to counter participants' tendencies to hear what they want to hear and see what they want to see. Structure the meeting to make sure they hear what is actually being said and see the reasoning behind it.

If he went about it correctly, Jed could engage the creative talents of his direct reports while minimizing misunderstanding and counter-productive activity. To do this, he needed to create a responsible meeting structure that demanded enough group discipline to produce actual consensus and not just an illusion of consensus.

Meeting Structure

Jed had to reconsider his preference for all-day meetings. They can produce the illusion that intensity correlates with results, that denying access to the restrooms produces wondrous revelations. Most "all dayers" are like glazed donuts. They look good. They smell good. And after you've eaten them, the lump in your stomach tells you it was a mistake. You swear them off, but four months later, you are eyeing them again, convinced that this time, the experience will be worthwhile. Breaking the process up into digestible pieces that build on each other tends to produce a better product.

This isn't to say that an all-day meeting can't produce results. It's just a much more challenging approach. Setting aside the lack of content absorption time and the compressed space for decision-making, consider the distracting pressures a high level session like this can have on the meeting members. The dynamics of group participation and leadership in a marathon meeting can make or break a reputation, possibly a career. Participants are pushed and prodded in many directions. There is no time or place to reflect, to take a measured position, to understand others' positions. You're out there displaying each spontaneous thought for critical comment. You're out there constantly shifting, choosing to play the diplomat, the politician, the reconciler. You have to avoid inadvertent pretense, zealousness, and self-aggrandizement. You can't appear to be scavenging for approval. You're boxed in to choosing sides, and choosing again. You lobby and support. As the pace picks up you have to move deftly among various roles without losing your balance. All the while, you watch the most powerful people in the room, gauging and anticipating their positions. Who has time for substantive content? It's all about rapidly timed performance.

There is merit in using the collective brain to produce ideas and solutions. And a setting devoid of day-to-day distractions that helps focus on the issues of the moment is fine. But in my experience, successful planning and problem-solving sessions require more than an off-site location and half-day meetings. They require:

1. Preparation.
2. Facilitation.
3. Anchoring.
4. Mutual commitment and individual responsibility.

Meeting Preparation

I once worked for a rapidly growing corporation notorious for its poor meeting habits. Managers and professionals ran from one session to another, often not sure with what agenda they would be dealing. It was a sign of influence and status to be invited to a multitude of meetings each day. Forget that almost nothing was accomplished through these meetings.

At the time, I had responsibility for a variety of human resource departments. In this role, I once attended a cross-organizational meeting with the supposed agenda of creating mutual support and cooperation for a major technical integration plan that would affect various corporate interests. A few minutes into this technical presentation a new colleague, responsible for employee relations, slipped quietly into the room and sat next to me. As the meeting progressed, he nodded when the rest of us nodded, frowned when I frowned, and all the while studiously scribbled notes on his legal pad. Halfway through the session my colleague turned to me and whispered, "Why am I supposed to be here?"

"I didn't know you were supposed to be here," I whispered back.

His eyes widened. He clicked his pen and quickly left the room. An administrative assistant had mistakenly put his name on a list. That list merged with other lists, and soon he was running between buildings attending all the wrong meetings. These meetings were so poorly structured that distinguishing relevant participation from irrelevant attendance was not easy. Had someone calculated the cost in terms of wasted productivity, the humor surrounding this frenetic dance would have quickly faded.

Good meeting leaders make sure everyone who attends has a written description of issues to be explored and objectives to be accomplished. The issues are framed clearly and not subject to a variety of interpretations. At the start of the meeting, the leader probes as necessary to ensure that everyone understands the agenda and their role.

The meeting leader is also responsible for supplying participants with all the initial information needed for discussion. The operative word is *initial*. During the meeting, new information or informational needs will surface. A death trap for a meeting leader is trying to anticipate all eventualities and providing too much information.

But how much is too much? I have worked with engineering and accounting firms that thrive on data. Their typical information expectations, both in depth of detail and span of content, would paralyze those in retail sales. If you don't know the tolerance of your organization's capacity for ingesting preparatory material, you are not paying attention to its culture. Look at the information (such as reports and articles) routinely routed through a work setting. Who initiates the distribution? Whose comments are in the margins? Check the pace of the distribution. Are people actually reading the materials or just passing them along? Where are the bottle necks? Is the information acted upon and by whom? Examine how non-routine information is introduced into environment. How formal is the preamble? Is it just a note on top, or a meeting introducing the subject? What do readers say in casual conversation about what they are being asked to review and the nature in which it is disseminated?

Successful leaders learn from history. Keeping in mind participants, time frames, and leadership styles, what preparatory information processes have been effective in meetings with problem-solving agendas? Consider where data landslides or the paucity of information has lead to disaster. Failure can often teach more than success.

When in doubt as to how much is too much, err on the side of restraint. Distribution of information should always indicate what participants must read, what they *should* read, and what peripheral data will add to their ability to participate more fully in the agenda. It is the responsibility of the leader to clarify and connect every piece of preparatory material to the meeting's deliverables.

There is power in good preparatory information. Take care that it conveys the message you want participants to receive and discuss. Will the information have the effect you want it to? Will it stimulate a further objective exploration of options, reinforce an existing direction, or counter current trends?

Meeting Facilitation

Facilitators are not group leaders. They don't call the meeting. They don't form the group's goals. They don't provide opinions or make any recommendations with regard to the content assessed or the decisions made.

Facilitators are freeing agents, owing their allegiance to the goals of the meeting. They exist only to allow the group to function effectively in pursuit of those goals. They keep the process moving forward. Their interest is in establishing and maintaining a quality process. They must ensure that the outcomes of the meeting align with the agenda and its stated deliverables. They make sure the group stays on target.

Prior to the session, the facilitator meets with each player and establishes a level of familiarity and comfort. It can be initially awkward for some teams to have a stranger in the room, interjecting, interrupting, pushing, and pulling them through the day. Knowing, in advance, the facilitator and the facilitator's goals can help move the group into a productive mode more quickly at meeting time. Although some facilitators actively participate in shaping the preparation process, they are very careful to be seen as a messenger and not as the leader of the upcoming meeting.

During the meetings, facilitators use a variety of techniques to:

☆ seek input from all participants.

☆ check participation, keeping specific group members from either dominating or being dominated.

☆ manage the movements of the 800 pound gorilla in the room (the group's dominant member).

☆ establish balance.

☆ ensure that everyone understands what others are saying.

☆ restate and focus decisions and assurances the group makes to itself.

☆ reflect on what the group has agreed upon and how it fits the stated objective.

Facilitators understand the dynamics of the group's leadership: Who are the organizational leaders, who are the social leaders, how do they behave; what can be expected of them, and what brings out their best qualities.

Facilitators are excellent listeners. They hear the group. They hear the individual. And most importantly, they hear what isn't being said. And they utilize this attribute to keep the participants moving toward a positive conclusion.

Facilitators have the analytical and process skills to form a context within which the group can plan and problem solve. Some believe that planning is a sequential process from vision to action. Others feel planning has to be more pragmatic and mirror their perception of reality, juggling, testing, and validating multiple directions simultaneously. The facilitator has to have the experience and facile skills needed to align the desired approach with a process that meets the comfort level of the group.

Facilitators debrief the group, collectively and/or individually, on how the meeting process is unfolding and how it can be improved. Most importantly, they gauge each member's perception of what happened and what they anticipate subsequent meetings will produce.

Facilitators are the group's historians, keeping track of what was agreed upon and what subsequent actions are to be taken.

Facilitators manage the traffic that intersects the group meeting. It is not uncommon for problem-solving and planning groups to call on the expertise of outside content professionals. It is often best to do so through the facilitator to ensure that the experts stay within the parameters of their roles and don't accidentally become meeting participants. Experts are often position advocates and are called upon to make recommendations. Facilitators have to prevent the passion and conviction of an expert from disenfranchising the group members through the force of those recommendations. The experts are there to identify and clarify. The participants are there to question, reflect, and conclude. Facilitators have to ensure that each issue receives balanced consideration, and to continually guard against experts voting by hidden proxy.

Participants in strategic planning meetings tend to be managers. They are disposed to making decisions, usually with constrained time and information. If the facilitator puts too neat a package of alternatives before them, they will morph from explorers of options to judges of direction—from jumping beyond what are the alternatives to how best to get things done, from examining the issues to ruling on them. When this happens, the planning session is over. Something else has taken its place. The activity may appear expedient, even satisfying, but it is not planning. It is the facilitator's responsibility to keep the group from jumping over deliberation to premature decision-making.

The facilitator also needs to be sensitive to participant biases regarding both the issues and the other group members. This may be the facilitator's most-important and most-challenging role.

While everyone brings history to the table, and everyone has likes and dislikes, what they do with their biases during the planning sessions is the facilitator's concern. Opinions and subject biases are essential content components as the group wrestles with ideas and issues. They shouldn't be repressed as much as they should be placed in perspective. Get them out, get them clarified and sorted, address their parameters, and move these biases into the appropriate context to be dealt with as part of the decision-making process.

Personal antipathy is another matter. Meeting lore is fraught with examples of undermined and destroyed processes that were not the result of the actual meeting agenda, but individual dynamics based on past acrimony. If the group is to function as a team, there is no room at the table for behavior that detracts from the mission. It has to be assumed that every member of the group, based on their experience, perspective, and skills, has a critical role in deciding the direction of the organization. The facilitator should make clear that behavior counterproductive to the goals of the group will have consequences. It is irrelevant whether team members subordinate their personality biases for the greater good or for fear of negative consequences. It is irrelevant whether that subordination produces some form of cathartic revelation. What counts is clearing the table so business can move forward. That's the facilitator's responsibility.

Anchoring

Before anyone leaves a planning meeting everyone has to be clear about the tangibles that will also be leaving the meeting. These tangibles are the anchors that keep everyone tethered to the planning process. Bullet words on a flip chart are not anchors. Outlines of direction are meaningless until the group owns them. A facilitator can write down what has been agreed to, but unless each member of the group buys into it, the anchors are just lead weights.

Once the group demonstrates genuine ownership through its energy of involvement, a record of these shared agreements should be on each participant's work desk as soon as possible (usually within two days of the meeting). The record should include:

☆ Meeting notes.

☆ An account of specific decisions and how they fit into the agenda.

☆ Next-step deliverables that include measures and timetables.

☆ Outstanding action items—who is responsible for what, and when.

☆ Any expectations to be met and specific preparations required of each group member before a next meeting, if there is one.

Anchoring confirms the success of the process. It is the group's legacy, defining where it has been and where it still needs to go. It is also part of the inertia that keeps the process on target.

Team Building

It is good to:

☆ see oneself as a respected and critical part of a larger group.

☆ feel that real success is only measured in group terms.

☆ support all the other team members.

It is not good to:

☆ go along to get along.

☆ use the team for personal gain in conflict with the team's best interests.

☆ allow any team member to carry less than their share of the work.

Meeting participants should be committed to the process and to each other if the outcomes are to be successful. They need to be a team. Embedded in the act of commitment are the underlying intentions of each participant. How do you know if the intentions of the individual will benefit the results of the group? How does a leader know if he or she is managing a team in more than name only? Although being a team player is a cliché, some positive and negative elements of team play have obvious applicability in organizational life.

☆ Is there demonstrated mutual respect for each other's time and energy? Is that reflected in the day-to-day workings of the group?

☆ Does the group tend to support each other or take shots when the opportunity presents itself? Are the shots taken publicly or privately?

☆ Does everyone pull in the same direction? Is everyone pulling their own load? What is the behavior of those who *are* pulling toward those who *are not*? Is the behavior publicly displayed?

☆ Do each person's actions promote collective success?

The greater the sense of team, the easier it is for the group to stay on target and achieve its deliverables. Where there is less of a team ethic, the planning and problem-solving processes, and their related agendas, are usually more structured. The facilitator has to work harder at keeping everyone on point.

But the facilitator can, and should, do only so much. It is up to each individual to come ready to play. Individual responsibility and commitment go beyond being prepared for the meetings. Being a responsible participant means being aware of how you listen, how you participate, and how you help further the goals of the group.

Being a responsible individual and part of a successful group does not, however, mean having to subordinate your personality.

Sports have endless examples of dynasty teams comprised of unique, sometimes legendary, individuals able to function together successfully. Think Yankees, Celtics, and 49ers of decades past. Even the most elite special operations units in the military take pride in being independent thinkers who can function effectively in a collective team setting. Everyone has to contribute to the team to be considered a member. Actions go beyond individual contribution. Teams are not about the player who always takes the shot or the defender who sacrifices team objectives for personal stats. Teams are not about the CFO who runs an outstanding finance area, but sits quietly at management meetings, preferring to kibitz, one-on-one, with the CEO at a later time.

When executive management becomes aware that a planning team's collective commitment and personal responsibility fall below a functionally tolerable line, they need to:

- ☆ size up all aspects of the situation to determine the reasons for dysfunction.
- ☆ make modest allowances for the lone wolf.
- ☆ consider team-building outside the planning process, being aware that such a longer-term solution will not remedy their short term needs.
- ☆ assess individual intentions going forward.
- ☆ take immediate action, perhaps even disbanding the planning team.

If the group is teetering on the functional precipice, the facilitator may be able to cobble together commitment by discovering and building on core mutual values and ethics.

Lone wolves do not herald team disaster, provided their number is extremely small, one or two at the most, and their actions compliment the group's objectives. There will always be the eccentric who has been with the company since before electricity, and whose behavior is tolerated for what he or she contributes to the organization. These lone wolves do not present any impediment to the team function. Such outliers are managed inclusive and exclusive of the team. They are felt to be part of and yet unique within the process. They parallel the solitary defensive back that never enters the huddle and always covers his receiver one-on-one. Because lone wolves almost always prevent a receiver from catching the ball and often intercept a pass, the defense adjusts to this behavior rather than the other way around. This arrangement benefits both the individual and the team provided that the lone wolf does not violate the group's goals and ethics. If those lines are crossed anyone becomes expendable. The same should hold true for the corporate lone wolf.

Team play is a learned behavior and takes time to develop. Bad teams can get better. Good teams can get better. Team building is ongoing, subject to constant improvement. If a company wants to initiate or accelerate team building, the CEO had best be prepared to fully support and participate in the effort, or it will never have a chance of success. And everyone should be prepared for the long haul. Team building to a level of productive functionality takes time, achieves success in small increments, and is tested and tempered during crisis. Team building rarely starts with as massive an agenda as strategic change.

Team Building Failures

Some organizations just can't foster a genuine team ethic. Awareness of that reality can prompt leaders to take alternative and more expedient decision-making routes.

I have worked with a handful of second-generation companies whose majority ownership is in the hands of the founding family. Management consisted of a group of professionals (with or without some modest equity stake in the organization) and a group of family members involved either in the strategic end of the business or being trained in the bowels of the company with the objective of someday ascending to the executive ranks. I have observed two phenomena consistent with these family-owned businesses that present significant challenges to sustaining any kind of team ethic and commitment.

☆ There are multiple and often conflicting ownership agendas at play.

☆ The third generation often does not share the long-term desires of the second generation.

In "My Way or the Highway, Inc.," the owner's son and daughter were nestled in mid-management positions, learning the basics before being kicked upstairs. Professional management was paid well to implement, but the equity granted to them was purely symbolic. They were excluded from strategic planning, from any feeling of psychic ownership in the vision and direction of the company. They were mercenaries and behaved accordingly. This was just a stop for them on their way to a better goal. There was no passion in their work. Yet the owner often wondered why his managers were indifferent or even resisted change.

The "Who Knows What the Hell is Going to Happen Company" had a more inclusive style. The second-generation owner had given each of his direct reports a meaningful stake in the company. Not enough to collectively override decisions made by the family's ownership, but enough to care about the long-term performance of the firm. The owner wanted a group of strategic thinkers who actively participated in the design and direction of the company. Here were the makings of a solid management team.

Enter the "Who Knows" children. With the owner desiring to retire in a few years, his two sons had increasingly immersed themselves in the workings of the company. They had diametrically opposed positions as to the organization's future. The first son was set on selling the company to the highest bidder and retiring at an early age on his portion of the earnings. Travel and family were his priorities. He felt that every action taken should be dedicated to boosting short term earnings, to creating a balance sheet and profit and loss statement that would be attractive to a potential buyer. Forget about asset accumulation and long-term debt. Sell off what the company didn't need in order to achieve immediate gains. Get rid of anything that would take too long to materialize bottom-line growth.

The second son wanted to create a more dynamic company by taking greater risks in the marketplace. He was in it for the long haul. He wanted the brand to stand for more than the modest, predictable firm their clients had always depended upon. His strategy was to increase research and development, increase marketing's budget, and look for better opportunities to maximize their resources, even if it meant entering tangential businesses. To him, long-term debt translated itself into a healthy investment that would pay dividends in the future.

Gridlock ensued when the professional managers pressured the owner to reach a sustainable agreement with his sons on the company's future.

For a host of emotionally driven reasons, the owner wouldn't take action. Team effort disappeared, and the company's vision flatlined. Everything stagnated until competitive forces compelled the owner to seek outside support. A buyout agreement was reached with one son as the other acquiesced to a more measured growth strategy. During the period of indecision, sides had been taken, and some mutual goodwill had been lost. Both the ownership and its management would spend a considerable amount of time reestablishing mutual trust before any meaningful team process could resume.

These examples highlight two Rubber Chickens directly effecting positive team effort. One is:

 Communication is irrevocable and irreversible.

Saying "I'm sorry," or "Forget what I just said," may slightly lessen, but never obliterate, what has already been said. The memory of what was said will linger far after the event and, to some degree (subtle or otherwise) influence future communication. The second Rubber Chicken is:

 Interaction is based on more than just the immediate event. It is based on the history all parties bring with them to every encounter.

That history will influence everyone's perception and reaction to the issues and events before them.

I knew a head of sales whose inattention to these two Rubber Chickens caused an insurrection that eventually led to the company terminating her. For all her other talents, she never understood the lasting affects of her behavior. She saw no relationship between her angry outbursts of one day and her staff's alienation the next. Each eruption and perceived belittlement had a compounding effect. Up to the day of her termination, she never understood why she had not been able to build a team and why everyone resented her.

It is not just a matter of subordinating your own counter productive interaction styles. It is being aware of the biases you and your team bring to every encounter, to every issue. You can't completely eliminate bias any more than you can successfully take back what has been said. But unless those biases are acknowledged and controlled they will get in the way of active listening and rational problem resolution.

This is uncomfortable territory for many managers. Some will dismiss examining and understanding the quality of interactions as just more "warm and fuzzy" crap. They attribute qualitative assessments such as this and subsequent remedial action with weakness in leadership. Sophocles said, "Nothing in the extreme." And then he died. I am not suggesting that any organization go overboard in uncovering the "why" behind their communication and interaction patterns, but am I also not endorsing complete ignorance as to the underpinnings of team behavior. This is a book about teams successfully achieving results using the tools available to them. Teams have been around since cave dwellers banded together for their mutual survival. During a period of time bad teams can function effectively and good teams can just as easily miss their mark. It is not about "good or bad," or about being "weak or strong." It is about knowing how to avoid failure. Fundamentally, the more you know the better off you are. Leaders need to know. That, in itself, is enough justification.

Team Alternatives

There are instances when a management team is not quite ready to function as a planning group. The team is too new and is still searching for a productive operating style. There may be too many distractions preventing them from functioning successfully as a planning group. Just their reporting on status without territorial posturing is a challenge. The team may be too old and set in its ways. Thinking outside the box becomes difficult to impossible. Each player knows what a colleague is about to say and the responses are typical, almost orchestrated. Finally, the team may be in disrepair and its broken pieces need to be snapped back into place before it can function again as a team. But that reconstruction may take too long for planning to wait its turn.

Leadership may have no choice but to continue the planning process in spite of the management team. In this situation leadership can bring together strategic thinkers from various departments in carefully structured small groups and solicit responses to pressing issues. Such groups do not have the latitude of a management committee, but their recommendations carry considerable weight with the chief executive. The management committee can become involved, individually or collectively, in reviewing the recommendations and commenting on them before the CEO decides what to do next.

When you enfranchise these strategic thinkers, whatever their roles, it has both developmental and retention benefits. A relevant Rubber Chicken:

 People respond to inclusion.

Knowing that management will listen and that management thinks enough of their abilities to include them in a high-impact process is heady stuff. The company gets to see the individual's potential and depth: the individual feels a new loyalty to both the direction and leadership of the company. If properly structured and facilitated, the situation is a win-win for everyone involved.

While the thinkers think and recommend, where does this place the management team? That depends on their state of evolution. If, through a separate group process effort, the team is finding effective and creative decision-making methods and improving the quality of their interactions, the CEO may well utilize their abilities to help further shape plan development. With carefully set expectations she may introduce them into the process in measured steps, going beyond review and comment to creative input and decision-making accountability.

If management team building becomes protracted, the CEO has other, more problematic, options:

1. Going it alone, where the planning process rests solely with the CEO.

2. Shuffling the management group, bringing in new players, and building a team from new cloth.

Both these options are time consuming, have limited to unpredictable outcomes, and create potentially negative residue in the company. They should be considered radical alternatives.

Overriding any consideration of team utilization is a constant sense of urgency. Each planning cycle is dictated by external forces bearing down on the organization. Management's constant challenge is to anticipate and stay ahead of its consumers, competitors, suppliers, creditors, and government agencies. That drum continues to beat and its rhythm will dictate whether or not there is time for the management team to be effectively utilized in strengthening the company's planned approach to these challenges.

The Big Picture

The Army taught me how to fire weapons for distance and accuracy. First, it was the M14 and then the M16. The learning scenario was similar, regardless. The range instructors always repeated the same directives: Sight. Relax. Squeeze the trigger. Sight encompassed everything from defining the target to accounting for all the variables between you and the objective: wind, distance, lighting, and human interference (as in others shooting at you). Once everything had been taken into consideration and adjustments made, you took a breath, held, and expelled. Then an instance of calm before you squeezed off the round. All of it was very mechanical, and was designed to keep you in control of the process in spite of external pressures.

Setting aside the morality of weapons and war, the method of hitting a target is quite similar to any organization's planning process: identify your objective and all its variables, move forward in a deliberate and calculated manner, and always stay in control.

There is a tendency among groups to lose sight of the target and to lose control. As time pressures and distractions increase, so does the urge to reach conclusions based on preconceived notions or half information. Always letting the issues take you to their logical conclusions and never losing sight of the target produces the best results.

In my experience working with business planning groups of varying sizes and dispositions, they all address the same fundamental questions to stay focused on the target. Their answers are a blueprint of where they are, where they need to go, and the challenges ahead.

☆ What is the company's overriding vision? Aside from providing investor return, what is our purpose for existing?

☆ How should the organization be structured, what competencies should be resident, and what kind of internal interactions and behavior will reconcile with their business vision and goals?

☆ Given where they are and where they want to be, what critical changes need to take place?

☆ What are the human implications of the changes for the staff, customers, and suppliers?

After those questions are answered, questions about the answers need to be asked:

☆ What facts and assumptions led to those assessments? How comfortable is leadership with the information that was used?

☆ How comfortable is leadership with their collective conclusions?

☆ What questions were raised that were not answered?

It is imperative not to gloss over that last question. If the group still needs to know something critical to help it evaluate current or anticipated conditions and the implications of change, processes have to stop until those answers are found. Once confident in the initial blueprint, leadership is faced with still more questions:

☆ How is it going to bring about the changes that will take the company from its current reality to its target?

☆ What are the alternatives? Which will work best given the culture, needs, and resources available?

☆ Do the alternatives raise more questions or indicate that the initial direction should be reexamined?

☆ Is the action plan complete? Are there any gaps in leadership's thinking?

When sighting on the target, effective planning groups build success steps. Success steps are actions broken down into workable, measurable segments that people can realistically accomplish relatively quickly. These steps are sequential, deliberate, and strengthen progress between challenging hurdles.

Even with manageable steps clearing the path, planning is hard work. It forces an organization to confront itself and dissect its weaknesses. Good planning can be all encompassing and at the same time laser-like with regard to goals and effect. The strategies and direction in the plan stand on a deep foundation of well thought out and examined detail. It is a foundation built through energy and organization. And once completed, the plan will initiate actions that will stimulate new thinking, new examinations, and ultimately another planning process. The cycle may be months or years away, but it will happen. All plans, all strategies, are subjects of time.

Planning is never-ending. Planners should guard against the mental break, the little pause that breaks produces inertia. It is human nature, after any exertion, to want to stop, to rest, and catch your breath. This inclination often occurs after the first planning summit has been reached. You want to give yourself a week before continuing the trek. You don't want to look to the horizon, to the seemingly endless summits before you. You just want a little time to enjoy where you are and how you got there. But your energy, your enthusiasm, and your focus will all diminish by the time you resume your trek.

I consulted for a major service organization whose chief operating officer had a one word sign that dominated her desk: Momentum. Her cadence was measured, deliberate, and continuous. Her direct reports called her the U.S. Grant of their industry, always keeping her troops on the move, always engaging the forces in front of her, always marching south. To her, momentum was the precious commodity that differentiated her company from the competition. By her will and authority, she shaped the corporate culture and kept it going. It permeated every part of the organization from sales and customer service through the internal support departments. Everyone marched in unison. Everyone marched to the same drummer. And nobody broke ranks to admire the view.

To this COO, momentum was the mantra of the planning process. Planning was a continuous series of events. Questions answered produced more questions. Decisions translated into actions resulting in more decisions and actions. Nothing was frenetic or unmanageable, and everything was unremitting.

The Professional Perspective

Jed listened to what I had said before asking, "Okay, so once my team puts a decent sales plan together, you'll be ready to design a compensation package for the sales staff?"

Almost.

Compensation, in its creation, structure, and rewards is a series of messages. It is not only a statement of the value an organization places on what is to be done, it is a fundamental statement on how an organization values the people who will be getting the job done. Those "personal, intangible, and often subconscious" messages can influence the relative worth the doer places on the tangible values contained in the reward program.

If you give most compensation consultants a business plan, they can whip up a mechanically compelling design in no time. But I don't work that way. I find that reward programs implode much less often due to the mechanics of their design than due to the inattention given to the context within which that design must function.

Untested assumptions or ignorance of the framework within which the sales pay and reward program exist can shatter the best design. Yet even an average design can produce amazing results if it emerges from a thorough understanding of the eight keys to compensation design that enhances a solid business plan.

Before shaping a plan or doing any modeling or piloting, before anyone closes a sale, the management team should address eight central issues honestly and fully. In fact, these eight issues are key to any reevaluation of a reward program.

The Eight Key Questions About the Eight Key Issues

Answers to these questions form not only the building blocks of effective sales compensation and reward plans, but also the foundation from which the company manages change and growth:

1. How are sales objectives communicated?

2. How do you make sure that new products or services reinforce the organization's vision, strategy, and operating style?

3. What critical information does management need about how the marketplace rewards comparable delivery teams?

4. What is the key to getting the most from sales rewards?

5. How can the organization maximize sales management strengths and minimize weakness?

6. How does the company engage its sales representatives?

7. What departments other than sales should participate in designing sales compensation?

8. How can an organization minimize design complexity?

The Three Categories of Response

When I offer these questions to clients before engaging in any work, their initial responses usually fall into three categories:

1. Wrong answers
2. No answers
3. Relevant answers

Here are examples of each, from executives with whom I have worked who manage sales of $3 million to the sales of Fortune 500 corporations.

1. **Wrong answers** (and in this case there are wrong answers):

    "Our sales staff is paid very well to do what they are told. We are a fast-moving company with little time to convince our people that we know what we're doing. Our success proves that we know what we're doing. If they don't like it, we can find people do."

    "We pay for loyalty, teamwork, and putting an all-out effort into work. Measurements are fluid. Success is relative. It is not as important to us how successful employees are as long as they support the team and keep trying."

    "Our vision changes every few months to keep up with the changes we are facing in the marketplace. You've got to be flexible around here. Adapt or go the way of the dinosaur."

    "We pay our salespeople exorbitant amounts of money to keep up with our competitors, but I honestly wish we didn't have to do it. They don't really make that much of a difference. The product sells itself."

2. **No-Answer answers:**

    "I don't know what the answers are," followed by silence and the accompanying blank stare.

    "I never thought about some of these questions," followed by a sheepish smile and another blank stare.

    "Those questions aren't important. When can we roll out the plan?"

3. **Relevant answers:**

Although relevancy is always specific to the client's environment, the answers furnished are consistently:

▸ honest, detailed responses to every question.

▸ responses that reconcile with the values and direction of the organization.

The Short Answers to Sales Success

Strong sales managers inherently know the eight answers to a winning sales program:

1. Develop measurable and challenging result expectations that reconcile directly to your business plan.

2. Ensure that sales objectives reinforce the organization's vision, strategy, and operating style.

3. Let what defines you as a company be the determining factor in considering your external information needs when establishing sales rewards.

4. Link sales rewards to challenging, realistic, and achievable goals.

5. Hire and develop strong, gifted sales managers.

6. Establish a climate of mutual trust.

7. Demonstrate how interdepartmental support serves the common good and meaningfully reward such mutual collaboration.

8. Reconcile each reward component with each sales strategy's intended outcome.

Together they address the persistent mega-question, "How can our company increase sales?"

Recap

When planning change, be it as global as organizational direction or as specific as annual goal setting; manage expectations by clarifying the planning group's objectives and setting a commonly understood starting point of view.

Ensure the objectives and the parameters of participation are clearly defined well in advance of any team interaction.

Assess the management group's ability to function as a team—their collective commitment to the goals of the team, their personal responsibility to contribute and constructively in support of their team members, and the quality of their interactions.

Don't be hesitant to continue the planning process in spite of dysfunctional management teams by enfranchising other strategic thinkers in the company, while the management team rebuilds itself.

Prepare for planning and objective setting success by:

☆ Providing meaningful advance materials that are attuned to the operating style of the participants.

☆ Using a facilitator charged with keeping the meeting process moving forward, debriefing the group, keeping track of agreed upon actions, and recording planning outcomes.

☆ Never losing sight of how the big picture affects your goal setting; that is, your company's overriding purpose, needed competencies and organizational structure, anticipated changes that influence current decision making, and the human implications of change.

☆ Building success steps: sequential, workable, measurable actions that represent interim progress toward longer term challenges.

☆ Maintaining momentum.

Once your objectives are defined and your goals established, ask yourself the eight key questions that form the building blocks of the reward program that is to be developed so productivity can be influenced in the desired direction.

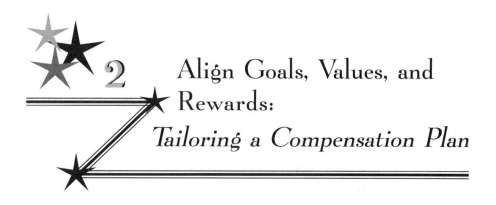

Align Goals, Values, and Rewards:
Tailoring a Compensation Plan

Observations of an Urban Tracker

Obseving is more than an academic exercise, more than just something to do while you wait to be summoned into the catacombs beyond the lobby. Anyone entering a new office area would benefit from taking in what the initial environment has to offer. Good consultants as well as good salespeople are always looking for alignment; they want to know if what they see matches what they hear, or what they are about to hear. They want the added advantage of being prepared for any disconnects they may come across on their journey into the target company.

First to appear on the corporate horizon is the receptionist. Much the same as a restaurant host, the receptionist sets the tone for all subsequent company encounters. Are you greeted with indifference or hostility? Or is it one of those lost in space characters who can't quite fathom why you are standing in front of them? Better yet, are you considered a nuisance, getting in the way of a much more interesting conversation with a passing employee? Is there a magazine between you and the attention of the receptionist? Does your pulse rate mysteriously climb to match the number of gum-crushing chews being rendered by the person seated before you?

Still waiting, you listen to the receptionist's phone technique. You observe his demeanor with other visitors, staff moving in and out, and delivery personnel. Flirtatious? Demeaning? Is there public gossip going on at the front desk? Does it appear that the receptionist is bored and searching, although not very hard, for something else to occupy his time? Even if this initial negative experience is followed by a positive meeting with the person you were scheduled to see, you can't help but wonder why good management would permit their front line to be staffed so poorly. Or is the experience positive? Are you greeted professionally, kept informed as to the status of your pending meeting, offered water or coffee? Does the receptionist set a welcoming tone? Are you made to feel welcome, expected, and valued?

You take a seat and look around. Is the area spacious or confined? Is the furniture functional, stylish, threadbare, or compiled from unrelated sources? What decorates the walls? Are there generic prints hanging, original art, safety posters, or perhaps inspirational messages? What kind of magazines are on the table? Are they industry related or eclectic in variety? Is it testimonial literature? How dated are the materials? Have they been donated to the table by the same folks who dragged in their patio furniture? You stare at walls and shelves lined with awards too small to accurately decipher.

What is the general atmosphere permeating the area? Do people appear tense as they silently dart from one door and through another? Or is there too much casual banter? I have seen what would be considered confidential counseling sessions on most planets, take place in the reception area. Visibly exasperated managers have taken out their frustrations on staff or vendors in the view of strangers. I have overheard the voices of poorly positioned sales staff and customer service representatives as they aggressively went about their business behind thin walls and open doors that did an inadequate job separating the public from the private.

Why make a conscious effort to assess all these elements when entering a business establishment? Because all that you see and hear is telling a story about the priorities and history of the organization you are about to encounter. The observational messages gleaned from these initial encounters have resonated so strongly with some managers with whom I have worked that they have regularly sent trackers into their own reception areas. Much like using "shoppers" in retail stores, they found it to be an informative exercise. Consider debriefing your own "designated visitor." How much in the telling would be a surprise and how much would be predictable? Would it be a narrative you would enjoy hearing?

The Mission Behind the Mission

Nothing is more telling than that icon of most reception areas, the mission statement. It is the written testimonial that the organization publicly and willingly unveils. In language designed to be peppy and motivating, the mission statement reveals the company's purpose for being and the values with which it subscribes. These are the values that are seen as critical in achieving a successful purpose. The document is rarely engaging and usually underwhelming.

I have formed a theory. The size of the frame surrounding the company's mission and values, and the number of words housed inside that frame correlate with the size of the company's human resource department.

Human resources departments are relatively new in the pantheon of business. Someone, somewhere always kept the records; the legal comings and goings of personnel. And of course, there were payrolls to distribute and benefit costs to calculate. In all but the largest companies, an office manager, a finance manager, or perhaps an administrative manager was charged with supervising the paper trail. But the fundamental people decisions of hiring, counseling, training, and determining pay rates were always the sole purview of the line manager.

As staff related laws of the 1970s became more extensive and employees more litigious, more personnel departments came into existence. Still, their primary responsibility was to keep the file cabinets in order and provide the data needed when asked. It was a reactive role. Some of these departments assisted managers in screening applicants for low- and mid-level job openings. Some counseled (in a rudimentary sort of way) those same staff members when something went awry.

Nice people whose main stream business acumen was found wanting often made their way into the ranks of the personnel department. For every management partner whose counsel and guidance was sought, who participated in staff planning and development, there were at least a dozen other personnel specialists who were kept very much out of the loop.

A couple of decades ago three rivers of activity met to form the Human Resource function. An evolution of the historical personnel related support tasks that included processing and orienting new hires, training staff in specific tasks, and gathering and analyzing all manner of people- related data merged with a body of scholastic thinking that deemed management a behavioral science, and both flowed into a business community that was becoming increasingly larger and complex. Human resource professionals emerged from the goop with expertise in developing organizations and managers, designing reward systems, advising leadership on optimizing employee relations, and running interference for socially ill equipped department heads. All these activities were rationalized to be critical to a company's productivity and "purpose for being."

"Purpose for being" gave birth to the cottage industry of defining vision, values, and mission. The exercise seemed straightforward enough: Put together a statement the staff could proudly march to and sprinkle in enough about the company's operating climate to make outsiders either feel envious they didn't work for the company or privileged that they were doing business with so forward thinking and enlightened an organization.

It is unfortunate, but many human resource folks are their own worst enemies. Their desire to be of value is offset by their difficulty tolerating simplicity. To many of them, nothing is worthwhile unless it can be beaten into submission with an excess of words, media, and meetings. So, a group (who still can't read an annual report, functions reactively, and generally speaks in a language alien to their constituency) goes about decorating the public halls with placards attesting to the company's chosen way of life. Too often this relatively sound idea is wasted, slipping into a morass of faded written muck.

But even faded muck sends an unintended value message. Still sitting in the reception area, I look at the clichés. I read over the same vague phrases trying to fathom their meaning. I get lost in the volumes of values and visions purported to be the foundation upon which the organization's purpose for being has been built. The same message always comes through. Someone endorsed the relevancy of creating this public vision and value statement. Someone chose the creators of this icon. Someone approved that which hangs on the wall. Someone is telling people more about the company than they are aware of. Someone is reinforcing two Rubber Chickens:

 Rarely do the swift engage the plodding.

 Rarely do good leaders hire weak subordinates.

So what is the harm in a little corporate dribble staining the wall? It is an opportunity lost. It is a potentially powerful public statement that tells the world, "This is us! This is why we exist as an entity. This is what we value. And everything we do is designed to further our reason for existing and reinforce what we think is the proper way to conduct our business and ourselves. This is our yard stick. This is what we should be measured by each and every day." It is a codification of direction and purpose. It should be as important and revealing as a financial statement. It should be a vibrant, working management tool. Most of the time mission statements are just so much wall covering.

Purpose for Being

Regardless of what is, or is not, written and framed in the corporate entry halls, every company has a very visible internal and public face. Healthy companies offer a consistent outlook regardless of which face is viewed. That consistency is governed by a singular purpose for being and a set of values that transcends specific transaction. A healthy company's purpose for being is reinforced throughout its environment and reflected in all its behaviors. You see it in the reception area. You see it in the company's treatment of customers and suppliers. It is there in every staff interaction. It shows itself in how the company supports the community.

A company's purpose for being, which is another way of describing an organization's vision, typically goes well beyond just making money. Whether profit or not-for-profit, it's a given that an organization cannot survive without generating the capital needed to operate. Investors don't invest and contributors don't contribute unless they are assured the organization can multiply its financial resources. But if the company's only purpose is its financial well being, it is placing itself at a distinct disadvantage in the marketplace.

Corporate culture has been blasted by the cynical as a warm and fuzzy abstraction. These are the same folks who have a binary view of life; everything is black and white. To them shades of grey are for the touchy feely crowd. There is right and there is wrong. There is telling it like it is, and if you don't like it, either suck it up or get out. It is an oversimplification of reality devoid of sensitivities and nuance. Relationships are patterned as if everyone is a child, parent, or sibling. Typecasting by race and sex abound. It is a reactionary's dream. And it is stone cold out of date. These folks are deaf and sightless in their own environments.

Every organization has a style of operating, a method of decision making, a way of confronting people and problems. Every company has unique interaction patterns that overlay the business agenda. All organizations, sometimes covertly and sometimes overtly, reward for desired behaviors and penalize for out of bounds activity. Whether written down or learned informally, these elements comprise the corporate culture. Within these elements are principles that guide accepted behavior and reinforce the culture and, ultimately, the company's vision. An effective mission statement threads these principles and values throughout the vision. They bring the deeper mission, the one beyond providing investor return, to life.

How many people do you know who are driven to work for a company principally because of its ROI, its earnings ratio, its stock rating? Even if there is an assumed sharing of the wealth in a financially flying company, its effect is transitory. Monetary rewards have a shelf life. Eventually it is never enough. Small bumps in remuneration result in more immediate dissatisfaction. Bigger bumps have a longer time frame before the fire has to be rekindled. In climate survey after climate survey compensation is rated poorly relative to other environmental factors. On a scale of 1 to 10 it is usually a 4. Great compensation packages score a 6 or 7.

People work for companies for a variety of factors that circle around the concept of purpose. Doing something that is perceived as meaningful, that one can take pride in, is a common bond that brings individuals together. They identify with the brand; they identify with the vision; they feel good about the company helping, making, improving, or leading. They want that sense that they are in the right kind of place surrounded by others who have a similar passion for the work, for the vision.

This is not to advocate that the purpose of a company has to be altruistic or benevolent. A former client was very clear about his company's purpose. He was transforming the landscape of the country by obliterating his competition. He saw himself in a fight to the finish. Ultimately he envisioned his company would be the last of its kind standing. He would not only provide his service at a better cost, he would undercut his margins to drive other suppliers out of the market. He focused as much on his competitors as he did on his clients, looking for weak spots to exploit, recruiting away talent, offering enticements to the competition's client base. He sacrificed the short term for a longer-term objective. Customer satisfaction was just a means to an end. Real satisfaction came when a competitor closed their doors for the last time. And when he drove another company under, it was framed as one of the inevitable outcomes and risks of an unregulated free market. It often sounded as if I were interviewing the Godfather, "Nothing personal. It is just business."

What he didn't anticipate was that his steamroller approach to market share often generated a corresponding mission from competitors and peripheral businesses. The monolith, who offered pre-packaged goods at a low price, was now challenged by the smaller customized and personalized alternative. They might have been in the same general industry, but they had entirely different purposes for being.

Focused Vision/Compatible Values

Big versus little, finesse versus heavy handedness, and customized service versus low cost supplier are all relative approaches to doing business. None are inherently right or wrong. The important point is that successful companies of all shapes and dispositions, whatever their value structure and culture, seem incredibly focused on their mission. Every action they take is consistent with achieving their goals. Every action is measured against its effect on the company's purpose. And they never lose sight of reconciling action and vision. For them, that consistency equals organizational sanity.

The benefit of consistency of vision goes beyond the clear line of sight it establishes between action and result. It goes to the heart of productivity and satisfaction. Anyone deals far more effectively with predictability than laying themselves open to random chance. Consider the people for whom you've worked. It is much easier to adjust to someone whose behaviors are consistent, given the same stimulus, than those capricious and unpredictable managers who "love to keep people off balance." Swings in purpose are just as disconcerting as swings in mood.

How does one channel ones passion and motivation when the organization's purpose is a moving target? One day the vision is grand and glorious. You are changing the quality of life for those using your product. The next day corners have to be cut and you are a low cost leader even if the quality of your customer's life is adversely affected by product malfunctions. The following day you are adding on loosely connected products and services in the hopes of attracting a larger consumer base that may or may not see the life, changing benefits of your product. In these scenarios vision has been replaced by fear of failure. The belief system that drove the organization's initial purpose appears fragile and weak. The values that created and governed the company's operating style are also suspect. Nothing is nailed down. Everything is up for grabs.

Companies with visions that appear to be the most motivating seem to be the ones that are located on the virtually unreachable horizon. They can withstand the vagaries of the market. They are fashioned to be overarching, to transcend the immediate. And they have a special quality that captures their staff's attention and imagination. It may be oblique to the outsider, but if you work for the company you get it.

Adhering to purpose and consistently reinforcing the behaviors most prized in the organization, the ones that support that purpose, takes discipline and a day-to-day commitment. It also requires a strong belief system that, within your frame of reference, you are acting right and doing right. An ongoing commitment to any belief system is not an easy task. But there are steps an organization can institutionalize that will help keep it on course.

Recruit and select job candidates who are inclined to support the vision and its values.

You don't want cult fanatics with myopic sight. You are looking for talent that can independently think and who can creatively adjust to conditions without losing track of your company's over arching goals. Of all the management disciplines associated with staff, the hiring process seems to be conducted in the most incomplete and haphazard fashion. In essence, there is very little discipline. Hiring "right" significantly decreases employee relations problems, equity and pay parity issues, as well as development and succession challenges. Yet during the progression toward selection, too many managers go with their guts, ask the wrong questions, talk too much and listen too little. In-house and professional recruiters often worry less about fit and retention than they do about quickly filling the requisition. Rarely does anyone think ahead.

Based on the resumes they review and their discussions with specialized employment support, managers should be prepared to meet prospect employees with a dozen "what" questions. "What can you tell me about…," "What examples do you have of…," "What did they value in…," "What role did you play in…" A manager may not use all his preplanned questions, and she may add more as the discussion flows; but they should be ready to go.

It also helps if multiple interviews can be conducted with the same candidate, bringing together a variety of points of view. If something was overlooked in a past interview or required further exploration, the next interviewer should be prepared to probe and uncover. Good selection takes time—not wasted time, just time. The long-term payoff is worth it.

Collectively and continually reinforce the company's vision and values.

This should so be so pervasive within an organization that it becomes habit. Everyone should be continually asking themselves and each other, how their actions compliment the direction and culture of the company. Just as important, staff should be looking for opportunities to demonstrate how someone else's behavior or results help move business' visions forward.

Reinforcement rituals should be looked at as valuable internal marketing. It can take on many forms and venues. Companies use their mission mantra on letterheads, e-mail headers, and posters strewn around the worksite. It can be in the form of questions, references to past accomplishments, emphasis on upcoming milestones, or stressing overall goals. Reinforcement can go on during one-on-one planning and performance assessment sessions, at group meetings, and at formal presentations. An indirect benefit of brand advertising, where the company's image and implied values is featured as opposed to informing the audience on the merits of a specific product or service, is to increase the staff's pride of association. Often companies internally preview these advertisements for just that effect.

The key is to capitalize on each ritual. Build on each event. Have the employee population begin speaking in the language of the company's values and overriding purpose. Phrases and abbreviations take on specific and special organizational meanings. "KRABNITZ" may mean nothing to an outsider, but to the company staff it is a priority message. Although these efforts seems contrived, and initially they are, forced behavior eventually gives way to habit; habit becomes institutionalized. Everyone takes personal ownership in perpetuating the company's vision and values.

Design a reward system that sends value messages aligned with the company's vision and culture.

Much of this book is dedicated to this hypothesis, as it relates to the sales staff. It is a theme that subsequent chapters will explore in depth.

For purposes of this section, it is important to point out that many companies continue to discount their most critical message drivers for ones that reflect competitive forces or historical practices. Too often compensation plans are designed to emulate another organization's approach to pay. Why? Either because leadership or staff came from that company and they understand and are comfortable in its workings, or the company is perceived to be a sales leader and imitation becomes more than just a form of flattery. It becomes a perceived retention tool. "Why go to work for Frobish when we can pay you the same *and* in the same way?"

Both rationales for such emulation are usually fallacious. Sameness does not ensure retention and familiarity often does not translate well into a company with a different purpose for being and one that may stress different values. Rather than the message driving the reward plan, the plan obfuscates the message. Worse, the plan can become the wrong message. Short-term gains will eventually succumb to longer-term confusion and productivity challenges.

Designing a reward plan around a company's purpose for being requires asking a series of fundamental questions before anyone begins crunching cost numbers. In the case of remunerating the sales staff, ask yourself:

- ☆ What is the company specifically rewarding the sales force for generating? New business from new sources, new business from existing sources, and/or continuing business from existing sources? Are we rewarding for the kind of business emphasis that is in keeping with our stated mission?

- ☆ Should any reward distinction be made as to how the business is obtained, where it comes from, whether accounts are actively managed, and who is creating the business? Does rewarding for any of these distinctions compromise our stated mission or values? Are we not rewarding for distinctions that reinforce our direction and operating style?

- ☆ How does the company's environment, management, territory distribution, and training affect sale performance and, in turn, sales rewards? Are any of these elements creating conflict between what we are and what we wish to be as a company? How can these elements positively and simultaneously affect our productivity and our vision and values?

☆ What reward mix (base salary, commissions, bonuses, and/or non-monetary rewards) will attract the selling skills the company requires? Is this mix in keeping with our sales emphasis, our culture, and our vision?

☆ What reward mix will continue to stimulate improved performance? Is this mix in keeping with our sales emphasis, our culture, and our vision?

☆ What is the sales staff's sense of the economics that drive the business? Is their sense of economics consistent with the company's sense of economics, with the economic assumptions that drives our vision?

☆ Are there relevant windfall issues, or other business conditions that affect the perceived fairness of rewards? Do these issues conflict with our company's overall sense of what is fair and correct behavior?

Bottom line: Do the answers to these questions indicate some repair work is needed before determining how best to reward the sales staff, or are staff expectations consistent with leadership's view of company priorities and conditions?

Celebrate the achievement of each mission milestone. Acknowledge those who represent the best examples of this achievement.

Celebrations are not only a way of reinforcing the company's purpose, but also a way of getting the staff to take a breath and decompress. A lot of mileage, in the form of memories and motivation, can be gained from celebrations well done. We will look at the value of celebrations as a form of sales reward in another chapter. Whether the reasons behind celebrating are based on reinforcement of values or recognition of achievement, there are a few key rules of which to be mindful of when considering the use of this powerful approach.

Acknowledge significant achievements. Don't discount the event by giving equal weight to small and large accomplishments. Two more Rubber Chickens:

 People are not stupid.

People, consciously or sub-consciously, are always searching for the meaning of things.

Your company has put together a plan consistent with its purpose for being. You have pre-established goals and milestone steps to indicate whether you are staying on course. You measure your actions and results against those goals. You have intentionally over-communicated intent, objectives, results, and reactions to those results. Everyone is focused in the right direction. And then you go off and celebrate something that has nothing to do with any of that. Do you think your staff is a bit confused? Do you think your staff is going to try and figure out why you are celebrating the newly painted office rather than the launch of a new product? You betcha. And if you do finally celebrate the launch with as much gusto as you did the lime green walls, do you think your staff is really going to continue to be confused? Absolutely. Let's go back to the previous Rubber Chicken. In the presence of confusion, poorly validated assumptions tend to surface and people attempt to explain the unexplainable. Those assumptions born in a vacuum of information can drive behavior in exactly the wrong direction.

I had a friend who met a young lady and immediately fell in love. One night, shortly thereafter, she turned to my friend and told him she loved him. He was ecstatic. Ecstatic until he got to know her better. It seemed as though she loved him, and the trees, and her drapes, and just about everything else with which she came into contact. There was so much to love. It all seemed to make sense to her. But to my friend, love between them had taken on a new, and substantially diminished, meaning. Organizational leadership has to be careful with what they fall in love with and how it manifests itself in the eyes of their staff members.

Recognizing talent and achievement is always subject to editorializing. Someone will always feel that the wrong person was chosen, particularly if it is not them. Perhaps it was the right person, but for the wrong reasons. Any such kibitzing distracts from the intended objective: to both recognize the achievement and to stimulate continued excellence on the part of those watching the proceedings. If your intent is to motivate staff, you best choose examples that only fringe elements would criticize. The best achievers should be universally recognized. Personality aside, these stars are respected for what they produce and how they compliment the overall mission of the company.

Once stars are selected, management should reflect on how they market corporate heroes and prepare them for the show. I use the term marketing in its most positive sense. How does leadership maximize the message? How do they avoid having the festivities blow up in their faces because an important part of the celebration was not prepared?

Everyone gathers around to hear the recipient tell her audience it was nothing; anyone could have accomplished what she did. Then there is the "other" star. It was about time management recognized his brilliant achievements; he is the only one in the area pulling his weight. Or the group is presented with the mumbler, who sheepishly nods, quietly slurs some words, and slides his way off stage right. With recognition comes the responsibility of acknowledging the team, of reaffirming the worth of the endeavor, and the purpose of the company. Stars need to show genuine enthusiasm, and, if the audience is lucky, maybe even humor. Stars shouldn't walk off the platform until they have pledged continued attention to the standards being adhered to.

Being the center of attention and basking carefully in the light of such recognition does not come naturally to everyone. Whether this means first praising a potential star in private and pumping them up for the big event, or pointedly coaching them on how to be gracious and constructive in their acceptance is dependent on the rapport a leader has with the individual. But preparation is vital. There are exceptions: staff whose responses can be predicted and maximized, but don't allow the event to fall flat for lack of preparation.

Having stated all this, preparation is worthless without sincerity of action. The leader, the recipient, and the participants who are gathered all have to believe in what they are part of. Such belief is not the product of an overnight epiphany. Sincerity is borne from a history of positive reinforcing experiences, maybe even inspirational events. Management should look back within the history of the company and use the past to reinforce and put context to the present.

If management is new and initiating celebrations for the first time, or there has never been a history of celebration, a leader is going to have to sell their beliefs and the reasons for celebration. One rarely can make others truly believe what you believe in at a first encounter, or first celebration. That's going to require the reinforcing factors of time and consistent behavior. But even in a first encounter, an effective leader, a genuine communicator, can make the audience believe and respect the sincerity behind those beliefs.

If leadership has a sense that not all the players within this triad of presenter, recipient, and audience are on board, celebration becomes a secondary agenda. A new and more pressing concern has surfaced; authenticity of intent. What is the underlying reason for any skepticism? Can it be fixed before the celebration? Does it require action, through voice or deed, on the part of leadership to reaffirm the belief system? If the chasm is substantial and a bridge can't be built in time, the celebration may have to be postponed. We will talk later, and at length, about two fundamental ingredients in any successful team: trust and respect. For now, if either of these ingredients is missing or damaged within the team, and in their absence cynical and counterproductive behaviors have surfaced, management is facing a flashing red light set squarely in the center of the road being traveled. Forget about celebrating anything. There is a major misalignment in play that will derail any attempt a company has for moving its organization ahead in unison.

But let us assume, for the present, that trust and respect reign and there is enthusiasm for the pending celebration. One last element has to be added into the celebratory mix; the context of culture. A company should be entertaining, perhaps even unique in its celebrations. Staff should leave the event satisfied, motivated, and looking forward to the next reason to rejoice. But all this should occur with in the bounds of what an organization's operating style can tolerate. Be entertaining, but not to the point that the entertainment overshadows the reason for celebrating. Be unique, but not to the point that the audience becomes more focused, and possibly uncomfortable, with form than with content. Don't try to be "in" when your organization is "out." Don't play to a demographic that doesn't exist within the participatory group. Don't use the celebration to "shake things up."

Ensure that the vision and values of the company can withstand crisis.

Crisis behavior is said, by some, to be genuine behavior. Anyone can act the role of the captain when the seas are rolling smoothly below the ship. Everyone on board the corporate vessel can easily crew together when distractions are limited and the journey is progressing as planned. But what happens when the sea winds cease to blow and the ship is dead in the water? Or a hurricane unexpectedly lashes out from the North? What then? Will it be control or chaos in the midst of pending calamity?

It is tempting in crisis to let go. It is a compelling reaction to forget about what has been learned and practiced and to drop back to forms of behavior more visceral and primary. However, the damage when falling back is significant.

The Frobish Company was in the midst of a perfect storm. Within the week sales across the board, for reasons that report data or vignette could not explain, had taken a sharp downward turn. Careful inquiries indicated that its competitors were not experiencing a similar fall off. One of the best sales representatives in one of the most demanding territories had given notice, effective immediately. Her reasons were vague and progressively more inexplicable as management attempted to understand her sudden desire to leave. There was no room for reconsideration. She was gone. And there was no one in the succession plan ready to fill the void. They would have to go to the outside for candidates. Something the staff would not be happy about. Finally, a major supplier had just announced they were recalling components discovered to contain a major defect—components critical to Frobish's leading product. Production would have to be shut down until the defect was corrected or another supplier could be contracted. Either option meant a significant wait time with staffing implications throughout the company.

Two years prior, in the midst of corporate prosperity, the management team had worked with an outside firm to better define their values and mission. In their eyes, it was affirming the basis of their success. It was the beginning of a reinforcement process that extended throughout Frobish. And then came the perfect storm.

Balancing the quality of life between work and private pursuits went out the window with the founder/CEO's demand for a meeting of his direct reports over the weekend. Everyone was to be there, no exceptions. The CEO's messages were clear: he wanted action. He was frightened, angry, and he wasn't about to hear any excuses. The participatory team behaviors to which the group had grown accustomed evaporated with each subsequent mandate. The HR Director was to get the star sales representative "back." The CEO didn't care how it was done or what it took. "Just do it. And I don't ever want to hear about our top people leaving again." He glared at the head of HR, "Your job is to keep our best people. Do your job!" The operations head was next. "You get on a plane tonight and meet with Franzens. This recall is unacceptable. Get them to come up with a supply alternative and fast! I don't want any of their typical double talk. They screwed up and we aren't going to suffer because of it." Then he wanted to know what was wrong with marketing. "What kind of an operation are you running?" he asked without waiting for a reply. "How can sales tank and we don't have a clue as to why? I want answers by Monday."

The CFO and IT managers tried to put the problems in perspective and tried to rekindle those beliefs and direction under which the group had operated. They were shut down by the CEO's last words. "Obviously we have grown too complacent. We have forgotten what brought us success in the past. We just can't suit up, go out on the playing field, and expect our opponents to let us run over them. It is back to basics. Everyone does their job of blocking and tackling, running and catching. I call the plays and we execute, just like we used to. Every day is a day in the trenches. No let up. No more surprises. Am I clear?"

Silence.

The CEO mistook the silence of shock for the silence of agreement. Team action uncoupled. Honest communication and productive problem resolution left. Silos began being built. Success was no longer defined collectively. What they had established as governing principles, a style of operating, a mission, and purpose for being was no longer relevant.

During the next few months, the company would sort itself out under a new banner. Several areas embraced the change. They raced to survive. Survival meant deflecting blame on others with equal amounts of self- promotion. Inordinate time was invested in the politics of positioning. Opportunism replaced strategy and common purpose. The culture fractured. The HR director headed a list of staff who resigned and were replaced by those who were more comfortable with the game as it was now being played.

The change was not the result of the crises that occurred. The troika of events was the catalyst that showed how frail the stated vision and values of the company had been. The company's belief system was shallow and wanting, without provision for withstanding the blast of its CEO. It allowed underlying harsh values, very much not in keeping with intended images and practices, to surface and dominate.

Worthy purpose and worthy values are worth supporting. The test of a culture, of its true validity in the organization, is not during routine and predictable times. The test of vision and values occurs when pressure on those beliefs is enormous. Sustaining a desired culture requires both practice and faith, in that order. Or stated another way, "Fake it until you make it."

Emergency service personnel, people subjected to crisis situations on a regular basis, practice what to do and how to do it. They practice over and over again, until the exceptional to the rest of us becomes their norm. Adrenaline is managed by reflex action, by automatic response ques. Companies can consciously practice their values and operating style in "what if" situations. If crisis, then what? What if the CEO, or any member of the leadership team, reacts counter to the beliefs being perpetuated, then what? Are there catch words, images, meeting protocols, previously agreed upon actions to be taken to short circuit "other culture" behavior? At first, practicing crisis mode may seem artificial and self-consciously awkward during the drill. It is after that first real crisis, when the organization acts within its expected context and rationally applies itself to the situation, that the practice shows its value.

Faith in an organization's belief system and related operating style remains intangible until tested. It is an esoteric exercise until challenged by some form of reality. Behaving in accordance to a belief system in the moment of its greatest challenge is placing a great deal of trust in chance outcomes. But if that behavior is grounded in experience, practiced or real, it has a much better probability of being replicated under the most trying of conditions. And from that experience develops faith. It is pragmatic, but it works.

5 Values

There is universal acceptance that the concept of an organization increasing its impact, when there is a stated, focused, aligned, and understood business purpose, has merit. There is also power in acknowledging what behaviors the organization values and shuns. Sound companies have adopted these concepts and acknowledged their behaviors almost from their inception. The scribing process may seek to tailor the words and images to keep them simple, dynamic, and succinct. But the fabric of who they are, how they operate, and what they value is already out there; none of these organizations wordsmith from blank cloth. The fabric of who they are, how they operate, and what they value has been established way in advance of it being institutionalized in writing or symbol.

For as long as there have been organizational consultants there has been a mound of intellectual gelatin floating around that continues to define and redefine what a company should have on its cultural shopping list. And there are always enough readers eager to either compare their organizations with each new list of super companies and/or attempt to emulate their approach to doing business. It is not the purpose of this book to comment on the lost cause of mimicry or provide a statistical opus on what purpose a company should or should not have.

In my years of empirical observations I have observed five commonalities among long-term successful organizations that are worth noting because of how these behaviors manifest themselves in equally successful reward systems.

1. These companies all invest in their people.

They spend the time and money developing skills. They reflect, in one fashion or another, the worth they place on staff. No one working for these organizations has the feeling that they are there for the near term, that they are easily replaceable, or that they are being used. The investment is not solely focused on the interests of the company. People develop and learn based on their needs and future aspirations. The process is meaningful, often rigorous, and never taken for granted.

2. These companies enforce a balanced perspective regarding time dedicated to work.

No one is lauded for drowning themselves in their work. Time and resources are made available for community activity, for growing oneself out of the office. There is an appreciation that someone working too long and too hard will eventually lose sight of what is critical and what is not. Before they burn out, they will wreak havoc on the rest of the crew in a host of counterproductive behaviors. Somewhere along the line they will lose their sense of humor as well as perspective. They will be miserable and the company will be miserable. And all too soon the company will have to return to the time consuming and expensive recruiting well.

This is not to say that all successful companies dedicate themselves to maintaining the exact same degree of work intensity as another, but all are clear as to what their individualized intensity expectation is. And all who join buy into the unwritten contract.

3. These companies foster communication.

There is active listening—sincere desire to promote dialogue. Most importantly, communication results in action. People are encouraged to express themselves through constructive, well-thought-out processes. The ground rules vary with the culture of the company, but everyone in these organizations knows that they are expected to contribute to the exchange of ideas and points of view. Everyone knows that something productive will come from that effort.

4. These companies have great managers who hire talented staff who are constantly being strengthened.

Strong people want to work for managers who will support their growth, who will stretch them, and who will allow for learning through mistakes as well as achievements. Great managers see themselves as managers first, and as content specialists second. Management is their profession. They see management skills as transferable across industries and are not encumbered by historically imposed restraints. Their source pool for leadership talent is as large as they can build it. They work at making their staff successful.

5. Most importantly, these companies see the behaviors as fundamental to their existences.

Development, work/life balance, communication, and professional management are ingrained in their daily routine. Habits have been formed around these behaviors. Every opportunity has been taken to reinforce these characteristics. Even in the most stressful situations, these companies hold true to their ways.

Design Is All About Purpose

Whether one chooses to decorate the company with statements of vision and values or leave the walls blank is less relevant than considering the issues which have been raised. And the Zen of it all is that, if one doesn't consider these issues relevant and decides to make no statement and take no action, that is making a statement and taking action. Those mute on the point of their purpose for being are broadcasting in their silence as loudly as the most ardent adherent. Whether it is acknowledged or not, no matter how muddled, every company has a style, every company has a purpose. Those who avoid dealing with these issues, who avoid consciously aligning tasks and structure with purpose and style have made their statement. During the long term, the marketplace and their own staff, will decide the consequences of avoidance.

Putting together a sales reward program is a journey, a major hike in the corporate forest. From that standpoint a defined purpose and operating style forms the frame of the backpack that will carry the design process forward. Everything that goes into shaping that design from sales objectives to reward plan administration is going to have to fit comfortably into that backpack and within the confines of that frame if it is going to survive the journey. If the reward plan is too complex for the frame, or if the plan's objectives do not fit the frame's structure, the program will be of little value.

In designing sales reward programs you reconcile the plan elements to the purpose and style of the company, not the other way around. It is an obvious theme that is violated so often and so randomly that it bears repeating.

☆ Companies force fit plans borrowed from their competitors. Newly hired managers bring along plans that worked for them in previous assignments.

☆ A manager demands that the new plan has more at risk pay. Why? Because while on a transcontinental flight he read that the only good plan is a highly leveraged plan.

☆ A manager demands that the new plan have little pay at risk. Why? Because he equates having pay at risk with turnover, and although turnover is presently modest, he wants to keep his best people.

☆ The company's stated purpose is to provide a full range of services to each of its clients, to be a central resource the client can go to for every need related to the field. That same company does not reward its sales staff for cross selling or deepening the relationship with a client. A new product sold is a new product sold, regardless of whether it is to an established or new account. The value placed on the sale is the same. It is simple to administer and easy to track.

☆ The company sees itself as a collegial, inclusive organization drawing on the creativity of its staff to solve problems. The sales manager, based on unspecified pressure from above, has arbitrarily changed the sales compensation plan's criteria and payout structure three times in the last two years.

At best, these illustrations reflect a detachment between the way a company feels its purpose and behavior should be and the way it is. The often-heard excuse explaining this divergence is that pressures, demands, or even "the important stuff" draws the organization off target and requires it to behave and prioritize differently. There is a belief that someday, when everything "settles down," the company will get back to adhering to stated messages. But someday never seems to happen.

At worst, some companies see a stated purpose and operating style as just a required public face, something that is competitively necessary, but not to be taken seriously. Visitors can read about commitment and direction, about behavioral values and priorities, and gain some comfort in the thought that went into the process of company definition. The staff knows what the company is really all about. It may take a period of acclimation to figure it out, but eventually everyone on the payroll understands what really counts. And then they can choose to continue with the organization or leave at first light.

Alignment, Alignment, and Then More Alignment

If the words on display in the lobby are not the words that are going to be used in designing change, the task of alignment becomes that much more problematic. Alignment of purpose and values can be dollars saved and loyalty gained. When a company's purpose and behavioral values are solidly linked and that linkage is vibrant and apparent, reward packages can leverage a distinct competitive marketplace advantage. A reputation of being exactly what you say you are can make the difference in recruiting and retaining staff.

People come to work and stay at work for a series of compelling reasons, not the least of which is to be rewarded fairly. But money alone as a reason is often subordinate to the issues imbedded in the direction of the company and the kinds of people who are drawn toward the company's values. In sought after environments, compensation is competitive, but rarely excessive. The worth of the position is packaged around the additional premium offered in its contribution to purpose. And from that contribution can flow a comprehensive reward structure.

And What of Jed?

Our CEO of the previous chapter had been busy. His new theme has become, "Planning for Success." He had been working on two fronts: developing an aggressive business plan and articulating the vision and values that drive his company's operating style. He felt satisfied that he was able to answer a fundamental question that had been nagging him for some time. *What keeps his employees coming to work?* In a quick climate survey the staff reaffirmed the importance of working for this company with its sense of purpose, where leadership exhibited strong ethical practices. They valued the participatory nature of the environment, and, most compelling, working directly for a supervisor they respected and with whom they had a rapport.

Jed felt comfortable that the business plan he and his leadership team had devised aligned with both the company's overarching vision and its operating style. Implementation of the plan would leverage the relationship between sales staff and their first-line managers, allow for participatory goal setting input, and stay true to the values reflected in how team members viewed each other, their customers, products, and service levels.

The objectives of the sales plan reinforced the behaviors Jed wanted to reward: individual initiative, supportive team work, client perceived strong ethics at all levels in the sales chain, and relationship building.

When we next met, the plans and next steps were clearly documented and in place. The organization's values and priority behaviors had been defined and linked with its sales goals. Jed felt the organization was ready to move on and develop an aligned reward system for the sales staff. After reviewing the actions he had taken and their results, I agreed. It was time to let the journey begin.

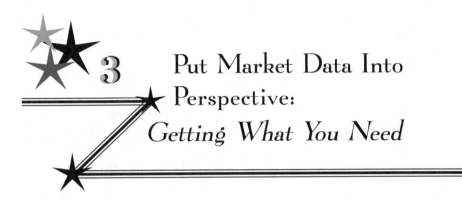

3   Put Market Data Into Perspective: *Getting What You Need*

The Need to Know

It is a typical day. Jed has read two papers on the way to his office just to get a sense of what's been happening since he went to bed last night. Has the world shifted in any way that will affect his business plans or results? Once behind his desk, Jed brings his computer screen to life. He drains his first cup of coffee while checking the cash flow report, the receivables report, and the production and backlog reports. Then there's the sales forecast to actual comparison. Gears switch. How does all that information reconcile with the financial figures that have just arrived? It's time to check the profit and loss statements.

Then there are the meetings: status presentations on the employee satisfaction survey, the product development project, and the legislative initiative his company supports.

Within the next nine hours Jed will have read one more paper, a trade journal, reviewed an economic forecast survey, and referenced both a university and a specialized service Website comparing information on his public (and sometimes privately) held competitors. The information gained throughout the day (and in some cases the lack of information) will generate constant activity within his organization, all of which is geared toward decisions that will prompt even more information. And each day will build on the next.

We are surrounded by information. If there is not a binder within reach, a screen to be pulled up, or a database to reference many people feel somehow incomplete. We love data. Successful managers attribute where they are in an organization with their ability to acquire and analyze information. It is how we grow up in business. It is a fundamental.

A manager's brain is always deciphering—determining credibility, assessing timing and applicability, and distilling the complex into the workable. If there is a new idea, a new proposal, let's see the numbers. But, accidentally or otherwise, numbers can lie. Statistics can lie. We have all experienced the effects of conclusions drawn and actions taken based on poorly formed samples or projections made from initially flawed premises. The ultimate in quantitative frustration is not being able to trust the base data itself. How do we know if the information is complete? Or accurately replicated?

And knowing the vulnerability of information integrity, how do we react once the numbers are shown?

I worked with an organization whose culture was data happy. If you couldn't fashion a complex "what if" formula on Excel or develop a compelling query on Access, then you weren't in tune with the driving forces behind decision-making. If the data you presented wasn't linked through a labyrinth of source files, you weren't really trying. The basic premise might be wrong. Even the data might be flawed. But oh how they loved their screens of numbers. Each analysis would uncover a bit of minutia that could be wrestled with for hours. And each wrestling match took them further away from engaging their management challenges and deeper into the twisting and self-satisfying world of analysis paralysis.

A new sales manager joined the company. Discovered and mentored by a senior executive, this new face became a source of wonder. He could create and analyze data bits with the best of them. He had a firm grasp of the workings of management data technology, yet he chose not to immerse himself in pools of information. Instead, he asked few, but pointed questions. Instead he challenged the very nature of the information being gathered. Instead he took information to the high ground, constantly testing its worth against the pressing needs of the organization. He started drawing people's attention back to the fundamentals of the business and reconciling everything, including information, against those fundamentals. If it didn't answer a driving question or provide insight to help make a strategic decision, he moved away from the screens and reports that were hypnotizing others.

He took a risk. He was initially seen as an oddity—definitely not the stereotypical sales type. He projected an "executive in training" demeanor rather than someone who was retiring in place. His management and coaching skills were average, but not his sense of vision and direction. They were outstanding. He focused his sales unit and kept them on the targets his questioning and analytical skills were able to uncover. His risk paid off in results. Executives listened to his insights and began to understand his thought processes. The Board listened as he aligned his unit's actions with the company's purpose for being. Most telling was when peers and subordinates began acting as he did. Soon managers were being praised not for generating reams of information and analysis, but for the impact and implications of their analyses. Those who sought answers to the right questions and those who knew to *ask* the right questions prospered. A wide swath of harvested data gave way to a more narrowly focused, but highly productive, collection of management information.

Not everyone in the senior levels of corporate America is arithmetically literate. And there seems to be a correlation between the quantitatively lacking and the bluster and passion they can create.

Twenty accomplished professionals spiral a board meeting into confusion when one of their members, fixated on what he perceives to be numeric imprecision, has disengaged from the substance of the agenda to proclaim he has found a flaw with the numbers. While others have been discussing the merits of a particular proposal, he has been adding the numbers. They don't add up. The back of his hand slaps the papers for emphasis. The summary sheet and the presentation's appendix don't reconcile. "What's going on here? What are you trying to get us to approve?"

Doubt momentarily floods the room. Opponents of the proposal begin to marshal their arguments, using the data confusion as justification for a complete reexamination of the issues. Chaos is averted when another board member points out the discrepancy is due to rounding. An uneasy calm returns. The gremlins had almost been awakened. The board was almost at a dizzying precipice, just about to examine the potentially frightening process behind the figures.

Source Data

Source data is the brick and mortar upon which information and ultimately conclusions are built. What rational leader wants to put the weight of their organization's goals and objectives on a foundation of source data that could be poorly designed, or even more devastating, flawed, or incomplete? And yet companies do it every day. And deep down we know that it is a constant possibility. What is our defense against this inevitability? It is the sanity check. Sure, the data is telling us one thing, but does it make gut level sense? We know that speed and carelessness are always in competition with accuracy for first place in affecting conclusions. We sense the potential for error in both information origination and fabrication. So we call on intuition shaped by experience to make the final determination. It's risky business.

For whatever reason, human resources, strategic planning, and IT all reported to one executive who reported to the COO of the company for which I worked. Weekly, I would troop over to this executive's office with information on a variety of situations, conditions, and possibilities. He was a tall, lanky engaging man in his mid-60s with an incredible background in business and public service. His office was always at sea with wave upon wave of binders and folios. He was a strategic thinker, always two steps ahead of most of his peers. At the end of a particular session, he asked about a small project. We had good data on it and based on that information moving in one particular direction seemed the most prudent approach. He looked at the data. "No, I think we should move left instead of right." I wondered why.

"I just feel that it makes more sense."

"Why?"

"I just have this feeling."

Even though all the information was saying one thing, he wanted to go the other way. Unfortunately he couldn't articulate why. Gut should be based on something that is at least within the realm of explanation. So, we went left—right off a cliff. If the data is fundamentally sound and its preparation for analysis is solid, intuition should play a limited role. The question then becomes, how do we make sure we are on firm ground before we are forced to trust our instincts?

If something appears wrong with financial or sales conclusions, more often than not, we can backtrack the analysis to its source data. We can verify the building blocks and uncover the flaws that led to our disbelief. We will push and pull until the tolerances for error are reduced sufficiently and some form of data coherence returns. In these situations, the sanity-check alerts us to a possible disconnect and pays off through our diligent investigation.

Grains of Salt

When we are confronted with compensation survey documentation, whether or not our gut is telling us that something doesn't add up, the road back to source data typically ends around a blind curve. The bricks that go into forming these survey reports are fashioned by hundreds of different hands using similar (but hardly ever precisely the same) criteria, fired in an equal number of different kilns, and sent to one location to be smoothed, refined, and assembled. The final product is taken on faith and is beyond validation. If you can't examine the source data you have no way of reconciling the distance between what you feel and what you see. The security we find in other kinds of information and the rituals that we have generally adopted to test that information don't apply to compensation surveys.

This is both good and bad: bad because time and money have been spent on something that may be of marginal management use; good, because it forces us to go beyond the data and make judgments based on internal as well as external considerations. In this way information becomes a qualified resource in making decisions and is not permitted to make the decisions for us.

Without "N" There Is No Survey Business

It is important to appreciate that not all compensation surveys are poorly put together; just most of them.

Survey companies are in the business of selling surveys. To a degree, depending on the survey company, they feed upon our insecurities by reassuring us that, for a fee, they have the answer to that most desperate of questions: Am I paying competitively? It is very tempting for the survey supplier to ignore any responsibility to educate and instead pander to the black hole of ignorance that surrounds this question. They not only assure us that they have the answer, but after throwing a pile of data at the question, they then massage it into a digestible executive summary. They have taken a complicated question, surrounded it with confusion, and then dummied down their supposed answer. In most cases, they have also created an answer that is simplistic and meaningless.

Of course not everyone can access the treasure trove of survey information. Not without paying for the privilege. You have to share your data before you can examine information supplied from all the respondents. And therein lies three major problems related to survey process:

1. Marketing participants.
2. Who actually supplies the data.
3. Answering questions that can be answered (as opposed to asking questions that should be asked).

Again, one must always remember that survey companies are in business to sell surveys. A survey product needs to have enough of the right participants with enough of the right jobs to appeal to all its buyers. The buyer is looking for representation of key comparators and key jobs. The survey company needs those comparators and those jobs to perpetuate its business.

If the survey company can stimulate the need simultaneously from all parties it can create the survey. Deals are made. "Right jobs" takes on a qualitative hue. The survey company allows for slight wanderings away from the benchmarks being examined. If a company has a job a little different from the benchmark, input provisions are made to modulate the response. Big companies and little companies are included, differentiated by revenue, asset, and/or staff size cuts. Often, these differentiations are not really telling. Is the job less complex or require more skills to perform if the company's assets are greater? Is the job worth less if the revenue stream is less?

In the survey business, more is always better than less. And with more equivocations the survey discipline is almost always compromised. So, the company offers to slice and dice the data in every way suggested. It offers the supposed ease of computerized input and display. Anything and everything is done to give the appearance of easy input, customized analysis, and digestible output. Above all, your company will be included with those you most want to know about. But what will you really know?

There is an inherent and obvious motivation on the part of the survey companies to keep their business viable. Rather than hone the survey process with better questions and a more meaningful contextual relationship between jobs and their organizations, an easier option is to crank up the volume. Therefore, the greater the number of jobs, matches, and organizations being surveyed, the greater the possibility of both economies of scale and sustained revenue. In this case one organization's profit could be another's loss. With larger survey populations comes the potential of combining unrelated information and driving down (and appreciably distorting) the value of specific positions. While accumulating more respondents guarantees survey company revenue it doesn't necessarily guarantee increased quality or usability of information. Formal surveys, as a group, provide little illumination on job values or the frameworks within which those values exist.

Formal surveys are a process of half-baked examinations, culled from a mass of questionable data that continually perpetuates information insanity within companies. Given today's technology, we are able to faster generate faulty thinking and informational compromises and disperse them easily. To better appreciate what is wrong with the end product it is best to walk through the process from its beginnings.

The Typical Scenario

A human resource professional, someone responsible for assisting in the positioning of salaries in the organization, is motivated to gather external compensation data. Usually the reason falls into one of four categories:

1. **Proactive Anticipation.** "When the boss wants to know what's going on in the job market, I had better have the data. And, if I can get salary information using the Smedley Survey, all the more credible."

2. **Ego.** "I got an e-mail from a survey company telling us that Kratzmar Corp is going to participate in their annual survey. They are really big in our industry. We better participate. It will increase our visibility and status to be included."

3. **Habit.** "This will be the 10th year we have provided data to this survey. It's no big deal. We have it down to a reflex action; can get this sucker done in one hour flat. This year maybe, we can do it in 50 minutes."

4. **A Question.** "I wonder if we are paying our sales reps competitively."

The survey input forms arrive. Generic descriptions are offered, often with titles or job classifications that are marginally recognized. Here is an example of what is found in a typical national survey:

Sales Representative III (SRIII)

Sells company products or services in assigned area or territory. SRIII is distinguished from SRII and SRIV by products or services of a highly complex nature which requires considerably more specialized training or in-depth knowledge than an SRII but less than an SRIV. The knowledge level of the SRIII is such that in hiring a replacement, candidates would require either previous experience or extensive knowledge and training related to the product or service prior to being able to call upon customers. To carry out the responsibilities at the III level typically requires a college degree or equivalent, along with sales ability, to be successful as compared to the SRII.

The HR professional takes a moment to reread the description...and then takes another moment. Finally, the survey is passed on for completion by an entry level HR specialist.

If an HR department is big enough to have compensation professionals, entry positions go through two rites of passage: evaluating position worth based on job descriptions and completing salary surveys. In the absence of a first line compensation analyst, a first line generalist is chosen to take on these tasks. It is much the same as the martial arts novice. Before you are taught complex sets, you learn balance, body position, and patience. First level compensation folks learn about comparable worth through completing and reviewing descriptions and surveys before they are allowed to design plans or influence structure. They also learn, as byproducts of dealing with job values, about their organization's functional hierarchy and its politics. Through time, they will grow to hate the drudgery and reality disconnects that come from reading and evaluating job descriptions and completing surveys. That hate will grow exponentially if they feel they are stuck doing questionable work.

One of two populations is now charged with completing the survey: the very new or the very jaded.

Problems arise when the analyst tries to determine which description applies to the company's sales specialists.

☆ SRIIs sell products or services that are of "greater complexity, which require more specialized knowledge." But both IIs and IIIs require the same background and knowledge.

☆ SRIVs sell to major accounts. But the company is small enough to consider all their accounts as major.

☆ SRIVs also sell to large accounts. Again, the company's accounts are all of similar size.

☆ SRIVs demonstrate "complete knowledge of the product or service *and* the organization's policies." Some of the company's sales representatives have complete knowledge of some of the products, while others have in-depth knowledge of all the products. Is there really a difference? And all have complete knowledge of the organization's policies.

At first, the analyst thought the company's sales reps fit the SRIII category. But now he is not so sure. The kinds of accounts and knowledge might lend themselves to the SRIV description. If he levels them using the wrong description the analyst could be under-reporting or overstating their salaries. Eventually the returned analysis would reflect them as being under- or over-paid with their peer group.

It's best to look at last year's input. Good gravy! The sales reps were reported as SRIIs! The individual who completed last year's survey left the company. There is no documentation to suggest why the leveling decision was made.

The analyst decides to report the position as SRIII. Months later, when the survey is completed and distributed, the analyst will find that his sales reps are overpaid as SRIIIs. *But are they really overpaid or were they reported in the wrong level?*

Additionally his input has affected both the average and median values for the entire sample population. The inflationary pressure of these numbers will cause other companies to raise the rates they pay their SRIIIs in order not to lag the marketplace. The dominos have begun to fall.

Next assignment: A key executive has been offered a job with a competitor. Can the company counter offer and still maintain parity internally and with the marketplace? What is the survey data telling the company? A quick analysis indicates that the position is paid competitively, within the 75th percentile of the data reported. Perhaps a slight adjustment can be made and still maintain some parity with the executive's peer group.

Not good enough says the CEO. "We can't afford a lack of continuity while we are going through a critical period in our company's history. We can't afford to lose this individual. The market data is not relevant.

The incumbent brings more to the job than the responsibilities indicate. And (pause for effect) she has a law degree." The degree is not relevant for either her current job or the competitor's position. Nevertheless the lowly analyst is told to look at the compensation rates for legal counsel and come up with a value factoring into consideration both jobs.

Exasperated the analyst mumbles to his superior, "Why not just pay the executive what the CEO wants and be done with it." Ah, but the compensation committee of the board would never agree to a raise without supportive market data. "But...but...but..."

"Now, now," comforts the HR manager. "Just put the data together and we will pass it up. Oh and be sure to reference the survey source." As to maintaining peer equity, the other executives are free to get a law degree whenever they want.

A Moving Target

As the previous section illustrates that pay rates based on marketplace data provide, at best, an imprecise frame of reference. It is equivalent to positioning a player on a baseball field. The shortstop is somewhere between second and third base. Specifically where between second and third depends on the hitter, players already on base, and the capabilities of the fielder and his teammates. No two shortstops will be in the exact same place even when the variables are identical. But you know an outlier when you see them—perhaps the shortstop covering second base when a shift is called for or playing too deep into left field to compensate for an outfielder positioned at the wall. If you saw the shortstop covering first base or crouched behind home plate, you might well wonder if there has been a titling problem. That, in a protracted analogy, is the dynamic you face when assessing market data: multiple measures based on a variety of situations leading to general conclusion—some of which are already out of date due to personnel changes.

Even when you have decided on a match, most surveys fail to surround the market data with a context that can be used for any pinpoint analysis. When one looks at pay rates for a position, rarely are the reporting organizations profiled with regard to variables that influence their value determinations. What is the revenue emphasis of the company? Are they focused on multiple or new distribution channels? Most importantly, what is their overall compensation mix? Little if anything is provided about compensation guarantees, sign-on bonuses, and non-cash rewards. One can sometimes find a benefits and perquisite summary appendix, but, frequently, it is high-level information and relatively meaningless.

There is an ultimate test to confirm my cynicism. Ask the person responsible for your survey input and analysis if they would stake their job on the accuracy of the data generated. When the CEO challenges the findings, when recruiters swear the job is at least 20 percent greater than what the printout says, when the incumbent threatens to leave for a similar position at a far greater rate of pay, how many compensation professionals will tilt their chairs back and point reassuringly at the screen in front of them? How many will blow reality off and stick with the data? Most will flinch. And when they compare the data with the actual salaries of incumbents in their organization, particularly at the higher levels, how many analysts will find confirming validity in the reports? Bottom line: Surveys make people feel good until they don't make people feel good. Then pay rates are changed, regardless of the surveys and regardless of the energy expended on their behalf.

How Can One Rationally Approach Pay Data?

Whether it is the results of a formal survey, a prospective applicant's assessment of fair pay, or rumors that a competitor has just raised the compensation hurdle for sale representatives, companies who couple sound, pragmatic decision making skills with a set of principle (in this case pay principles) are going to find it easier to put any information in the proper context.

Sound and pragmatic decision-making skills in action are an experience worth seeking out. It is the art form of business. Good decision-makers are fast, but not reckless. They don't rush to decisions based on anecdotes nor do they blindly accept all the data they receive at face value. They don't ignore what they hear; they just employ a discipline before reacting. They treat each narrative account as they would any other piece of business intelligence, always verifying the details, the context, and the source's motivation. They look as much toward what is missing as they do to what is apparent. Within reason they attempt to understand the full picture before choosing a course of action.

There is suppleness, a flexibility of approach. Good decision-makers can live with ambiguity. They appreciate shades of grey. Above all, they fight the urge to replicate and mimic when faced with uncertainty. They are creators of direction, and their decisions are always aligned with the company's internally grounded belief system.

What Are Your Own Pay Principles—30 Thousand Feet?

What in-house guidelines shape your compensation decision-making? Companies will answer the following questions differently, because each answer is aligned with a company's unique values and current situation. Your answers form a set of pay priorities that will influence the perspective within which you evaluate marketplace information.

1. Is your company's compensation expense based on each employee's individual contribution and value to the organization? Or is compensation seen by your employees as an entitlement based on some form of social contract?

2. Does your company determine pay criteria predicated on standards for success, and the assessment of the employee's productivity? Or is pay based on indices, such as relative hierarchy or seniority?

3. Does the staff self-assess their contribution?

4. Is compensation funded based on the degree of business plan achievement? Or is funding seen as a pre-established cost to be accrued for, regardless of company performance?

5. Are certain functions in your company paid differently than other functions even though market data or internal perceptions might think them similar? Is this difference based on their specific needs or perceived priorities? Or does pay equity preclude such considerations?

6. In the sales sector, are developers, renewal specialists, and/or maintainers of accounts given the same compensation importance? If not, what message is the hierarchy of importance sending to your sales staff? Is it the right message?

7. Are all sales team members (hunters, closers, installers, and customer service support) or segments of the team, compensated based on meeting collaborative goals? Or are they independently assessed and remunerated? Or is there some combination at play?

8. Is your sales team pay derived from the same source of funds, or do some functions find their pay at risk while others do not?

9. Is your sales pay uncapped? Or is there a philosophy that, at some point, compensation becomes excessive and those financial resources should be used elsewhere? If uncapped, is there any relationship between open-ended pay and the salesperson's ability to take their book with them from company to company? If capped, is there any relationship between defined maximums and sales based in large part on your company's brand identification, product quality, and service reputation?

10. Does your company compensate for windfalls: opportunities that seemingly fall from the trees as a result of the wind and not necessarily the actions of the sales staff? Do you discount these results when compared to other revenues generated?

11. What is the purpose of base pay in your sale compensation package? Does it reward for attendance and hygiene factors, skills and competencies displayed, results, behaviors that support the team, demonstrated loyalty, and /or meeting interaction expectations? Do your sunk costs (because base compensation is expensed regardless of company results and rarely decreases over the tenure of the incumbent) meet any of these purposes, all of these, none of these? Is base seen as irrelevant if your sales functions are highly leveraged or does it provide a symbolic binding to your company?

12. Does your company adjust salaries of current staff if the market demands that new staff be brought into the organization at a comparative premium? Or are competitive rates feathered into regularly scheduled reviews and pay events for more tenured staff?

The answers to all these questions reflect six major issues:

1. What behaviors your company values.

2. How your company perceives individual and collective results.

3. If, and why, your company differentiates job impact.

4. What parameters, if any, your company places on compensation values.

5. How your company uses various pay and reward components.

6. How your company perceives and acts on issues of pay parity and equity.

Examine these six issues carefully. Take a position on each point. Return to the 12 initial questions and compare how aligned your position is with the answers to those questions.

For example, let's use the first issue to illustrate how Jed, our CEO mentioned previously, would profile his sales organization relative to each of the 12 questions. (See pages 73–74.)

From Jed's notes he concluded that more could be done aligning this value through creating a better balance between individual and team rewards (more attention to team results) and by reviewing equity issues that might be undervaluing certain successful performers whose base pay may be out of sync with less experienced but newer staff.

After looking at all the issues relative to the questions, Jed had developed a deeper understanding of the internal drivers in his existing reward system. It was this frame of reference that would now govern his view of market data and affect any subsequent decisions made.

Drawing Market Data From the Right Pools

Pool #1—The Job Pool

The marketplace refuses to call an orange an orange. Before assessing any information, it is best to verify that what you think you are looking at is really what you are looking at. As elementary as it sounds, this is an often-discovered error in the analysis chain. If you are not comparing oranges, at least know what you are comparing. Oranges to tangerines is a more meaningful alternative than oranges to eggs. Rounded yes, but after that...

To vault the jargon of job classifications you need to know what the position is being compensated for; what factors are being valued. Managers should never let staff, particularly human resource folks, hand you a spreadsheet of numbers, a colorful graph, and then drive the agenda briskly toward recommendations. Stop the music. Ask what specific responsibilities, skills, knowledge, and experience exist in the surveyed jobs you are about to discuss. What do they have in common with the positions in your own world? Make sure any summary sheet you are looking at isn't clouded in

Issue	Question (paraphrased)	Response	Alignment of Issue & Response
Behaviors valued are: individual initiative, supportive teamwork, strong ethics, and relationship building	1. What is compensation based on—contribution, value, and/or social contract?	Performance-based sales results—new and renewals. Team component to overall rewards.	Reward indirectly for individual initiative, team work and relationship building by results achieved. Poor ethics penalized (termination). Good ethics recognized, but not substantively rewarded.
	2. Pay based on pre-established productivity standards?	90 percent pre-established. All based on productivity of individual and team.	90 percent aligned.
	3. Self-assessment?	No history of gaming.	Get input at assessment time—no desire to change; not necessarily aligned with allowing individual expression.
	4. Funding of comp?	20 percent base funding; 80 percent funding from plan achievement.	Aligned; all funding predicated on individual and team performance. Base only rises based on individual objectives met or market values.
	5. Perceived pay parity and equity?	Parity and equity based on relative value of positions and performers.	Aligned; resist outliers to internal values regardless of market indicators.

Issue	Question (Paraphrased)	Response	Alignment of Issue & Response
Behaviors valued are: individual initiative, supportive teamwork, strong ethics, and relationship building	6. All sales functions valued the same? Any hierarchy message?	Renewals valued less than new business.	Could put more emphasis on relationship building through customer service and renewals.
	7. Rewarded based on collaborative goals; independent achievement?	Combination; 70 percent of compensation based on the individual; 30 percent based on the team.	Team results rewarded too low to be aligned with values.
	8. Degree of pay at risk.	80 percent at risk for individual sales staff; less (30 percent) for customer service and renewal specialists.	Aligned with valuing individual; allows for greater reward opportunity for results; disconnect with team—softer at risk implications.
	9. Uncapped or capped sales pay?	Capped—sales individual not the only factor in securing sales.	Still reward very well for individual and team contribution.
	10. Windfall provisions?	No.	Could conflict with strong ethics value.
	11. Use of base pay?	Team and company focus rewarded through base; experience and knowledge gained rewarded as well.	Aligns with values, but not a major component of overall compensation; stronger focus on individual.
	12. Adjust pay equity between new and existing staff.	No overall adjustments made.	Some equity issues need to be addressed.

assumptions. Does the information collected differentiate those positions that are exact matches from positions that are less than or greater than? Are the differentiations substantive enough to cast a position out of the match pool? Something as fundamental as positions with senior responsibilities, regardless of title, being lumped into the same pool as journey level functions can skew the data so as to significantly and erroneously raise journey level values and decrease senior pay opportunity.

Pool #2—The Company Pool

Matching is a two-part process: (1) insuring that the appropriate jobs are residing under the same data umbrella and (2) having relevant companies reporting this data.

What is a relevant company? Determining relevancy can be a revealing experience. It is not uncommon for executives to specify whose data they want reflected in a pay survey. It is also not uncommon for the end result of this quest to be disappointing. Often success in securing data from desired companies has more to do with needs and perceptions than with job comparability. Assuming you decide to create your own survey or hire a third party to put one together, be prepared for the following:

☆ You want Company A to be in the survey mix because of industry similarities. Company A acknowledges it is in the same industry, but that's about all it feels it has in common with you. Company A passes.

☆ You want Company B to be in the survey because you lose staff to this organization. Company B acknowledges that it has similar types of skill sets and knowledge required to do its jobs, but doesn't see any similarity in industry segmentation. Besides, they feel they have a competitive advantage in recruiting your staff, once you've gone to the trouble of training them. Why should they reveal their pay rates to you? Company B passes.

☆ You want Company C to be in the survey because you acquire talent form Company C from time to time and usually at a premium. Company C is in a different industry and considers turnover a natural extension of their evolution and operating style. They are not concerned about losing staff and have no interest in your company or its positions. Company C passes.

☆ Company D has heard that you are interested in doing a survey and is most interested in participating. D is in the same industry and has jobs that appear to match. You know a lot about Company D's organizational history, or lack of it, and you are not too excited about their participation. They are undersized and too specialized. If they lose one sales person they have lost a 10th of their revenue generating force. From what you have heard, D negotiates compensation with little regard for parity. They deal in the moment. They are headquartered in Denver. You are headquartered in New York. You wonder what kind of coherent salary data they would be able to contribute. You don't return Company D's phone calls and e-mails.

You are back where you started—wanting to know more about Companies A, B, and C with nothing to show for it. Is that really a bad place to be? Is this the end of the survey road? No and no. There are ways to stimulate participation, even with resistant companies, and we will touch upon that a few paragraphs from now. But be careful what you wish for.

There are inherent dangers in relying too heavily on external comparisons, particularly if a comparison is an oversimplification. Comparators must be qualified matches in industry similarity and performance. The interested company competes for talent with the comparator organization. The wrong set of unqualified comparators can cause overall market values to creep in the wrong direction.

For example, if a company is performing lower than the 50th percentile of its comparator group but reports its staff compensation, particularly actual total compensation and target compensation, at rates that reflect higher performance, the median values of the overall survey are pushed upward. Overall compensation rates can escalate as a reaction to this information without any commensurate increase in actual performance. Careful compensation analysts and managers will look at surveys during an extended period of time to ensure that what they are seeing today relates rationally with past data reports from the same source.

How to Best Obtain Data

Never rely on only one channel of information. Data should be triangulated from a variety of credible and reliable sources that understand your organization's priorities and internal dynamics, and that can help you determine what role the marketplace can play in shaping your compensation structures. The best sources are always those with a perspective.

The Trusted Compensation Professionals

The best alternative to the standard production survey is the use of trusted third-party compensation professionals. I don't use the term "trusted" casually. These are compensation types who have been in their fields of business for extended periods of time, who relate well to a company's human resource, sales, and management leadership who covet their reputation and who would not compromise their ethics for any fee.

These specialists can customize materials to meet the collective needs of all the participants. They can solicit the best group of comparator companies and use both their adaptable process and their ability to tailor the survey to entice participation. They can prepare the materials relevant to data gathering so as to ease the pain of data collection. They can provide a process that flexes as concerns are added or modified during the data gathering and reporting phases. They can establish crossover participation between different industries with common jobs by establishing and controlling the data from participant pools desired by all surveyed parties. Company B participates with Company A because Company X is also included. And company X participates because of Company A. A credible third party can keep everyone at arm's length, avoiding any impression of collusion or impropriety.

Similar to any production survey, third-party-generated surveys require a significant number of participants and positions to maintain confidentiality of the responses. Most professional survey developers will not report any data with less than five matches. They are also cognizant that the larger the number of respondents reporting the greater the chance that the values reflected will be depressed. The looser the sample becomes and the more oddities are thrown into the pot, the more unraveled and irrelevant is the data. There is an art and discipline involved in arriving at a meaningful representation. A survey should have a tight weave to it, good matches, and a tailored number of participants. The survey should have a meaningful focus with questions that paint a picture participants would not get through a standard production source.

Third-party-generated surveys can be expensive when compared to the standard data surveys. As mentioned, they require a significant number of participants to maintain the confidentiality of the responses. But their completion timeline can be at least half that of most standard surveys and the specifics they provide are more usable and comprehensive. Cost for the first survey cycle may be borne primarily or entirely by the company initiating the survey. An effective third party will establish a community of interest that will transcend the initial survey cycle and lay the ground work for continued information sharing. In many cases, the relevancy of the data being sought and the quality of the process outcome will stimulate cost sharing among the participants, thus lessening the long-term expense for all.

Trusted Recruiters

Another credible source in triangulating data is the trusted recruiter. Note the term "trusted" again. These are not the dramatists who reflexively add 15 percent to the overall cost of talent. These are not the folks who can't differentiate between the skill sets and experience of the Chairman of the Federal Reserve and the manager of the accounts receivable department. These are not the recruiters who just get the job specifications right. These are the ones who are continually finding talent way beyond the company's short-term needs.

You can easily tell who the poor recruiters are. They charge a bundle, provide too few or too many candidates, and offer little in the way of practical counsel. To them candidates are a good fit because of their demeanor and resumé. There is no analytical discipline in their recommendations. Their screening process is incomplete, vague, and purely qualitative. They avoid asking penetrating and specific questions because they don't know the job or understand the environment that well. Their listening skills are average. Most often they have good hygiene factors, are well spoken, collegial, and have other people doing their basic screening and selection. They are big hats with no cattle. The after-the-fact confirmation of their lack of skill lies in the retention of the individuals who are chosen from their pool of candidates.

But they are only half the problem. Somebody in the company selected their services and hired the mismatches they offer. Somebody in the company has the wrong perspective regarding recruitment.

Trusted recruiters listen to their clients, the potential candidates, and the marketplace. They want a win-win situation in the end. They want their candidates retained, motivated by their new environment, performing beyond expectations and rewarded accordingly. They are people who keep confidences. You can be sure that what you are saying to them is not being said to others. You know this because they don't gossip about others to you. They use their sense of the market in the judgments and information they provide when reconciling both pay and overall compensation.

Recent Hires

Recent hires are another good source of intelligence, provided their observations are free of data-altering filters. Know the circumstances under which they left their previous employer. Determine how it will influence their view of compensation and the comparator. Without violating previously signed confidentiality agreements, did their position in the former company provide them a credible vantage point of information that could help in assessing external compensation values? Do they have a healthy perception of their current pay package, or did they assume their role with misgivings about the compensation offered? Can they extend your network of information objectively and accurately?

Production Surveys

Rubber Chicken:

 There are exceptions to every rule.

Given that axiom, production surveys must exist that are comprehensive and descriptive enough to cover the basics and step gingerly into the more advanced pools of information. If one is found, covet your participation.

The Basics Market Data Should Tell You

Once you have a meaningful set of commonly recognized jobs and relevant other-company participants, once you have assembled credible sources of information, and once you have a solid grip on those internal issues and values that drive your operating style and decision-making, you are finally ready to examine the data that can be provided.

At the very least, outside compensation information on the target positions should provide a manager with the basics considering mean, median, and weighted averages, such as:

☆ What is the position's total compensation?

☆ What comprises total compensation (cash, health benefits, retirement benefits, capital accumulation plans, non-cash recognition, and reward programs)?

☆ What percent of total compensation is cash?

☆ What percent of total cash compensation is base salary?

☆ What percent of total cash compensation is annual variable compensation (bonus, commission, or incentive)?

☆ What percent of total cash compensation is being accrued for a longer term variable plan?

☆ What is the pay rate distribution for each component of cash compensation for each position being examined? What is considered the 25th, 50th, and 75th percentile of values in the marketplace for each component?

☆ What other compensation and perquisites are provided the function?

These basic questions help you understand the larger value picture. A company cannot position its own compensation components intelligently or competitively until it knows the tendencies in the marketplace, until you know to what degree the sales positions being compared are compensated for risk (variable pay).

The compensation data on a position is usually segmented along a range of values. That segmentation has meaning when comparing the marketplace with your own staff. Typically, the 25th percentile of compensation, along a range of values, pays for individuals who have the skill, but relatively little experience in the job. The 50th percentile represents the journey level compensation rate for someone with both the experience and skill to start producing after a short orientation period. Compensation at this level assumes the individual will require less supervision and oversight than a novice. Pay at and beyond the 75th percentile is considered premium pay. Individuals in this end of the value spectrum bring a great deal of demonstrated past experience and proficiency to the position and require very little management support or intervention. With premium compensation comes premium performance expectations.

Allowing for a reasonable sample, comparing average compensation to the 50th percentile for the same position can give one a sense of value distribution within the population. For example, where the average is appreciably higher than the 50th percentile one can assume that the distribution is skewed toward the higher values. The converse is true if the average is lower than the 50th percentile. These spreads allow you to make some assumptions about the length of service and/or level of experience of the staff being reported. Experience rates may provide a clue as to the type and implied difficulty of goals and challenges that feed into the compensation payouts for this group.

Beyond Basics

More penetrating information is usually harder to obtain, and there is a reason for this. Gathering this information provides a more complete picture of the compensation rationale behind the numbers. You tread on revealing ground when sourcing this data. It may provide more in the way of how an organization operates and prioritizes its activities than it is willing to reveal. However, obtaining the answers to these questions can prevent you from replicating and institutionalizing previously unexamined and flawed practices. It is a coup when you can uncover a more detailed representation of the comparator group. It is the nut that every third party compensation specialist looks forward to breaking.

Look for Vertical Hierarchy

Who do the positions report to? If the position is supervisory, what positions report to this job? Is compensation data available for these connected positions?

Why—The vertical picture of an organization, through its reporting relationships, provides you with a clearer understanding of a comparator's value system. The pay differences between the position and those it reports to, or who report to it, can hint at their relative impact and possible overlap or wide separation of responsibility. It can point to the reason why a position is highly paid or paid well less than peers.

For example, a 30 pecent spread between functions in a reporting chain does not lend itself to smooth promotional patterns. Is this the result of poor salary management, a historical anomaly, or significantly disparate skills, knowledge, or experience that would preclude movement between these functions regardless of their similar classifications?

What functions does the position really supervise or manage? Is the pay rate predicated on supervising positions with appropriate heft? Do sales managers supervise other sales supervisors and professionals? Is the sales-team leader supervising sales staff, installers, customer service personnel, an administrative assistant, or all of the above?

Focusing on each function and its pay structure separately, without linking that information to its relevant functional connections, does not provide you with a clear enough picture to reconcile the data you are examining.

Look for Kinds of Pay-at-Risk Programs

What kind of variable plans are used by the companies surveyed? What are the actual payouts as a percentage of their target compensation? Does variable compensation begin to pay out after dollar-one-revenue is generated, or are there performance thresholds that must be achieved before any incremental payout occurs? Are there "windfall" provisions that moderate variable pay? If so, when do they go into effect and how do they dampen payouts? Is variable funding accrued on an ongoing basis, or is it funded only at the close of the plan cycle and based on the resulting performance outcomes?

Why—The amount of variable opportunity as a percent of base or overall cash compensation indicates the risk philosophy of the organizations being looked at. Defining how that opportunity is structured, without revealing actual company performance figures, further refines the indication.

Bonus plans typically imply a collective result with rewards dispersed based on the notion that everyone had some affect on the final outcome. Incentives usually measure individual results based on specific and unique measures. Both may have performance thresholds that pay a portion of the target amount when achieved. Knowing how close to target pay those thresholds are, can provide clarity of the challenging nature of the target and the expected performance of the participants. As a general rule the higher the threshold payout, the higher the actual performance threshold. No threshold payout may indicate that the company expects a good portion of its sales staff to meet target goals. In this case, the goal may be more achievable than challenging.

Many plans have payout ladders predicated on commensurate results. Some ladders are capped, or decrease in proportional payouts as certain higher levels of achievement are reached.

Plans with a healthy distribution of payouts imply managed motivation and challenging performance standards. Plans where all participants make or exceed target imply sloppy goal setting, lack of challenge and recognition for exceptional performers, and/or poor utilization of compensation funds. A solid variable plan will typically have 10 percent of the participants out of the money, 15 percent of the participants between threshold and target, 60 percent around target performance, 10 percent somewhat above target, and 5 percent far exceeding target. It is valuable to know if certain functions always achieve target where other seemingly related positions do not. Is there an entitlement ethic evident in the payouts reported or the funding process?

Structures can tell you about the cultural messages worth recognizing in a comparator. Bonus participation may imply the promotion of a collective team ethic. Incentive structures may signal a focus on specific tailored targets with a more competitive sense of recognition at play. Knowing if bonus plans extend to a wider audience or to positions lower in the organizational hierarchy may indicate whether the bonus plan is more symbolic than productivity focused. By examining the payout potential at various levels and positions within one structure you can identify whether the company pays variable opportunity that is more hierarchical than functional. Or put another way, whether the company promotes a "have" and "have not" mentality.

Whether the company pays commissions from the first dollar of revenue generated, or pays after base costs or some other expense criteria have been recouped, may reveal how sophisticated they are in use of funds, or whether the positions are valued for an individual's impact on the sale versus the company's impact on the deal.

Equally telling is a company's reaction to "windfall" sales. Is there a form of discounted commission or does the sale go completely unrecognized? Are there provisions for lead generation or shared sales? The degree to which a company will identify operational conditions that affect sales and align those conditions with their compensation programs may be an indication of their planning acumen and experience.

Look for Maximum Payout Opportunity

Is variable compensation uncapped? If not, when is the ceiling reached as a percent of target payouts or a percent of performance expected at target?

Why—Capped plans can often indicate how much is too much when compared to shareholder dividends or reinvestment needs. It can also speak to the company's view on how much impact the functions have on the results generated. Caps may reflect whether revenue growth at a certain level is seen as a product of brand identity or relationships beyond the skills and actions of the plan participants.

If the plan is uncapped, how meaningful is the distribution of payouts beyond target? Is the program paying a real or perceived premium for performance? Do competitive capped plans actually payout similar to uncapped plans? There is great leverage in promoting sales plans without caps to staff. Substantial mileage can be achieved from marketing a plan that has unlimited potential, when, in reality, performance and pay never exceed competitive levels.

Look for Hidden Compensation

Do the companies reporting offer hiring bonuses, or guaranteed variable compensation in the first performance cycle after employment? Where is this reflected in the compensation data being reviewed? Do companies reporting provide safety nets for their new sales staff? How is this feature being address in the compensation data?

Why—Identification of hiring bonuses, guarantees, and safety nets will help correctly size and qualify the compensation being provided by the target positions. These provisions are often lumped into variable pay lines distorting both pay rates and performance reflected in pay. This is particularly prevalent in emerging and high turnover businesses.

Look for Staff Experience

What is turnover like in these positions? What are the promotional patterns like in these positions?

Why—Turnover information will help reconcile data reported by various percentiles. Reactions to turnover can become visible in pay rate contradictions. Environments with high turnover may staff at the 25th percentile or drive the market up by providing premium pay for incumbents that would be otherwise considered journey level. Such actions are often telling as to an organization's pay philosophy and development depth. Rates that are negotiated in a moment of stress can affect both the general market and parity within the organization. You can avoid overreacting to escalating pay if you understand the motivations behind paying on the high end of the spectrum and reconcile those behaviors with your own priorities and operating style.

Look for Employee Perceived Compensation Value

How does staff value the various components in their compensation mix?

Why—Employee perceptions about their compensation can tell you more than just the quality of the plans offered. Companies that invest in marketing their compensation, particularly those elements they feel will resonate with the staff, will often generate an employee mindset that may have more to do with emotional satisfaction than logic. I have seen the phenomena firsthand. Individuals who understand their company's compensation philosophy, how each component fits into the overall scheme, and are provided substantial amounts of information and dialogue opportunities will tend to value their packages more than employees in other companies who actually have better compensation programs, but who do not understand the workings and relative value of these programs.

And there is also the "care" benefit associated with over-communicating compensation philosophy and its programs. Companies who market their programs effectively are seen by their employees as caring and concerned. This generates a sense of pride and loyalty that reaps retention, recruitment, and performance advantages.

If you are too far away from the factory to hear the whistle blow, then you are too far away from the factory.

External compensation data is just one piece of guiding information that shapes a company's reward program. Establishing a relevant and realistic compensation structure with components that produce the behaviors the company wants and provides meaningful messages to its participants is more about internal factors than it is about the conditions of the marketplace. Your strategies, goals, operating style, vision, and people values all have to align with the types of and size of the compensation opportunities you make available to the staff.

Compensation design is an active, conscious decision—not a reflex reaction to what others seem to be doing. It is important to know what is out there so you can rationalize your decisions within a complete framework of information. The better the data accumulated, the better your sense of the playing field. But ultimately it is just information, easily jaundiced and to be viewed with appropriate skepticism.

External practices are not an undeniable force to bend toward. In its absence you are still going to be compelled to move forward. As a manager, if you find yourself going left and you feel good about the decisions underlying that direction, even if there is a data void or if information exists telling you that others are going right, go left vigilantly, but go. That's what management is truly all about. That's why you are in the chair.

Provide Realistic Sales Rewards: *Controlling Expectations*

Getting It Right

If you subscribe to the philosophy that there is nothing that money can't buy, or to the philosophy that there is nothing that money can't fix, skip this chapter. People with these philosophies do compensation a disservice. To them compensation has properties similar to an opiate: Inhale deeply and all will be made better; at least for the time being. Complaints, performance challenges, and organizational concerns will all be met with the same response, subtle or otherwise. "You're being paid very well. So well, in fact, that we expect you to tolerate whatever work conditions exist. Just suck it up and get on with the job." Each time the stresses increase, their response will crescendo, "Get over it. Keep moving. That's why we pay you the big bucks." These distributors of largess forget two very important Rubber Chickens:

 The effect of pay, used as a pain killer, always wears off.

Eventually you need to administer larger and larger doses to forestall the inevitable. Pain will return. Issues of organization and performance will remain unhealed.

Compensation isn't just action taken; it is a message.

It is about value. The value of the individual's contribution as perceived by the organization, and as the organization wishes the individual to perceive him- or herself. It speaks to cause and effect, to behaviors and outcomes that are aligned with overarching vision and concrete objectives.

I am reminded of a regional manager I encountered who couldn't understand why he was having such high dysfunctional turnover—dysfunctional in that the people he didn't want to leave were always exiting. Turnover *can* be healthy. Some jobs dead end and the move internally to other positions requires too great a leap between current skills, knowledge, and experience and expected tools to perform effectively. As companies mature and change, people mature and change. Often these transformations are not compatible, and it makes sense for people to move. Turnover for these reasons can be slightly disruptive, but predictable. It offers others opportunities, keep the organization vibrant, and eventually serves everyone's interests. Dysfunctional turnover never meets those criteria. It is a surprise to management and always very disruptive.

The regional manager was paying his departing talent in the 90th percentile of the marketplace, often based on the slimmest of rationales. When I asked if the challenges of the job were too daunting, expecting 90th percentile pay to be reflected in equivalent performance expectations, he discounted that as a problem. "We want the best and are willing to pay for the best. Hell, if I knew what the 100th percentile was I'd pay that—top dollar, nobody would be making more anywhere. We're after rainmakers."

It turns out these rainmakers were never allowed to make rain. They were kept busy maintaining existing accounts with little prospect for increasing sales. Renewals, which were relatively automatic, were all the new business they had to look forward to. The company was always on the cusp of exploring new markets, but could never put their plans into play. The rainmakers were kept at arm's length, never part of planning or problem resolution, kept in reserve until the "right" moment.

On the other hand, this regional manager's safe performers, those who met the minimum expectations of the job, were happy with the upward trending income they reaped as a result of the high salaries paid to their supposed peers. Although not as generous as the monies received by the rainmakers, it eventually became impossible for the safe performers to leave without suffering the consequences of the downwardly adjusted compensation packages they would be offered by wiser minds.

Good people are never satisfied with just money. Good people will leave while mediocrity clogs the career pipeline. Good people, by their absence, will send a message.

This chapter is about doing it right, about utilizing the elements of compensation for what they were intended, and avoiding the traps that confuse and undermine staff behavior.

Putting Compensation in Perspective

Jed felt prepared. He and his management team knew their organization's direction and had reached a consensus on what operating style made the most sense for them. They had deciphered the compensation marketplace and selected what data was useable and reasonable with their values and their reference points. The foundation was laid and the framing built. They were ready to determine what to pay and reward, how to structure pay and reward, and when to pay and reward. They had two objectives:

1. Provide the shareholders with maximum compensation effect for dollars allocated.

2. Ensure that employees knew they were remunerated and rewarded fairly, for the right reasons.

A subtlety has crept into this discussion worthy of note. Why distinguish between remuneration and reward? For our purposes, remuneration will address those components of compensation that are provided out of competitive necessity—elements such as a living wage, health, and welfare benefits. Reward components emphasize compensating for achievement of goal measurements and, in some cases, behaviors related to those goals. Rewards take the form of variable pay (incentives and bonuses) or non-cash programs. Remuneration is a fixed cost. Rewards should thrive or vanish based on the incremental gains they produce. We will explore why it is supremely important to use the right form of compensation to stimulate the right effect.

When all else about pay and rewards fade away, this Rubber Chicken's searchlight should continue to sweep the horizon:

 Compensation is always and only defined in the context of your organization.

Without the organization to give it purpose and to shape its meaning, it is an abstraction. An abstraction is the peg that won't fit into the hole. Abstractions are thrown against the wall in the hope that they will stick. The annals of compensation history have too many tales of good companies assimilating the good plans of other companies and then failing to maximize their own compensation value. Good companies taking someone else's compensation approach and throwing it against the wall. Replication may be a form of flattery. In compensation design, it is a formula for failure.

It Takes 30 Minutes to Stop an Aircraft Carrier

Another Rubber Chicken:

 If your company's expectations and operating style are not aligned and consistently applied to the day-to-day workings of the organization, your compensation program, is going to go nowhere.

The difficulty is hardly ever in conceptualizing how things should be aligned, but rather lies in getting history to stop repeating itself. Depending on the density of a company's pattern of reinforcing past behaviors, its current hierarchical structure and its management's disposition toward constructive confrontation, change can be daunting. Often, and unfortunately, change is the byproduct of crisis. What could have been planned for and feathered into the existing organization is often hurriedly crammed through the corporate grinder to prevent impending disaster. Just as often, and just as unfortunately, half-hearted attempts are made to align fundamental behaviors with strategic expectations. Temporary patches are applied and reinforced with vague intentions in the hopes that something will change on its own accord. Unwanted people will self-select out of the company. The marketplace or some superordinate act will precipitate required changes. Maybe a key management committee member will win the lotto and boogey. Both approaches, super-aggressive and super-passive, become a profound statement of the company's actual culture and its leadership.

Leadership teams that can actually create whatever necessary changes are required to bring about the necessary organizational course corrections are rare and highly valued. They have an appreciation that it is not all about them.

In the course of redesigning a sales compensation package for a large national corporation, I had occasion to attend several of their senior management meetings. The CEO, a charismatic and technically competent executive, had an item not on the agenda that he needed to cover immediately. He told his direct reports as assertively and precisely as possible that certain counterproductive behaviors pervasive throughout the company had come to his attention through the customer relations area and were to cease immediately. He emphasized that it was critical to the overall direction of the company that a shift in emphasis be made, and these behaviors were standing in the way of that shift. Once he was satisfied by his team's responsiveness to the issue and their reassurances that changes would be made swiftly, the CEO continued with the meeting's agenda.

At the next management meeting, two weeks later, the CEO was livid. Nothing was changing. It was apparent through their quantitative reporting process that behaviors were not changing. It was also apparent to him that his directives were being ignored. He told each of his executives that he would not tolerate any further delays. Again he received affirmation from his staff and promises of immediate corrective action.

The CEO's frustration caused great anxiety among his subordinates, but had no real effect on the situation. Sheer force of will never wins out unless it sticks to the right people and drags them along. Each executive at the meeting cascaded the directive down to lower level meetings, which in turn continued to pour the information down until it pooled at the level most likely to take meaningful action. While senior players were jumping up and down, the real change agents were identifying themselves and trying to translate directive into action. Dialogues were being generated up and down the line. Questions, confusion, clarification, actions, and remedial actions began taking place. Two months from the initial CEO directive a corrective process was taking hold. The CEO had assumed the force of his personality could stimulate immediate action. He now began to appreciate that, for an organization of their size and to engage changes as substantive as he envisioned, command presence alone was not enough.

An aircraft carrier takes longer to start, maneuver, and stop than a patrol boat. The proportional distance between the wheel, the rudder, and propellers is a simplified way of explaining the complexity of mass coming to grips with inertia. The CEO, previously mentioned, was in command of a corporate carrier. The distance between his turning the wheel and change being effected was taken up by a series of management layers. The command was subject to repetition. The quality of that repetition, the understanding by the crew, any vested interests at play, and the reinforcement by each subsequent layer of management all contributed to the final product: change.

If the CEO wanted change to manifest itself at the speed of a patrol boat, he was either going to have to temper his change expectations to the physical realities surrounding him, reorganize the way his carrier set about sailing the high seas, or more rationally move on both fronts. Ego alone would not propel his vessel forward for any sustained period of time. His management team, functioning in isolation, would be equally ineffective. It is an obvious management principle often ignored by those who can least afford to.

Choosing Carefully

Getting your compensation programs to go somewhere specific, as opposed to everywhere at once, is made easier if one remembers that each form of compensation is intended to drive unique behaviors and provide unique rewards aligned with those behaviors. One should also remember that the creative mind is never at rest. Someone is always compelled to design a hybrid compensation approach that intertwines multiple forms and behaviors in an effort to further distinguish their brand of remuneration and reward. The result of this creativity can be confusing and can often miss its intended target.

You can't keep some people from trying to fix an unbroken wheel. However, you can keep them from making one of artificial complexity's most egregious mistakes. *If a company chooses to use a variety of compensation approaches to value one outcome, it must never inflate the worth of that result by having the remuneration from each of those multiple approaches exceed a reasonable total value.*

The reasons for compensation are finite. You can divide the pie for maximum effect by choosing to emphasize one approach over another.

But a 9-inch pie, no matter how many ways you slice it and how different the portions may look, is still a nine inch pie. The compensation messages have to be reconciled with the compensation available. You shouldn't have a 70-percent message funded by 30 percent of the dedicated resources, nor should you have a 30-percent message funded by 70 percent of the pay available. And in all cases you shouldn't have 100 percent of the message funded by resources exceeding your allocation. It is amazing how otherwise financially astute managers will adopt a resigned attitude when told they are overpaying for a particular behavior. They often resort to standard reflex answer number one, "It's the marketplace." No it is not. No one can tell a company how to mix its compensation. And certainly no credible survey will tell you to pay 130 percent of total compensation for target performance.

Forms to Choose From

Hybrids aside, there are four basic forms of compensation, each with a different emphasis and application: base pay, benefits, variable opportunity, and non-cash compensation. A brief synopsis is worthwhile so as to establish common reference points as we proceed on.

Base pay provides security in exchange for the individual adhering to standards of conduct in dealing with internal and external business relationships, and remuneration for baseline performance results. As mentioned previously, it is a fixed cost. In all but the rarest of occasions it either stays constant or increases based on longevity, cost of labor, individual performance, or a combination of these factors. The elimination or decrease in overall base pay, usually the result of downsizing, can be both organizationally dramatic and individually traumatic.

Benefit offerings constitute the other portion of security-based compensation. Benefits (health and welfare) covers a wide range of potential programs. In most cases, it is the least-understood form of compensation to both staff and management. The programs are expensive, in some cases complicated, and generally over-managed and under marketed. Effective programs are demographically sensitive, tailored to maximizing the population's needs and perceptions. Health plans emphasize wellness maintenance and illness prevention as well as conventional coverage for routine and catastrophic events. Retirement related plans are diversified and positioned to afford the participants maximum understanding and control of their investments. There also exists another group of programs that are often categorized as benefits. These include community-related activities such as employee-directed or matching contributions, sabbaticals, and various forms of paid time off.

Although increased costs have brought about a universal increase in benefits, most programs continue to remain reactive rather than proactive. Company benefits administrators, those tactically focused on the mechanics of plan workings, and the financial specialists from accounting exert a disproportionate influence on the design of these programs. Typically their cost-reduction approaches do not take the strategic impact of benefits as a behavior driver into consideration. It is not how much the company offers that is important. It is what the company offers and how well the employee understands the trade-offs and decisions involved in arriving at a particular grouping of benefits that is critical. A customized package, employee sensitive and fully marketed, can provide the staff with a source of corporate pride that goes a long way toward employee productivity and retention.

Variable pay is designed to promote motivation, job satisfaction, and a sense of psychic, if not tangible, equity. In some instances, it also offers the possibility of capital accumulation. It rewards for focusing on the achievement of company priorities. These rewards should be funded from the incremental gain produced from the successful attainment of those priorities. Variable pay is the single most powerful and cost effective change vehicle in the compensation arsenal. There are two basic types of variable pay: short term and long term.

Short-term variable pay encompasses commissions, quarterly and/ or annual bonuses, and incentive programs. The plans developed in this category keep the staff focused on the critical and the immediate. They reinforce positive achievement as close to the event as possible, and evaporate when results or timeframes fall below expectations. They are the manifestation of careful and achievable planning. They provide substance to the company's direction.

Longer-term variable pay adds retention to the list of intended purposes by offering the opportunity of substantial capital accumulation based on the company's gains within a time horizon typically ending three years from the program's inception. Those who participate through the duration of the plan are rewarded with a portion of the gains achieved. Some programs offer vesting in a portion of the reward proportional to the participant's longevity in the plan. Others have cliff vesting, where the participant has to be employed and remain a part of the program on the last day of the plan to reap any reward. Variations on vesting are predicated on the specific challenges to be attained, the motivation messages, the timing that management wishes to generate, and the economics related to the goals being measured.

The classic longer-term program has encompassed company equity. There is no doubt that the use of equity has been abused in some organizations and there has been substantial debate about the usefulness of the changes that have been made to the accounting practices associated with option programs in stemming that abuse. Option programs, indexed effectively to selected companies and allocated prudently, are powerful tools in aligning the participant's interests to those of the organization. It is unfortunate that a viable alternative has been diluted because of a relatively small group of managers whose behavior has generated a disproportionate amount of oversimplified press. Past option abusers are going to manifest their behavior through other compensation vehicles. People in positions of power who are motivated by greed will always find a way to meet their compelling needs. The key is to preserve programs and eliminate the abusers.

Although somewhat crippled, option programs will still be utilized, or in some cases replaced or supplemented by other forms of equity accumulation. Performance shares and restricted stock are but two of a variety of alternatives that can be used to achieve the objective of sharing in the appreciation of a company's value.

Privately held companies, and those publicly traded businesses that are gun shy of extending equity programs to a larger employee population, offer cash-based long-term plans. These plans have historically been less robust in their award potential, but their motivational and productivity messages are often linked to more substantive performance measures than stock price. Using these indices better defines both the real gains of the company and the participant's real contribution. Cash-based plans can be seen as less of an entitlement than the "granting" of equity shares and more a product of actual achievement. Good longer-term plans, just as good short-term plans, pay for themselves without offsetting any earnings objectives. Whether equity- or cash-based, all longer-term plans have features that take into consideration the impact of taxable events at the time of vesting with many plans allowing for differed payments to avoid untimely constructive receipt of funds.

Non-cash compensation takes many shapes, all designed for extraordinary recognition and motivation. The alternatives chosen should reflect the values of the participants and not the leadership who put the programs together.

A CEO initially squelched a plan to award outstanding sales results with a specific and unobtrusive pin, suitable for lapel or blazer. It was "too hokey." After an inordinate amount of prodding from his heads of sales and human resources, he reluctantly agreed. On his subsequent travels to the company's various locations he not only noticed the pins being worn by his top producers, but many made a point to thank him for the recognition it brought them from both peers and clients. It became a goal for other sales staff to shoot for. It was a small investment generating a large return. The key, as in selling, is to always know your target audience well enough to anticipate the impact of your offerings. And if you don't know this, the key is in trusting those advisers that do.

Organizations, depending on their culture, see personal development, real time off (as opposed to leaving the building only to return to work that has been neatly piled up awaiting your return), travel, recreational opportunities, visibility situations (where those recognized meet with executive management or are selected to participate in taskforces or on committees, the results of which are reviewed at the highest company levels), or perquisites (special car allowances, parking accommodations, club memberships, organizational memberships) as worth the expense for the goodwill and productivity they engender.

A guiding management Rubber Chicken:

 People are not stupid.

They know when they are being jerked around. In the case of non-cash offerings, they have to be genuinely offered. If you are doing something because you feel compelled by competitive forces to provide this form of perquisite, don't slather it with false platitudes and images of sacrifice. If you are not comfortable recognizing people, either be careful of the format in which you do it or have someone else do it.

One of the great visuals I have is of a company president decked out in a peppermint-striped apron and celebratory cap scooping ice cream at a sales rally for his corporate staff prior to launching a new product line. Some others of his rank could have pulled it off, but not him. He felt ridiculous and it showed. He couldn't wait to leave, and that showed as well. This was a man very adept at engaging small groups in casual conversation. He engendered a sense of true concern for his staff and genuine interest in their personal aspirations. Someone else should have been scooping the ice cream while he worked the crowd. It was an opportunity lost.

Pop and Its Evil Stepbrother Entitlement

Whatever the form and however it is structured, the end point of any compensation package is for it to have "pop." The right form of remuneration or reward at the right time in the right context provides that pop. The antithesis of pop is entitlement. Entitlement blurs vision, dilutes efforts, and disengages the staff from the goals to be achieved.

Countering the entitlement mentality associated with base salary is pretty much a lost cause. Even when increases to base are not considered automatic, the increase amounts are so small as to negate any performance impact you can attach to them. I still marvel at how many organizations spend incredible amounts of time and mountains of paper dissecting the relative contributions associated with base pay. Performance assessments for the purposes of development and recognition are one thing. But one can only wonder at the reams of paper justifying a 3.5 percent versus 4.1 percent increase to base, rebuttals notwithstanding. It has to be one of the highest levels of company bureaucracy.

Equally goal-disengaging is the arbitrary adjustment. A typical example of this was embodied in the practices of an international company I was asked to assist. The company had created a rather elaborate sales incentive program with a myriad of weights and modifiers attached to too many variables. Nevertheless the staff understood the program's general parameters and aligned their behavior and results to the challenging goals articulated in the plan. Prior to determining final payouts for objectives accomplished, each participant's results (the basis for their payouts as reflected in the documented plan mechanics) were subject to the Presidential Compensation Factor, or PCF. Days would pass until the participant knew the final rewards for performance achieved. After a period of "reflection" the CEO would either adjust the individual payouts or leave them alone. Actions were predicated on criteria that were never clarified before or after the decision was made. But any adjustments made were final and irreversible.

Was the CEO a control freak? Was he dissatisfied with the criteria governing the plan payouts? Was he using the plan to reconcile other forms of compensation given to the individuals? Did he feel justified in exerting his influence on the plan outcome by virtue of his ultimate accountability? No one knew. Whatever his reason, as far as the participants were concerned, the PCF was the real measure of their standing in the company. No matter how well they performed, no matter how effective they were in achieving pre-established sales goals, their annual assessment came down to the PCF. If they barely achieved threshold results and their predicted payout rose through the black box phenomena, they were cautiously elated. They were doing something right. They were never sure what that was, but they weren't going to complain. The crumbling would come the following year when their cache went down even though their results went up. Those who were unaffected by the PCF suffered a different malaise: perceived neglect. Didn't the CEO care enough about them to do something to their pay? Even negative attention was at least attention.

The annual scenario of doubt and revelation played out for six years. Everyone tolerated the condition because a significant majority of the participants always received healthy incentives. Perhaps some were not as generous as initially anticipated, but significant enough for the sales staff to gloss over the process. Bonuses can have the same effect in an economically upward situation. No one is sure how results entered into the final consideration, but there it is. A bonus check received for a "job well done." The company is obviously healthy, so there is no need to worry about the details. Smile, be happy, and let's keep those checks coming. An entitlement is born.

Entitlements and indifference to arbitrary behavior remain fairly benign until the company's performance starts to go south. Then the questions begin, with the ultimate question being, "Why didn't I get what I was expecting?" As the company's revenue and market share slipped the PCF became a focus of ridicule and anger. The scales were tipped from difficult situation to crisis when two high achievers slammed the process and left the company. PCF, and all that it represented in poor performance focus and management, could only be remedied by going back to basics. The situation required examining leadership's operating style, designing a plan that clearly and openly articulated all criteria influencing the assessment of awards, and ensuring those rationales aligned with the organization's values and priorities.

Compensation is not about surprise or keeping the faith. Compensation can be a powerful contract between everyone in the organization. It is a contract that results in both achievement and commensurate reward, but it needs to be defined before the parties agree to live within its bounds. Arbitrary behavior or entitlements connected with variable pay or non-cash compensation have no contractual linkage. There is no understandable cause and effect. With each passing cycle the fundamental focus that binds staff and management to a common goal fades away to be replaced by administrative shadows, guess work, and the potential of gains realized, but not achieved.

Compensate Selling: Not the Sale

Sales compensation defines success through visible and tangible measures that are linked directly to margins and revenue. The direct line of sight between the event and the economics of the company provides for special opportunities of pay emphasis and timing that compliment the nature of the sales mentality. Sales people are steeled to withstand a degree of rejection, demonstrate perseverance, initiate independent action, and possess active listening skills. All these characteristics can be incorporated in structuring effective sales compensation programs.

Before one jumps into the development of sales compensation using base pay, benefits, variable opportunity, and/or non-cash compensation, it is prudent to appreciate factors that both influence the kind of compensation a sales job merits and the nature of the selling experience itself. Selling is affected not only by the universal considerations of organizational history, company practices, and expectations, but also by the quality of the product or service offered, the company's follow-up support capabilities, and the latitudes a sales representative is given with regard to pricing, market timing, and territory penetration. All of the above can influence the success of the sales result, regardless of the skill and experience of the sales incumbent.

There is a fundamental question that needs to be asked prior to developing any compensation plan: is the job really a sales job? And if it is a sales job what kind of selling is required? The answers to both questions will determine what compensation can effectively do to drive behaviors and reward results.

Salespeople are paid for what they do at the point of influence. Too often people are paid as sales staff when they have little or no influence on the sale. If the lights go on, the doors open, and the customers flock in, you have an environment ready for order taking. An order taker's behavior can adversely affect the course of a sale and flatten repeat business, but their persuasiveness and initiative does little to influence sales. Poor behavior and customer service is appropriately dealt with as performance issues that affect base salaries. You don't reward personnel for meeting the acceptable standards of the job; you pay them an appropriate salary. The exception to this scenario are sales personnel expected to use the order as an opportunity to cross sell, sell up, and or package products into a single sales ticket. Some form of variable pay plan, perhaps an individual or team bonus, will help focus behavior and reward for results that go beyond ringing up the order.

Order takers come in all sizes. Consumers see their distracted faces planted behind registers staring past them toward distant lights. This species can sense impending work before it arrives and are able to quickly scurry away from their station and disappear among the racks of product just as you are about to approach. Because consumers don't come to them, large corporate account ticket takers rely on phones, meeting for coffee, or staged events to secure the business. Because of their gatekeeper role, even the most passive ticket-taker rings up business. They stand between demand and distribution. The customer has no option but to go through them. And there is the telling differentiation between selling and securing a sale. If company reputation, product quality, uniqueness, and/ or pricing initiate the sales activity, and all that is left is answering of routine operational questions and the facilitation of closing documents, your representative is not really a salesperson.

Whenever variable compensation is introduced into the pay equation management has to ask itself if providing the job with a commission, incentive, or bonus will produce significantly different results than paying straight salary.

False Expectations

Some organizations create a false sense of influence, decrementing the individual's base salary and creating a "feel good" offset in variable form that virtually always pays out based on sales volume. In reality, sales would have been generated regardless of the compensation emphasis.

The pay message is irrelevant to the end result. The individual has little influence on the sale, but both parties feel good about the pay outcome. The company either breaks even in overall pay or saves on the fixed cost of base salary in those cases when sales activity drops and the variable component pays out less than planned. In the majority of cases, the individual feels a sense of accomplishment for running the race, a race without a great deal of sweat. An award for good attendance is wrapped in the guise of recognition for selling achievement.

Besides being inherently deceptive, the "feel good" approach institutionalizes potentially expensive pay structures while simultaneously anesthetizing individual motivation. Variable compensation provides for high-end rewards commensurate with high-end achievement. By acknowledging ticket takers as sales staff, companies are compelled to play the game as if there is a real sales staff at work. To remain supposedly competitive with jobs in the marketplace that carry the same job titles, structures are devised that allow for payouts beyond target. In some cases targets are reduced to provide a false upward opportunity. Someone achieving 120 percent of target goals is really achieving expected results. They are being paid what the organization anticipated; it just looks better than paying for predicted outcomes. Occasionally, truly high end targets are set. Motivation is deflated when ticket takers realize these goals can never be met by their own efforts because theirs is not really a job of influence. The participants have no control of the outcome. A telling criterion for whether a job is really selling.

In all cases, these programs are administratively more burdensome than managing base salary compensation. Everybody knows what's going on and it does a disservice to all involved.

Aligning Selling Focus With Compensation Reinforcement

Sales compensation should be tailored to differentiate between the various types and conditions of selling. The event horizon and the type of influence generated in relationship selling during an extended period of time are far different in transactional selling. The same holds true with regard to techniques when closing the sale or selling up. Sales derived from customer service or support contact is different from cold call selling. Initial persuasion is different than seizing an opportunity from a previously sourced and established relationship. As a rule, the greater the degree of persuasion required, the higher the variable opportunity.

The test of a well-put-together sales compensation structure is its ability to provide the shareholder and investor a concrete alternative method of understanding about what the organization is paying for, and of what each individual sales result brings into the company. The investor should be comfortable that the company is paying within boundaries that are reasonable for the revenue generated and the costs incurred. This should hold true whether expecting results at target performance or rewarding for and from the incremental gain derived from results beyond expectations. Said another way, a balance exists between the reward and the magnitude of the result.

A well-put-together sales compensation structure recognizes that, although not every sales person will achieve results beyond expectations, each should have the potential and should be striving for that achievement. It is important to differentiate that management is not asking the individual to be the best sales person in the group, but the best sales person they can be against a standard—a goal. Although it may appear that they are competing against each other, sales staff should always be competing against themselves. This prevents the best of the worst from crowing about substandard accomplishments and avoids the worst of the best from feeling inadequate when their performance was actually within the boundaries of stellar.

Sales staffs thrive on all forms of genuine reinforcement. Reinforcing behavior and focus are imbedded in compensation. Paying as close to the sales event as possible is key to reinforcing positive action and enhancing floundering performance. The time between result and pay in transactional sales is primarily a product of the economics associated with record keeping and operational efficiencies. Most companies are able to stay within two weeks of the event.

The direct relationship between when results occur and when reinforcing payouts can be awarded is often less immediate with regard to relationship selling and sales that are residual in nature. It is intuitively less desirable to pay a relationship seller full incentive at the time the sale is booked and revenue flows. That time frame surrounding that sale, from initial call to contract signing to revenue generation, can encompass a year or more.

A reasonable approach is to divide up the variable opportunity among several milestones leading to the sale's culmination. For example, paying a small portion of the variable opportunity when the relationship goes beyond the formal calling stage (perhaps when a presentation is made to key staff beyond the front line gatekeepers), another larger portion paid when intentions are clarified and meaningful negotiations begin between key staff in both companies, an even more substantial portion paid once the contract is signed, and a final payout provided once revenue is booked.

The rising structure of variable payments should stimulate aggressive behavior toward the close of the sale. Any pay realized prior to offsetting revenue is based on the supposition that the upfront risk to the company is mitigated by the number of sales that actually will be consummated. After a specific number of failed attempts and subsequent coaching, the company is going to have to reconcile its compensation losses by removing the salesperson. Employment at risk is always the necessary and timely counterpoint to generous sale-based compensation.

Residuals add another wrinkle to the variable pay fabric. No company wants its sales staff retiring in place, finding no compelling reason to bring in new business, and comfortable enough with pay derived from a continuing revenue stream that was the product of their initial sale. If the salesperson has performed a significant and unique role in continuing the relationship and revenue stream between the customer and the company, residual pay cost justifies itself. In a relationship role, many sales personnel remain the primary source of problem resolution and establishing comfort between the company and the customer. Although this may detract from the individual generating new sales elsewhere, retaining critical business for the long term may warrant an additional reward beyond base salary.

Organizations approach residual pay in various ways. Those who utilize a descending residual rate during a specified period of time discount the value of a salesperson's impact on the revenue stream as the customer increasingly interacts successfully with the company through other members of the staff. A variation of this theme runs the residual at a constant rate for a lesser period of time before it is discontinued. As mentioned, not all companies provide for residuals. They consider any non-revenue generating customer service support included in base compensation.

If the sales staff feels it is being recognized and remunerated fairly for specified actions that contribute to retained business and increased earnings, and those actions are a pre-agreed upon part of the job, the means of compensation, whether residual or a component of base pay, becomes incidental to them. The issue for the company becomes one of aligning the economics of the revenue stream with fair compensation that sends a message balancing needs for retained and new business.

Team

Residual compensation, usually poorly conceived residual compensation, often surfaces a discussion about who is doing what for the customer. If sales compensation is predicated on influence, what then is the influence, if any, of the larger organizational universe? Do several interconnecting roles share in the persuasive process? If everyone who faces the customer is expected to renew business, generate customer interest in other products and services, and/or refer interested customers to a salesperson, should they all be eligible for variable compensation consideration? The answer is as much a product of the organization's culture and sense of participation and team as it is about economics.

As mentioned previously, a company should not be paying full value for each form of compensation if each of those forms is used to recognize the same result. The same premise applies to multiple players as well as multiple forms of pay. Companies have been known to lose control of the multiplying effect when paying for the referral, the sale, the renewal, and the cross-sell. Everyone who touches any aspect of these dimensions gets some form of variable recognition. Some even pay a collective bonus or incentive predicated on effective customer service. In the rush, to have everyone reap rewards for focusing on specific results, a company can forget to balance the sum of the compensation awarded to the involved population with the revenue and margins these actions generate. This is not to say that awards should not be given for exceptional behavior. But if extending the sale is inherently an expectation of the job, the persuasion required to achieve the result has to be put in perspective, weighted, and made part of the position's reasonable and targeted total cash compensation. And if two positions have the same target expectation, the total remuneration for success should be divided accordingly.

A brief word about indirect selling, and selling to resellers: Indirect selling is a hybrid of relationship and transactional selling. The distinction lies in the indirect seller's ability to maintain a productive relationship with the reseller to forecast appropriate product sales as well as provide a timely flow of goods through the channel. Indirect sellers should be compensated not for the ongoing sale of the product (for which they have no control), but for minimizing return shipments that are the product of poorly anticipated demand. Offering the reseller the appropriate products and supply ensures a healthy and lasting relationship between both companies. Selling only occurs in this function to the extent that the indirect seller can influence the size and mix of the reseller's buy.

Controlling Expectations by Establishing Parameters

Best practice compensation designers constantly keep these Rubber Chickens in the back of their minds:

 Always size the value of a sale before determining compensation for that result. Value should reflect an acceptable net of all expenses (to include compensation).

 Pay at risk (commissions, incentives, bonus) should be predicated on the degree of persuasion required.

 Commission pay should only be used when there is an expectation of volume.

 Total sales compensation for a sale should encompass all parties rewarded for influencing that sale.

 Factor benefits and participation in any longer term pay program when valuing the total being paid.

 Utilize appropriate (demographically and culturally aligned) non-cash recognition events and programs whenever possible. Factor the "value" of these opportunities into the total compensation value being attributed to sales.

The following summarizes the discreet behaviors associated with the various forms of selling and the method of compensation that most effectively rewards related results:

Aligning Selling Tasks With Compensation Forms

Type of Sale	Associated Tasks	Form of Compensation
Transactional—Customer Initiated	Efficient processing of the sale.	Base Salary.
	If required to cross sell, sell up, sell to a contest.	• Incentive pay for multiple sales or specific sale category targets met. • Possible team bonus for achieving sales targets in associated tasks
Transactional—Customer Initially Ambivalent	Determine customer needs, present options, close sale—low volume traffic.	Base salary and bonus for achieving overall sales targets.
	Determine customer needs, present options, close sale—high volume traffic.	Commissions for each type of sale made.
Transactional—Cold Call	Generate leads, secure interest, present product, negotiate specifics, close sale—low volume traffic.	Base Salary and Bonus for achieving sales targets.
	Generate leads, secure interest, present product, negotiate specifics, close sale—high volume traffic.	Commissions and possible commission accelerators or bonus for exceeding sales targets.

Aligning Selling Tasks With Compensation Forms (continued)		
Type of Sale	**Associated Tasks**	**Form of Compensation**
Relationship—Lead initiated or cold call	Qualify potential buyer, secure interest, present product, negotiate specifics, close sale, coordinate installation, manage process flow, service follow up, renewals, offer new products/ services.	Base salary and incentives for achieving specified targets in each of the designated selling processes.
Indirect to Reseller	Expediting orders, minimizing product returns based on poorly forecasted needs, offering new products for the channel.	• Base salary and incentives— account based. • Additional bonus for aggregate results when influencing solid reseller purchasing decisions.

Note: *The distinction between commissions, draw, bonus, and incentive compensation as well as individual and team awards will be discussed in more detail in Chapter 8.*

Preparing the Sales Staff for Bounce Back

Much remains to be coded once alignment has been achieved between determining the type of selling occurring and the type of compensation that will stimulate productivity without losing control of the value message or the economics of the sale. Most that remains will be taken up in subsequent chapters. One issue that is germane to sizing the amount of compensation awarded and managing staff expectations can be touched upon here, and those are sale reversals.

Not all sales are final. Not all contracts are lasting. A company's policy on how it wishes to treat returns or breach of contract with regard to recouping sale compensation sends a message about its values and performance expectations. Every company provides allowances for material defects, ambiguous marketing, buyer remorse, fraud and defalcation, and/or operational breakdowns. These allowances have to be factored into sizing any cost of sale but they may not necessarily reduce the compensation value of the sale.

The sales role is accountable, shared or otherwise, for qualifying the customer, ensuring that the buyer is clear about the goods or services being offered and the conditions under which they are being sold, and for mitigating any pressure or techniques that the company would not tolerate as ethical or professional. The consequences of a broken sale caused by anything outside the scope of the representative's role should not fall on that representative's compensation.

That said, if the sales representative has culpability for a busted sale, depending on the reason, the consequences can be severe, including termination. If the reasons for a sales reversal are a product of poor training, novice behavior, or a legitimate misunderstanding, it is appropriate to recover compensation. It is equally appropriate to develop procedures and documentation that safeguard against continued vulnerability on the part of the representative.

The method of recovery is also an important consideration. Draconian recovery approaches can not only reverse the sales representative's tangible fortune, they also significantly dampen the individual's emotional drive toward achieving success. The message has to be balanced. Responsibility for past actions needs to be coupled with consideration for future accomplishment. Passive behavior on the part of the company is equally dangerous. If no one is accountable for the net effect of their behavior, if no analysis and follow through is done, conditions that could eventually damage the company's reputation as well as its bottom line may become imbedded and extremely difficult to reverse. Selling is not an indiscriminate rush to daylight where the positive is accentuated and the negative glossed over. Selling is a measured and deliberate process with accountabilities that promote a solid cadre of staff who take pride in their achievements and responsibility for their disappointments.

Marketing Expectations

Once you have decided what you are paying for and how you are going to go about doing it and when, don't just publish a plan document and have your managers hold a series of early morning question-and-answer sessions. Market the hell out of your sales compensation program. The key is to continually link the staff to the desired outcomes of the plan. Companies should generate psychic equity on the part of their sales staff; an appreciation of how their results affect not only the revenue stream, but also the company's ability to invest and grow. The marketing message encourages sales personnel to adopt a business (not greed) orientation to their work.

Much of what follows assumes an open corporate culture. The Rubber Chicken here is clear and primary:

 It is a reality of business that if the staff distrusts management in one aspect of their work lives, there will be a compelling urge to distrust management in all aspects affecting their work lives.

Trust closes the distance between expectations and the unknown. If there is uncertainty as to the level of trust the staff has and the levels of management that affect them, address and dispel that uncertainty before moving on. If your climate is not what you want it to be, clean it up before implementing any compensation changes. Without the clean up, changes most likely will not be well received, regardless of how compelling they may appear to an outsider.

Marketing your compensation begins before the roll out period. It begins when you engage your core sales staff in the development and operational logistics of the plan. (There will be more on this in Chapter 6.) For purpose of marketing, "core" staff references those individuals who are mature, experienced, objective, and excellent to outstanding performers.

You want the core group to represent the issues that will concern the good to excellent performers on the sales staff. You want the core group to reinforce the merits of the plan once it goes public.

Prepare prior to publicizing the plan and orchestrate the sequence of communication; who says what to whom. Select the best media for your target audience when you present the plan. Don't cheapen the plan's impact by cutting corners or assuming knowledge not yet revealed by the audience. Go over extended scenarios of the plan to ensure your presentations illustrate how expected performance is rewarded. Use the core group to raise questions that may be asked by the sales force. Make sure all the communicators of the plan have the same answers for each question.

Immediately prior to publicizing the sales plan, contact your best producers one on one. Make sure they understand the intention and workings of the plan. Gauge their reaction before going public. It immeasurably enhances the company's credibility in the eyes of your elite sellers when their comments are taken to heart and adjustments made. It is equally impressive when management acknowledges and reflects upon the comments of their best performers and clarifies through discussion why the plan will go forward as initially conceived—"discussion" being the operative action. Never hesitate to rethink any aspect of the plan or its communication before the final product is revealed to the entire sales team. Once the box is open, it's open. Damage control, at that point, will be confusing and distracting to the audience and reflect poorly on management.

When you are ready to go public with the plan, gear your communication towar dialogue. Don't slip in a CD, push "play" and walk away—figuratively or literally. Don't wait for the feedback to trickle in. Follow up immediately as well as after a brief period of information integration. Set a reasonable time period to discuss the plan before implementation. Deal with any and all issues openly and constructively without a hint of defensiveness.

Goal Setting Dialogues

One of the most passionate issues in a sales plan has nothing to do with structure and everything to do with results: goal setting. No matter how well put together a plan is, no matter how carefully the initial communication is organized, if the goals are unrealistic no one affected will be listening. It has to be crystal clear and credible to the sales audience why specific goals have been set and why management feels that these challenges reflect the best business information available, and, most importantly to the team, why they can be met.

Unfortunately, the tendency in recent years has been to low ball goals. Setting conservative targets appears to be the product of either poor planning or a desire to hop over a bar lying in the road and call it a jump. Management then points behind them at the inert bar and wipes the sweat from their brow. What a jump! Another accomplishment worthy of reward has been achieved. Another comforting report can be forwarded to ownership.

"We have met the challenge and it is us." In the short term earnings will be shored up by stringent expense controls. Expense controls are management's panacea. Even an average manager can figure out how to reduce expenses. For some managers, it is all they can do. In the long term, and fewer executives gear toward the long term, the organization's viability, its sales staff, and its management talent are all weakened. Goal setting is what management really gets paid for. Staff has to have trust and confidence in their management's ability to earn their pay.

Discussions around goal setting are an opportunity to refocus the participant's on the plan message as well as its mechanics. Provide information to the group as a whole on what was discussed and how each question was resolved. Don't fall short of your time schedule. Make sure everyone knows that after two weeks, for example, whatever still sticks to the wall becomes operative. Further modifications can be made at a later date, but for now it's time to start the sales engine and move on.

Managing Ongoing Expectations

Once the plan is implemented, look for any and all credible opportunities to reinforce and analyze results with the participants. Demonstrate that there is active energy at play. Assessments won't die quiet deaths. Each will lead to actions that continue to support the selling process. Success will be capitalized upon and weakness will be shored up. Results will be looked at in the broader scope. What role did sales, marketing, distribution, merchandising, customer service, and product development play in the outcomes? Use the broader scope to focus the sales staff on the interrelationships of the entire business. Work on that psychic equity.

Celebrate success, collective achievement, and individual contribution. This can be a delicate process. The celebrations have to be credible and well orchestrated. Credibility implies genuine success, not the wholesaling of the definition. The sales staff has to believe that the success marker was righteously achieved. The celebration should be timely, as close to the accomplishment as possible. It should be forward oriented: great work heralded in anticipation of continued great work. It is not a retirement event.

When celebrating, have the right people publicizing and recognizing achievement—people seen by the sales audience as having influence and stature. These people should be able communicators, sincere and effective. If they are unable to convey genuine appreciation and enthusiasm position them with someone who can. Script their roles for maximum smiles and minimum sound. If they are better in small groups have them mingle after the more public ceremony. If they come off as empty headed without a script, reverse the strategy.

Target the needs of those being recognized and not the needs of those doing the recognition. Rely on experts in the people skills business to maximize the celebratory event. This does not mean creating lavish parties or elaborate proceedings; it means reflecting your company's value system in ways that optimize the celebratory effect.

Celebrating collective achievement binds the group together. Celebrating individual achievement affords the group role models to emulate. The manner in which you recognize exemplary individual performance should give others a sense of what they can aspire to. Again, every culture is different. Individual recognition may mean discreet acknowledgements through a bonus in the pay statement followed by more public recognition in the form of a desired status symbol. The objective of public recognition is good will and enthusiastic aspirations, not jealousy and distraction.

Marketing the sales plan and its outcomes requires a continual review of the plan's expectations and results by all parties affected. The plan structure should undergo formal scrutiny annually. A good plan may require some minor tweaking as goals are adjusted for the coming sales cycle. Every three years, the plan should be examined to determine if it is still in alignment with the direction of the company and the needs of the sales staff. Baring any unusual circumstances in the market or the company, a good plan should remain viable for at least three to five years. That period of time will afford the staff some stability and provide management a reasonable period to assess its impact on sales behavior.

What It Is

Compensation reaffirms your company's objectives and your operating style, aligns direction and corporate values, and builds trust. Specific forms of compensation drive specific behaviors. Compensation is more than pay; it can be about recognition, development, and inclusion. And sales compensation should always reward influence.

For all the focus and energy that effective compensation can create, there is a flip side: Some companies refuse to acknowledge the limitations of compensation, feeling that pay will solve all problems and reconcile all challenges.

Compensation cannot select the needed strategic information, align it to the company's priorities, nor set powerful business goals. Compensation cannot coach the staff and remedy performance situations. Compensation can encourage recruitment and retention, but it cannot make the selection decisions nor develop the rapport that makes a sales person want to stay with the company. Compensation will identify exceptional pay or performance circumstances, but cannot apply judgment in administering the plan. Compensation may provide motivation, but it cannot counsel. It can reinforce expectations, but it is a poor stimulate of change.

Compensation will never ever take the place of management.

Motivate Sales Managers: Capitalizing on Their Strengths

If there is a theme that permeates this book it is one of interconnections. Successful sales compensation is not about any one aspect of the process; it is about the process as a whole. Good strategizing can succumb to poor plan design. Plans are inoperative if the sales staff doesn't understand or is incapable of delivering. Nothing works if you can't measure the results and assess who is doing what and when.

The process completely breaks down when the delivery system fails. By delivery I am referring to all aspects of the communication and guidance system related to compensating for sales. That system is in the hands of sales management. What they say, how they say it, and how they reinforce and manage the resources dedicated to sales can make or break any reward program. This chapter will explore why managers succeed, why they fail, and what executive management needs to do to ensure continued success.

From Whence

There is a theory that proposes that managers are born not made. Something mysterious resides in the chemistry of those who lead. I avoid this theory. These misguided folks could be confusing charisma with management or choosing to ignore the impact that past experience and environment has on individual behavior in the here and now. Perhaps, for whatever reason, they just don't believe in training and development.

Truth be told, I am also a voice in the chorus that groans skeptically at most management training programs. In 30 some years, I have seen very little in the way of formal training that has had a lasting, positive affect on improving management performance. Training programs suffer from several ills. They are usually separated from the reality of the environment. Even if they are laden with case studies and organizational vignettes, they are rarely integrated into the day-to-day workings of the organization. It is an away experience; physically or metaphysically. People are "sent" to formal programs. It is something done "over there," separate and away from the work scene, away from the manager's manager. The lack of connection to the daily challenges of the job can be palpable.

The first place prize is a week away training. Second place is two weeks away. One always returns to work piled higher than when it was left. Time away just means a steeper set of stair to climb to get back to where you were. Occasionally, a well-intentioned boss will ask the returning manager about the quality of their experience. The answer rarely penetrates the superficiality of the inquiry or the manner in which the organization behaves. Having sent the junior manager away to gather wisdom and technique, the boss feels absolved of development responsibility. Let's get back to work.

Definitely a Rubber Chicken:

 Development, whether it is through formal training, mentoring, or the natural process of supervision, has to be an accepted and integrated part of the workplace and a daily role accountability of every supervisor.

The Wrong Whence

Before you can develop someone in the role of sales manager, they have to be selected. People take on the role for a host of reasons. The supervisor's first challenge is selecting those who want to manage for the right reasons. This can become additionally challenging if the sales managers are already in place. Whether in the selection process or when introduced to an inherited management team, one has to be aware of the four basic *wrong* reasons people choose for managing sales staff.

1. "If anyone is going to manage this unit it is going to be me. I'll be damned if I report to someone with less experience than I have. Worse, it could be that young kiss-ass, Frobish. The only way to prevent the wrong person from getting the job is to take it myself."

2. "I am the rainmaker. There was never anyone like me before and they won't see my likeness again. I can shape and mold the staff in my image. All they have to do is watch what I do. My effectiveness will rub off on those I manage. They will never be as good as me, but they'll be good enough. One rainmaker guiding several drizzle producers; what could be better for the company? We will blow the socks off any targets we are given. It will be my legacy to the organization."

3. "Sales managers make a decent salary and get an override for the unit's sales. With a predictable base I can finally pay off those nagging credit card bills. With the override I can start to save for that new boat—the portable, collapsible one. I can take that anywhere. Boy, do I love fishing. I'll finally be able to get to those streams and lakes above Big Cross. I figure in six quarters I should be debt free and spending my weekends fishing with that new reel I saw in the catalogue and those hand-tied flies Bob talked about last week. Boy, do I love fishing."

4. "I can't wait to see Schmedley at the next industry association meeting. When I tell him I made sales manager he will bust a gut. I have to remember to let him know about my sit downs with Emerson and the other members of the executive committee. I want him to walk away with an appreciation of how I am influencing the direction of the company. Well, at least how I am hearing about the direction before almost everyone else. I wonder if I can get new business cards printed in time for Amy's high school graduation. That ought to shut up my idiot brother-in-law for awhile."

Issues of protection, insulation, security, and ego are all the wrong reasons for moving into a management role, but too often they are the motivating factors. Few are so inexperienced in the ways of organizational life as to verbalize these drivers. They will be sure to impress upon the selector their skills and abilities. They will emphasize what a good job they will do. But rarely will these candidates, after the proper management probing, surface the sustainable reasons for accepting the challenges of management.

The Right Whence

A candidate for the role of sales manager should demonstrate an enthusiasm and sense of urgency when it comes to analyzing, planning, and executing sales goals. At the very least, they want to be actively involved in the process. And they have ideas—ideas ready for discussion.

Potential sales managers are people who enjoy developing others, not in a paternalistic manner, but inclusively. They are eager to spend the time and energy it takes to work collectively on a common mission. Concurrently, they are always looking for strength in their staff. They can define strength in meaningful and measurable ways. They don't want a team dependent on them. They want professionals with the skills and attributes needed to generate independent thinking and well-thought-out opinions. They know that building a strong staff from a solid foundation will allow the team to multiply its effect, good sales managers derive their greatest degree of satisfaction by guiding a group toward sustainable achievements that are a product of the whole being greater than the sum of its parts.

Once leadership has found people with the enthusiasm, experience, ethics, and an orientation for the job of sales manager, how do you capitalize on these basics? The answer is *alignment*. Sales management needs to know the context within which it functions. Sales managers need to be able to articulate where the company has evolved as an organization, where it wants to be, and how it wants to get there. They must know as clearly and precisely as possible what behaviors and results executive leadership expects, and have agreement with that leadership on the actions that need to be taken based on those expectations. Sales managers need to be clear on the degree of planning, supervision and coaching the job requires. They have to be aligned with the company's operating environment. Are they to be team-oriented or emphasize individual contribution? None of this can be left to assumption. These are topics where it's okay for executives to over-communicate.

Another Rubber Chicken:

 Sales managers have to trust executive management's intentions and agree with their ethics.

These are the single most binding issues in fashioning a successful sales management core. Not only does this speak to establishing a history of interactions built on common values, but a deep knowledge of executive intentions and ethics that allow for an understanding of boundaries and of when and in what form independent action can or should be taken. Trust and ethical alignment will transcend and release any log jams that surface in most tactically challenging situations.

Sales management is the bologna in the sandwich, positioned between executives and staff. Sales managers provide all forms of essential information up the corporate line: changing conditions in the field, staff concerns, qualitative results of corporate actions taken, pre- and post-intelligence on what is and can work as it relates to the customer, the sale of the product, and the commensurate remuneration of staff. In the opposite direction, sales managers ensure that staff is informed and aligned with the mission, that every management action is explainable and complimentary to the overall objectives of the company. They provide the staff with a productive perspective as to what is taking place several layers above. Sales managers make policy and procedure credible.

It is very much a balancing act, balancing their advocacy for all points of view, including their own. Balance occurs when the intention of bettering the corporate condition for all parties is achieved. If the trust and alignment chain is broken in either direction, not only will the current operation suffer, but it will take inordinate energy and consistent reinforcement of what should be accepted behavior to slowly and gradually instill confidence in future interactions.

Maximizing Motivation

Jed, our long-suffering executive, and I were inching closer to establishing a comprehensive reward program for his sales staff. As he took inventory of all the necessary elements involved in putting together an effective plan, he was especially pleased with his team of sales managers. He leaned back in his chair and smiled. "Sharp. Focused. Know what needs to be done." Jed's comfort zone was only briefly occupied. He bounced up and began pacing again. "How am I going to keep them? They are a relatively new group. I pay them well, but, hell, there is always someone out there who can pay them more. I know. I know. Money isn't the determining factor." He looked my way. "So?"

"So," I challenged. "Answer your own question. Why are they working here?"

Jed thought about it for a moment before answering. "I let them manage. I give them the resources and the perspective to do the job. I am clear about what needs to be done. I listen to them. And I recognize their accomplishments."

That is a great deal more than many other organizations provide. Put another way, Jed had established a climate of trust, respect, recognition, and clarity of direction coupled with the resources needed to meet the challenges and achieve.

I Let Them Manage

Putting aside for a moment what component will most effectively reward which result, the following is an experiential list of proficiencies that compromise the portfolio of a successful sales manager. This list is not meant to replace, for better or worse, the prolific "how to" materials on being an effective manager that currently laden credenzas everywhere. Rather, this is just an overview of the critical aspects of the job I have witnessed that can cause the issue of compensation to become secondary to those of the sales team's basic survival. Each of these sales manager abilities is a key compensable factor to be recognized and rewarded either through base salary or incentive pay.

Mentor

There is an overarching message in being a mentor. It implies the primary focus of the sales manager, as it relates to staff, in building and enhancing each member of the unit. It is an improvement-oriented, advisory, and somewhat protective role. Mentors emphasize achieving through staff, of being valued not just for what they do, but what they bring out in others.

Mentoring is the essence of establishing a legacy. Good mentors create lasting and independent strength. They leave the unit's members stronger. It can be an exceptionally difficult role for a sales manager whose career has been predicated on individual success in selling. Effective mentors are able to subordinate their egos, and readjust their personal priorities. It is a discipline best learned by being or having been mentored.

Demonstrate a Candor About Their Deficiencies

A realistic knowledge of one's weaknesses and of those biases that influence counterproductive behavior is not only commendable, but necessary in any management role. This kind of information rarely occurs through revelation. It requires feedback from credible sources, and feedback requires an open environment where there exists trust when sharing. Even in a trusting environment, a manager needs to have enough self-confidence to hear about potential blind spots without overreacting.

Both the dynamic of feedback as well as the specific comments have to be evaluated. Neither can be discounted. Whether the sales manager identifies with the comments or not, whether it is based on actual events or implied behavior, the source and motivation behind the feedback as well as the quality of the information has to be acknowledged, understood, evaluated, and digested. This sorting process has to be done as dispassionately as possible. A strong reaction to any information will probably shut down any further information.

Candor is relative to each organizational context. There are political, emotional, and cultural boundaries in any company that defines sanctioned behavior. There is always the reality that what one person sees as a candid assessment of an individual's areas for development can be seen by another as weakness to be either exploited or expunged. Where feedback has not been a tested and proven behavior, inroads in establishing it as a mechanism for self improvement should be taken carefully and in measured steps.

All action under this umbrella of self-examination is done with the intention of improvement. That can be a powerful statement both up and down the organizational ladder. It also supports two fundamental Rubber Chickens:

 Never surprise your manager.

At all times, a manager functions under the scrutiny of multiple audiences.

Sales managers and their bosses may have moments of constructive disagreement, perhaps conflict. There are going to be times when one or the other, or both, are frustrated. But the impetus behind the vast majority of those issues is usually remedied over time and through constructive conversation. There is one behavior, particularly if repeated, between boss and subordinate whose potential for irreconcilability is almost guaranteed. A sales manager must never come to a boss with a piece of dated news too late in the telling. Worse, a boss should never be sitting in a meeting and discover a piece of critical information that should have been known beforehand. These circumstances constitute capital breaches of preparedness and are followed with a commensurate deterioration in the leader's trust in the individual charged with overseeing that aspect of the business.

All too often the sin of omission is the result of someone who is in over their head, a sales manager who has lost control. All too often, that same manager assured the boss that everything was very much in control. It is never, ever a productive strategy to tell the boss you "can do" when you can't, to assure your leader that it's "no problem" when it is. A second similar misstep and the manager will become a liability in the position. However, when the feedback process is fully operational, when both parties appreciate the strengths and challenges facing the sales manager, it is rare than an individual is placed in a situation where they unknowingly will create a surprise.

Counseling sessions, a personnel move, or a conflict between two employees are typically examples of situations that put a manager on public display. The walls of the conference room or the boundaries of the department are illusions. There is no confidential sanctuary where such business is conducted. Word gets out accidentally or intentionally. The reactions and behaviors of those directly affected are always judged by three distinct audiences: bosses, peers, and the sales manager's other staff members. Reputations are formed, for better or worse, by the viewing audiences. Credits are given and debits are deducted based on the way a manager handled each situation.

Knowing one's self well enough and being comfortable, confident, and open enough to work under conditions of such scrutiny are the mark of managers who engender confidence. A sales manager who appreciates the

Rubber Chickens related to their ongoing development and performance will build both credibility and interpersonal worth with others—two key elements in successfully weathering any future challenges.

Remain Sensitive to the Disposition of Staff

The manager who doesn't believe in the power staff can generate from being sideline observers to the flow of interaction weaving through the department is doing himself a dangerous disservice. Not only is the staff a constant audience to the sales manager's behavior, but it is never a passive audience. How these people react to the stimuli around them will shape the productivity of the unit. Successful sales managers adhere to another Rubber Chicken:

 Everyone deserves respect until they have failed to continue to earn that respect.

Attended to that axiom is the belief that people are not stupid and *everything is ultimately discoverable.* Therefore, the times one can deceive and obfuscate are rare and the consequences significant. Everything a manager does has to be built on a solid, credible, and explainable foundation. Every interaction a manager has with each member of the staff is an opportunity to identify and discuss those issues and concerns that are on everyone's mind.

Directly Educate Around Process

Selling is an art form. It is not uncommon to confuse order takers and customer service representatives with salespeople. The confusion is reinforced when we reward these folks as if they were really selling. If the product sells itself, there is no selling activity going on. Managing in such surroundings is primarily operational, dealing with volume and distribution.

In a true sales environment, the manager takes on the role of a coach, providing guidance in the nuances of the process. How does one approach a prospective client, qualify them, and present offerings that meet their needs, negotiate, and close the sale? A sales manager can observe, critique, adapt, and share methods and techniques that he or she has found effective. Raw attributes and skills can be honed and an appreciation can be gained for the finer points involved in the selling process.

Selling extends beyond the obvious target clients and into the sales representative's own organization. While most sales personnel are inclined to absorb the selling wisdom of competent coaches when it comes to dealing with clients, they often fail to see the relationship between good selling skills and corporate interaction. They fail to see their company colleagues as clients and customers. The sales manager has both the vantage point and responsibility of helping the seller connect the dots. The same skills being sharpened on the outside can help the seller work well with others on the inside, particularly in the areas of forming partnerships and resolving conflicts with staff that directly or indirectly share in the customer experience.

How often have we seen the Jekyll and Hyde in sales staff? Nicest guy you'd want to meet with the customer and an ogre when it comes to dealing with distribution and shipping, billing, or customer service. Effective insiders are seen by others as part of the company and not lone wolves darting in and out of the pack when it is only to their own advantage. Effective insiders are perceived as contributing to the whole, of providing support and understanding even when it doesn't directly affect their own material gain. Sales managers can shepherd relationships, prevent corporate collisions, and counsel their staff in the best techniques to further their interactions with others.

Manage Rumors

Rumor has been the subject of examination since the first grapevines took root in companies. Organizations have tried to stymie it, or manipulate it to their advantage. Some even believe the accuracy of rumor, its speed in dissemination, and the route it takes through a company can be a sign of corporate health.

Quite often rumor is nothing more than perception wired into a distribution network. There is an irritating axiom around perception and reality: the belief that perception is reality. It's irritating because mere perception, if believed to be valid, can close the door to further discussion or exploration of what is fact, half-fact, conjecture, and falsehood. Perception is reality only if we want it to be. If we trust that our perceptions are based on some degree of objective rigor, it is all well and good. But if one grabs a rumor in midair and gobbles it up as truth without examining its origins, what does that say about the corporate population, its trust in the company, and its predisposition? Why should the perceptions of ignorant minds whose ideas were formed from half truths (plastered onto too easily retained comic book venues) become my reality? Why should they be tolerated as anyone's reality? Whatever happened to getting at the truth of an issue instead of always looking for the easy way out?

For better or worse (and mostly worse), rumor will always exist—fueled by fear, greed, vengeance, a craving for influence or recognition, or a host of other less than desirable attributes. Rumor fills in wherever a communication vacuum exists, a vacuum of silence or one created by an excess of meaningless noise. In that vacuum lies the key to rumor management.

Rumors can be neutralized before they even germinate through the use of frequent, complete, prioritized, and proactive quality communication. The best, most credible source of that communication is the sales manager.

An effective sales manager is aware of the issues on the staff's collective mind and aware of conditions in the company. An effective sales manager is able to anticipate what needs to be known and time its dissemination, so that staff can incorporate new information as a matter of routine without being distracted from their primary mission of productivity. This is a tall order. It requires a good network within the company structure to maintain awareness of what is going on, all around active listening skills to catch oblique signals and ensure that messages are having their intended consequence, and a sense of the best media, setting, and emphasis when communicating. Above all it requires the staff's trust. All of these skills and attributes involve constant practice and exercise.

At some point even in the healthiest of companies, rumors will surface. In a positive environment staff will approach management for validation. Even in a less than optimal organization, staff will observe the manager's behavior to gain cues regarding the worth of the rumor. Managers whose demeanor sends a clear message that they are not going to get caught up in the theatre that is rumor mongering, go a long way in settling staff, strengthening their own credibility, and providing a forum for rational dialogue around the issues. As mentioned before, managers are always on display to multiple audiences. How they perform in the midst of rumor bantering is no exception.

Educate Indirectly

An effective sales manager gains an intrinsic high from the accomplishments of the sales staff in the absence of that manager. This is the ultimate measure of a manager's effectiveness: how staff handles a situation without cover of leadership. It comes as a product of teaching "why" as well as "how." It comes from watching while others learn through the "doing." It is attending client meetings as a coach and not as the lead representative of the company. It is about knowing when to let go and knowing when the salesperson has enough of the fundamentals to push out on their own without fear of self-destructing. It is about teaching problem-solving techniques and not solving the problem for the sales staff. It is about getting sales staff to see the underlying issues and which alternatives lead to the best decisions. It is also about knowing when to step in so as to avoid a pending disaster that could have motivational repercussions.

In addition to generating self-confidence in each sales rep and ultimately strengthen the unit as a whole, there is another byproduct to measured teaching; the staff knows where they stand and why. Micromanagers and active interventionists don't often realize the message they are sending. Salespeople who value independence and a sense of contribution will wonder if they are meeting expectations every time the sales manager swoops into a situation that appeared to be under control, or each time the sales rep's every action is scrutinized and reviewed. There will be a period of time where uncertainty and frustration will dominate thinking. That will be followed by the realization that the manager's over involvement is not a product of the rep's deficiencies, but rather the manager's. It is then the rep realizes he or she will never be allowed to fully flourish, that value will always be marginalized. The representative has two choices: give up or get out. The good ones get out.

Managers who educate leave a legacy of capable professionals who are able to handle tough situations. Well-trained salespeople know they are good because they have been given the opportunity to demonstrate their abilities and have had their successes reinforced through greater challenges and independence. The relationship that the staff has with its direct manager is one of the fundamental variables in staff retention. The respect and rapport generated through a collegial approach to learning can go a long way toward cementing that relationship.

Plan and Assess the Business Condition in Their Area of Responsibility

This is a basic role that some sales managers find painful. If they are disposed to being doers and typically function in the moment, it is understandable that taking stock through trend information or forecasting into the future are going to be challenging disciplines. But the essence of effective sales management requires that these fundamental roles be undertaken if for no other reason than the successful managers never have to go it alone. The nature of their job is to organize and maximize the resources available to them. That can only be achieved within the context of a plan and the realities impacting that plan.

Give a good sales manager a map and she immediately begins forming an intelligence gathering plan. What indices are required to best understand the territory and the clients? What are the best sources of information? How will information be gathered and debriefed? How will the intelligence machine be kept running so an ongoing assessment process can be fed? This manager will work with finance and marketing to clarify what best measures the conditions they wish to examine. Her sales staff will become both the final audit in validating the markers to be measured and the primary sources from which to gather the data.

Most sales staff are trained in supplying the majority of field information requested. The gathering process should not be haphazard or undervalued. The importance of the process in the future planning of sales has to be emphasized at the outset. It will have a direct impact on bottom line earnings. The collection instruments (whether templates in a computer, checkmarks, free response on a form, regular group sessions, weekly sit downs with the sales manager, or all of these) need to be devised, tested, and evaluated before being introduced into the process.

Assessments have to be framed for maximum effect. The media, the format, and the timing should be designed to capture the attention of those decision-makers charged with endorsing any next step recommendations or actions. Maximum effect needs to be qualified with the context of each organization. What is considered low key in one company may be seen as lights and sirens in another. Again, a good sales manager knows the target audience and knows what approach will best reflect the appropriate emphasis.

Effective sales managers anticipate. They know the follow-up questions most likely to be asked and the information they will need in response. They know the attention tolerance of their management and can predict the topic areas that will be probed more aggressively. Much of that foreknowledge will find its way into the measures and gathering process that is being developed well in advance of any presentation.

Know When to Act

We have all heard the term analysis paralysis. That condition surfaces rarely among sales managers. Most sales leaders see themselves as problem-solvers and, if anything, there is a tendency to load and fire simultaneously. The consequences from such exuberance can be problematic. At best the manager may solve the immediate problem, but the cost may be at the expense of strengthening staff, addressing related or longer-term conditions, and reinforcing their own calm and deliberate credibility.

There are those sales managers who feel their own worth in the organization lies in their ability to put out fires. These firemen are to be watched closely. You may often find them in the corner fanning embers and waiting for the flames to erupt. Only when everyone smells the smoke and sees the blaze will they save the day. Problem solvers can become problem creators or passive witnesses to events that could have been remedied prior to crisis.

It is far better to value and recognize problem prevention over problem resolution. Problem prevention can be achieved when the sales team has a clear understanding of what is critical and can interpret the signs that foretell of a problem in the offing. Problem prevention can be achieved when everyone on the sales team knows what their roles in problem management are, and when to inform and when to act. The sales manager is the educational and operational conduit in problem prevention.

But not all problems can be prevented, and that's when an effective sales manager is faced with deciding when and how to act. Most problems should be seen as growth opportunities for someone. The sales manager needs to place that someone at the fulcrum of the resolution strategy and actively coach them through the process. The time invested in working with others to arrive at lasting solutions is well worth it if future problems can be prevented through staff awareness or if the team is better equipped to independently handle any similar situation should it occur. Obviously, if the problem requires immediate or extraordinary action the coach becomes an active and decisive player. In these situations, a postmortem with the team is the best alternative to guiding others through the resolution process.

Provided that the staff member did not ignite the situation, problem prevention and resolution affords the sales manager with an opportunity to recognize staff not just symbolically, but meaningfully. Each problem prevented, each situation taken care of quickly and thoroughly is worth something to the organization in real dollars saved and time dedicated toward selling and away from fixing. A measured "well done" with an equally measured tangible remuneration can go a long way in cementing loyalty and longevity with the staff member and those observing the recognition celebration. Recognition should never be seen as an entitlement and any remuneration should vary in type. It may be a one-time bonus, or a special perquisite, or a travel opportunity, or a handshake from the CEO. Whatever it is has to be meaningful to the recipient, genuine on the part of the company, and proportional to the event being hailed.

Recruit Quality Individuals

At best recruiting is a crap shoot, which is to say that it is a gamble. But the odds are more in favor of the sales manager playing the recruiting game than in favor of those who are sitting in a casino pulling the handle of a one-armed bandit. And the odds increase when a sales manager knows not only the rules of the game, but how to put a little extra spin on the employment dice.

The game starts before recruitment and well before selection. There are two overused phrases that have been so abused they anesthetize the listener to their meaning and intent. I first ran across "employer of choice" several decades ago. A human resource manager kept adding this tag line whenever she mentioned the name and location of her company. It was an all or nothing statement. It was never just the XYZ Company. It was always "the XYZ Company, THE employer of choice in blah blah blah New York." She could never tell me why the company was THE employer of choice. Although I suspect it might have had something to do with the fact that it was the only company with more than 10 people employed in that part of New York.

I heard the other more recent idiot expression from a big city newspaper editor. His was a "destination company." Visualize people staggering across the mountains just to work for his tabloid. Why was it a destination company? "Because, we are the best of the best." Repeated attempts at defining "the best" proved fruitless.

Both concepts do have validity if they are grounded in specifics and are an accurate reflection of the company. Used carefully and meaningfully they can enhance the image of an employer. But if they are empty platitudes, parroted repeatedly by management representatives who haven't a clue why they are being used, the company is made to look like a refuge for idiots.

If people are seeking out your firm because of its management vision, if its results are envied, and you have an earned reputation for valuing staff as you value customers and investors, there will be more than enough applications and phone calls of interest from which to select future staff. If competitors and customers speak of your business in reverent terms, the word will get out to prospective employees.

Every company should have the "problem" of separating the best fits from a pool of ready applicants and never having to worry about where to find suitable talent. A truly desirable place to work has applicants at the ready in hot or cold labor markets. But a company doesn't become THE place to work overnight. Those previously mentioned attributes are based on a successful track record. What a company does day in and day out builds on their reputation. Every action, positive and not so positive, becomes part of their invisible recruitment brochure. The employment pool is being filled before you ever need to go to the well.

I leave it to the recruiting professionals to argue the merits of referred applicants. An obvious positive of a source referred by a known source is that the applicant is less of an unknown variable. A not-as-obvious negative of a referral made from within the company is the potential of institutionalizing similar employee characteristics. This may or may not be what an organization wants. Regardless, reality dictates that sales managers keep their feelers out in the marketplace in advance of any staffing needs. This has to be seen as a necessary part of the job. And such networking should be a planned strategy not a haphazard process.

Sales managers need to know what sales skills and attributes are transferable from other industries and jobs into their own environments, or what roles from other companies with a similar approach to sales will work in their organization. Relationships should be cultivated with these other companies through professional associations and business interactions. Such relationships only work when there is a balanced give and take from all parties. Sometimes it makes good long-term sense to recommend a candidate to another company. Besides the good will it generates, that individual may reappear someday to assume an even more critical role in your company. The receiving company who obtains a valued resource may reciprocate or refer another organization to you. Holding people back and coveting them never produces the desired retention result. Eventually everyone comes to realize what type of employer you are and makes tracks in another direction.

A good sales manager appreciates that formal reference checking, because of the liability associated with disclosure, is wholly lacking in needed specificity. With a measured degree of reservation as to the quality of the information, having a number of close contacts in the applicant's business sphere help triangulate a candidate's historical achievements and shortcomings.

Establishing connections with ethical recruiters is also beneficial. They not only act as go-betweens should recruitment become an earnest endeavor, but they also serve as intelligence gatherers on the general compensation practices within targeted companies. The term "ethical" is intentionally inserted. Ethical recruiters do not inflate values for the sake of increasing their retainer. Ethical recruiters do not overstate the skills and resumé of a candidate. Ethical recruiters dig deeper, ignoring the applicant's titles and looking for values and performance that align with your company. Ethical recruiters are seeking a lasting relationship based on their service. They are not going to blow that relationship by cutting corners or realizing short-term gains at the expense of ignoring a company's longer-term needs.

At some point, intelligence gathering makes way for direct contact. Formally or informally, the interview process begins. The selection process is perilous enough without drawing blindly from a stack of applications and going right to interviews. The more endorsements you have about the applicants, the more a sales manager knows about what each applicant possesses, the greater the likelihood for pointed and productive interview exchanges, aligned with both the needs of the company and those seeking the position.

Foreknowledge of an applicant is equally valuable in judging their interview dynamics. It is an oversimplification to assume that if anyone can sell themselves in an interview it is a salesperson. Every seasoned manager has met the applicant who pulls off an effective interview but can't find their way to the restroom and back on the first day of work, and their situation doesn't improve after a month. Interview is theatre and these performers have their part down cold: good eye contact, strong handshake, positive approach, and that well-spaced pensive look before the rehearsed, superficial response. They'll ask a question or two, harmless and non-confrontational.

They will leave with an impression of competence and compatible chemistry, but it is a one-act play. After the orientation period a demonstrated lack of content depth and decision-making ability will make you wonder why he or she was hired in the first place.

Conversely, we all know of people who make great employees but somehow blow their career opportunities at the point of interview. They are too understated or their confidence comes across a little too strong. They don't talk enough or they talk too much. They ask pointed questions, or they assume they know the answer and never ask the expected question. Fundamentally, they haven't been schooled in the art of the interview.

When stuck with a dud, who is to blame for the end result? In part it is the incompetence of the interviewee. In part, it is the interviewer not doing his or her job correctly. Even if the potential pool has been prescreened by someone in human resources, good interviewing takes work and preparation to differentiate the showman from the salesman.

Successful managers know what they want from an interview. They employ the same active listening and interaction skills they use with clients to dig into the motivations and work history of the applicant. They search for examples of a strong work ethic, enthusiasm, and a value system in line with their own company's. They look for personal confidence and pride in past achievements and potential challenges. They want specifics that will reflect content knowledge.

Sales managers know how to read the signs; ask open ended questions, use hypothetical situations, and watch body language from start to finish. They look for a sense of humor and perspective (how the applicant picks up on comments and the ease with which they express themselves). They project how the applicant will fit into the organization. They may have the applicant interview with a small cadre whose judgments and counsel the manager values.

Good job candidates will be watching and waiting evaluating the time it takes for the manager to follow up and eventually make a "go" or "no go" decision. An effective sales manager takes all the preliminary information that has been gathered, applies it to the interview, collects the thoughts of others involved in the selection process, and moves swiftly to make a well-informed decision. A successful manager wants the selection process to confirm and reinforce in the applicant's mind the positive feelings they have about the organization and its leadership. And after all that, it may still take six months to a year to confirm that the hire was indeed the right selection.

Ensure Bench Strength and Have a Depth Strategy

Good planning is interactive and ongoing. If you overlay the business, sales, and staffing plans there is symmetry. The business and sales plans will tell you what staffing is needed now and in the immediate future, not only in numbers, but in skill sets. All planning breaks down when symmetry breaks down—people spend too much time on the here and now and not enough time on the future and the "what-ifs." Staff planning breaks down when people avoid constructive dialogue around issues of competency and development.

More than compensation, the challenge of the assignment, the vision of the company, or its reputation in the market, the manager relationship can be the pivotal point in retaining staff. If that manager embodies the values and direction of the organization, if that manager can align those dynamics with the best interests of the staff, if that manager can be candid and open and positively oriented, then the employee has good reason to want to remain with this leader.

If a sales manager wants to keep good talent, that talent has to know how they fit into the plans of the company. No commitments or guarantees should be made, only a mature discussion of where current individual performance and projected personal development is potentially going to take someone (or not take them), provided that all forecasts are realized. "Here is where we see the business going. Here's how we see you fitting into our future plans. Here's what you and I need to do to get you ready for that future. What do you think?" It is fundamentally as simple as that; markers projecting the business progress, proactive assessment of staff, development steps identified around specific time frames, and dialogue and commitment from the incumbent. And then there must be follow-through.

Simple can always be made complex. Staff assessment and development can be taken to an extreme, orchestrated to run amuck. If your business and sales plans have a vitality that requires nimble fine-tuning as market conditions change, you should be wary of building an Institute of Training and Development. The Institute may do a splendid job of creating and structuring experiences that prepare staff for challenges, but the challenges may have long since changed. I have seen assessment practices that are ends in themselves, multifaceted permutations on a myriad of indices that over a series of weeks grind out voluminous evaluations. Such complexity comes with two huge historical problems: they take time and they disenfranchise the manager.

Then there is the avoidance factor. If a sales manager is really a manager, they are assessing, communicating, and developing on an ongoing basis. Not just out counseling the fellow who is not meeting his numbers—that's too proscribed. Staff planning is about engaging all the staff. It is part of the sales manager's job, day in and day out.

Developing staff is the most difficult and sensitive aspect of the management role and, therefore, it is the part most easily pushed to the side until there is no other alternative but to deal with it. And when there is no other alternative, it is usually too late to gain any mileage from the process. A good person leaves because they didn't know that the organization saw them as a key future player. Another sales member wastes time and energy developing transactional skills in an evolving relationship environment. The group begrudgingly carries one member, a nice guy who should have been redirected months, if not years, before.

And that surfaces another telling point. If the sales manager does not have their own development plan, it is highly unlikely that they are going to be working toward those ends with others. In some organizations, management functions under the false expectation that their competency is considered infinite, that they stand ready and equipped to assume any challenge. There is no need in addressing development—they are already there. There is also a macho executive ethic pervasive in some companies that serves to reinforce a lack of dialogue around development for the inner circle of players: "Real executives don't talk about such personal issues, you just get to tough out whatever is dealt you. You got problems with that? Well maybe you aren't cut out for the job. It's supposed to be lonely at the top." The source of these vacuums, whether ignorance or timidity, has to be countered from the highest executive levels and new ground rules established applicable to all functions in the organization. Without that action staff development will have limited credibility in the company.

But not all staffing needs can be satisfied through development. Sometimes the gap between current and needed abilities and experience is too great. Sometimes the required staffing needs grow too dramatically to be covered by the existing talent pool. Immediate needs can disrupt the conventional practice of promoting from within and hiring new staff only at lower entry points.

Appreciate the Perils of Filling the Void Externally

Although a practical solution under such circumstance, hiring experienced staff from the outside has implications that have to be considered before the selection process begins. Each new hire brought in above the established entry points sends potentially disruptive or distracting messages (intentional or otherwise), to the existing employee population. Comparisons are made relative to probable pay, career competition, shifts in company performance expectations, and opportunities for recognition and attention.

In the absence of dialogue, rumors will reflect the existing level of anxieties from the collective group and each of its individual players. It is not a sign of weakness or abdication to sit down with your current staff and ensure they understand why the outside hire is necessary and why the candidate selected will have experiences and skills that complement but are not resident with potential candidates already on staff. If anything, it is a sign of strength to be able to have an open discussion about staffing that invests the sales group with a sense of psychic equity in the direction of the unit.

If the manager has been candid with each sales member with regard to their strengths and areas of improvement or development, if each sales person understands what it takes to move ahead financially and career-wise, the discussion should be clarifying and reaffirming, not anxiety-producing or combative. If a staffing announcement produces an outburst of personalized frustration, anxiety, or anger, the ground work has not been properly laid and, quite candidly, the manager will get the reaction he or she deserves.

Compensation folks habitually do salary and range analysis to see where outliers fall with regard to correlating staff compensation to length of experience and performance. The exercise is done in search of parity. Senior players with solid performance records should be earning more than junior players in the same type positions with equally solid performance. Universally, such analyses point out that parity is rarely realized when comparing a senior player who has gained their experience through longevity within the organization to a senior player hired from the outside. The former outsider almost always has a higher level of compensation.

Managers grieve over the starting salaries for new incumbents, often begrudgingly paying more than they would like and using "market conditions" as their universal excuse. Without going into a discussion of the merits of creatively segmenting pay or extolling the virtues of promoting the total compensation package, it must be said that few managers consider the current staff in their new hire decision. The untested candidate starts out equal to or ahead of the veteran and, unless the veteran is promoted first, the gap is never made up.

At some point in time the veteran will come to realize the difference in compensation and often their only perceived remedy is to leave the organization and jump ahead in a new company. It is not only the compensation difference that stimulates movement away from the company, but a sense of betrayal. The trust relationship has been broken. The feeling that the organization was acting in the employee's best interest has been compromised and a bad message has been sent. But there is another reaction the veteran employee can have, and it is even more disruptive and personally destructive than departure: safe behavior. The veteran does just enough to avoid progressive counseling, just enough to behave safely within the performance parameters established for the job. Psychic equity has left the building. A sense of personal fulfillment has been replaced by the gaming routines associated with just surviving. People stop caring. This conduct focuses on another Rubber Chicken.

 Safe behavior mires and eventually kills a company.

It is harder to document, discipline, and correct safe performance than truly poor performance. But safe behavior has to be addressed, changed, or eradicated. It is that dangerous. It is that deadly. And it should never be given reason to rise up.

If a manager has to pay a newbie more, something meaningful has to be done to establish parity with the veteran staff. Shoot the first person who holds up the "it would be an exception to policy" shield and adopt a flexible approach to all reward mechanisms available; value the veteran in some meaningful fashion that creates that parity in the veteran's mind. If that can't be done, or salary adjustments can't be initiated, a gap will fester and the negative consequence will be far greater than the intended value the new incumbent will bring to the unit.

Bring Gravitas to the Table

Sales management is serious business, yet the too-serious sales manager fails in the role as often as the one who is too casual. Success comes through what could be best described as a catalytic collision. Success is the reaction of individual maturity, balance of perspective, self-awareness, sensitivity to surroundings, and confidence in engaging the uncomfortable, all constructively meshed with role expectations highlighted previously. No one can effectively mentor, educate, plan, assess, staff, keep order in the frenetic world of sales, and be decisive without bringing a calmness born from a seasoned and introspective depth of experience.

To Sell or Not to Sell—There Is No Question

Sales managers, even those who know what it takes to be successful, are all too often entangled in two nets which require help from their boss to untangle. The first net will attempt to ensnare them in their former role as a super salesperson. The second net will drag them down in a plethora of information.

Whether the organization asks or the individual wants to, sales managers who continue to sell as a regular part of their jobs often remain salespeople first and managers second. What appears to be a cost effective move on the organization's part brings into question whether the group really needs a manager or just a senior player who acts as a lead problem-solver and part-time mentor. Managers are paid to manage. As mentioned previously, there is a lot to being an effective sales manager both pertaining to the present and the future impact of the unit…and direct selling isn't part of that equation.

Some organizations defer, or abdicate, the decision of whether the manager should be selling. They let the manager decide for himself. There are new managers who will eagerly return to their comfort zone by spending time back on the line. But this division of focus, of being an individual contributor and a manager of others, is rarely effective. Managing is a full-time profession, a step in a different direction. If the sales manager isn't made to appreciate the distinction, the company won't get full value from the assignment and, ultimately, the individual will be less than satisfied with the role.

Logically, selling and managing simultaneously presents some interesting and practical challenges as to who gets what existing and new accounts.

If established accounts are allowed to remain with the sales manager the situation can build intramural resentment. Sales staff may feel they are denied an established base of income or the lack of opportunity to mine and develop these accounts properly. Keeping the more difficult accounts may cause the sales manager to spend too much time managing the relationship to the detriment of their other responsibilities. Instead of binding the unit, the sales manager with a divided role can create distractions and counterproductive behaviors.

Information Overload

Organizations expect managers to stay on top of prevailing conditions, to both correct problems and analyze trends. Additionally they are to assist in the forecasting of events that may affect product merchandising, staffing, pricing, and marketing. This can appear to be an overwhelming challenge to someone who has had to previously manage only one person (themselves). Even more intimidating is the host of reports and information being supplied from numerous staff entities whose existence seems dependent on the amount of paper or electronic files generated in a given month. Each entity is an authority on their seemingly critical piece of minutia.

The initial tendency of a new sales manager is to try to understand all the information being thrown at them and to stay on top of the data. The initial challenge of the new sales manager is to avoid analysis paralysis—more and more information leading to less and less action. The secondary danger in running this race is letting the information control management rather than the other way around. The question is not of what information I have and therefore what decisions can I make. The question is, "What decisions do I have to make and what information is needed to make those decisions?" Every other piece of scrubbed and polished data can be put aside.

It takes discipline and support from higher levels to stand up to the cost analyst in charge of report number 23.0002 and ask, "What has that report, or portion of that report, got to do with my current and future needs?" (and then to flush that report if the answer is unacceptable). Sales managers are not in business to justify the existence of information generators; it works the other way around. Data has to be put in perspective for the new sales manager, both in word and example. That is the organization's responsibility to its management.

Even with the right amount of information there has to be an established balance between tactical and strategic perspectives to keep sight of the target issues and key problems. Balance is a learned behavior that keeps the sales manager from overreacting, from pondering the abstract at the expense of the concrete, or from liking the muck over the high ground. Imbalance impairs vision and poor vision can produce collisions.

Compensating Sales Managers

Jed has the right management people and he has a leadership structure that makes sense for his organization. The topic shifts to compensation and how to pay sales managers. There are a few universal rules that apply in maintaining sound pay practices.

☆ Always think total compensation. Pay is just one aspect of total compensation. Don't forget the total value of health, welfare, capital accumulation programs, and other non-cash components when establishing values for just one element.

☆ Keep fixed costs, such as base salary, which are often not directly linked or measured by contribution, to earnings, and keep climbing year to year regardless of specific financial performance.

☆ Where possible, tie as much of your cash compensation levels to economic results achieved. This may encompass revenue generation, productivity enhancements, or expense reductions. Compensation should always cost justify itself.

☆ Don't overpay for the same result by fully compensating for that result in multiple components.

☆ Don't create a pay program whose elements are so detailed and so rigid that it takes the place of management decision making. Management is an evaluative judgment process. No pay program can replicate the human factor. Pay plans support managing, they don't replace it.

Cash compensation for sales managers falls into three broad categories:

1. Base Salary.
2. Bonus or Overrides.
3. Incentives.

Each exists to reinforce a particular type of performance-reward message. Mixing those messages and the pay vehicles used to reward achievement usually creates confusion and always results in a less than optimal utilization of funds.

Base

Base pay need not be just a vehicle to compensate for day-to-day management responsibilities or for demonstrating, through actions, the behaviors the organization considers fundamental to sound employee and client relations. Base salary can also be used to reward the baseline selling results achieved by the unit: those results that attain revenue or margin dollars which either cover the costs of operating the unit or meet minimal, but acceptable, returns. Base pay can recognize the manager's role in securing the fundamental earnings required of the unit to remain viable. Achievements beyond these threshold measures will provide the organization with results investors will find competitively sound; results where the incremental gains realized can be shared with management and staff through other forms of compensation without decrementing the profitability being targeted.

Bonus and Overrides

When sales goals are met or exceeded the primary reward vehicle for the manager is either through a bonus or an override. In either case the results achieved have to reflect the contribution the individual made through the management of the entire staff, not just the gains accomplished by his rainmakers. A sound bonus program avoids aggregate totals and looks to the median performer. How did each sales member contribute to the overall results of the unit? Bonus dollars should not only accurately reflect the sales managers' past impact, but encourage them to spread their attention throughout their entire staff in the sales cycles that lie ahead.

An override is typically used when sales managers are running a more transactional (as opposed to relationship-building) selling environment and where they have strong and frequent hands-on posture with the staff. Managers with overrides typically are paid lower base salaries. Their monthly income is predicated to a great extent on the transactions their staff secures, gaining as the unit excels. Overrides can be a percentage of every dollar brought, or become activated once threshold goals are achieved, with base salaries covering minimally acceptable unit results, or, in some cultures, overrides can be paid out predicated on a more formulaic process with ramps and slopes as certain sales targets are achieved by the staff.

Bonus is usually paid after semi-annual or annual results have been achieved. A relationship sales environment may necessitate a longer sales cycle between initial client contact and sales closure, thus making commissions and overrides unrealistic. As in overrides, bonus payouts can be activated after the unit has first met sales goals that are part of base compensation criteria. Some companies will divide the bonus opportunity among various events in the sales cycle. Leads that generate formal presentations or verified intentions by the client are rewarded, as is the closing of the sale.

The sales manager can share in residuals earned if the manager is involved in the client relationship beyond the signing of the agreement, and that relationship generates new sources of revenue not part of the original agreement. It would be a better practice and one in keeping with a desire for simplicity and fiscal responsibility to utilize base salaries for any sales management activity not directly resulting in revenue booked.

Incentives

Incentive pay criteria focus on strategic challenges facing the sales unit. The criteria address high-level issues that require an added measure of emphasis concurrent with these challenges. Examples include dramatically shifting the sales focus of the unit toward a particular product or service line, penetrating specific and exceedingly difficult or complex territories or markets, developing depth and coverage within the sales unit where there was a significant absence of attention, or sustaining aggressive trends beyond the sales cycle. The accomplishment of these objectives run parallel, but are not always dependent on the revenue results rewarded through bonuses or overrides. These objectives are also not directly related to day-to-day sales management, which is paid through base salary. Each incentive criteria has to be quantitatively measurable and sized as to its bottom line impact. That impact, when realized, forms the basis for an appropriate incentive payout opportunity. Because of their strategic nature, incentives are typically measured throughout a year's time. The nature of the objective, not the calendar, should always drive the time frame. For this reason, the precept of paying as close to the event as possible, which can be accomplished in bonus and override situations, is not always administratively possible with incentive pay.

The Comfort Zone

Not every sales manager is comfortable with the realities surrounding pay, either its components or target compensation. A former sales person whose orientation has always been to judge value only by the compensation earned may find it hard to reconcile the challenges of their leadership role with the fact that they may make less than the rainmakers they manage. They may have been the rainmakers at one time. They once felt in more complete control of their income potential. They sold, they earned. It was as simple and straight lined as that. Now they may feel that their income is dependent on others.

There are surely tradeoffs: the satisfaction of influencing events through others, career opportunities, and capital accumulation programs to include tangible equity in the company. Sales managers have to come to terms with the rewards and challenges of managing over the rewards of selling. As mentioned, previously the executive has the responsibility of laying out the role as clearly as possible and the candidate has the obligation of reconciling his or her past with a new future.

Sometimes a duck is really a duck, and not a swan. After repeated attempts, it is clear to all that the person holding the sales managers position is so out of alignment with what is needed that the gap cannot be closed, be it related to skills or disposition. In those situations, the executive in charge is doing the sales manager a disservice keeping them in the role. As devastating to the individual as it might appear to be, it is far more humane to move the manager out of the role than to have them continue to tread water trying to make a go of it. Everyone surrounding the individual in trouble stagnates as the process is protracted. The sales manager becomes a victim of the generosity of their superior. In the end, the delay only postpones the inevitable and time spent redirecting ones priorities, career, and potential life, is lost. It is a perfect recipe for fostering bitterness and hopelessness.

No Sales Manager Is an Island

As pivotal as the sales manager role is to the organization, it is always dependent upon its own leadership support to succeed. Strong, effective managers hire a strong and effective staff. Even strength requires a support network that is candid, that mentors, and that monitors and sets critical parameters that allow for latitude and growth. Managing managers requires time and energy and then more energy. But there is an overwhelming sense of satisfaction and pride on everyone's part when well-prepared and well-supported sales managers, who want to manage, succeed. The payoff to the company is loyalty, not only from the individual manager, but from the audience that views this form of commitment and productivity as a reaffirmation of a consistent approach emulated down the organizational line.

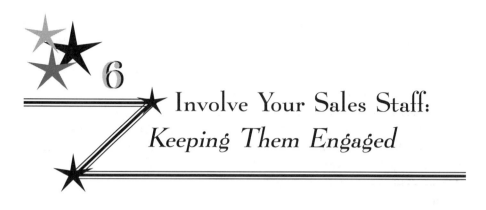

6

Involve Your Sales Staff: *Keeping Them Engaged*

For a time, the sales staff and its management got along well enough. No one really suspected the tension that was building. Jed would attend the semi-annual sales meetings and all appeared well. Jed was never too wild about being part of these contrived celebrations. He felt surrounded by a lot of glad handing, too much noise, pep-rally remembrances, more noise, superficiality, and even more noise. But it was something the sales staff appeared to enjoy. They seemed energized by the event and appreciative of the reinforcement they received from their sales managers. It was part of the CEO's job to be there and emphasize how important this cadre of sales professionals was to the company, talk about the future and how their continued energy would make the difference between economic success and failure, and pay special tribute to those that excelled beyond their peers. It was important to them, so it was important to him.

When sales started to flatten out the predictable grumblings began. It is rare that anyone complains with enough conviction and specifics to turn heads when business performance is going great. But when the numbers begin to freeze and trend lines start to point toward the wall instead of the ceiling, behaviors change. Issues that were waived aside in the past began ceaselessly buzzing around with no intention of going away. The wheels weren't coming off, but they were wobbling.

Jed wasn't sure if it was the meetings between sales and finance trying to analyze the root causes for the selling slow down, or the results of the company's first internal climate survey that brought everything to a head. Within a week of both events, the head of HR was at Jed's door. Some of their best and most tenured sales representatives were in deep complaint mode. A few were rapidly getting to that threshold where either they or the company were going to find the situation beyond reconciling. And a fair number of the regional sales managers were equally disgruntled. They were feeling increased pressure from the sales staff and a good measure of uninformed (in their opinion) commentary from the head of sales and the CFO on how to fix the plan to actual sales problem. Both agendas were related, and both required immediate intervention.

Both sides had reasonable positions. The sales staff felt the regional managers did not spend enough time with them on the road visiting clients and potential clients. The regionals wanted the sales staff to establish their own independent identities with the customer base. To the sales representatives their sales managers' unreasonable demands signified a lack of appreciation of the territories being worked. The sales managers countered that, if the sales staff would stop pontificating and start listening, they would better understand the economics of the business they were in and appreciate the reasonableness of what they were being asked to do. The sales staff couldn't understand why the concern levels were so high. They were effectively selling what they could. The sales managers criticized the staff for selling what they knew and avoiding selling what they should. Most sales staff blamed their leadership's old school mentality on the disconnects that were occurring. Sales managers bemoaned the new age thinking of their staff; low on disciplined concentration, analytics, and high on form, gloss and postcard level conceptual retention.

The intervention started with a set of questions that had to be answered by both functions (sales and sales management):

☆ How should sales management and sales professionals complement each other when engaged in the sales process?

☆ How well do they know each other's priorities/ predispositions?

☆ When are they a team and when are they a group of individuals, sometimes working at cross purposes?

☆ What are the dead zones or unspoken hurdles that keep sales managers and staff from functioning as smoothly as they would like?

The process was not about finding anyone's inner voice or extolling the merits of group bonding, although some of that would surface. The process was about engagement, about continuing involvement, about sales staff and management operating in concert.

This chapter is about those same elements building to the most powerful aspect of this type of engagement, collaboratively shaping a meaningful reward program for sales staff.

That all sounds good, and you've probably been exposed to stacks of team-building literature. In most cases, the warmth and fuzz they generate has a shelf life of about six months. Something stress-related usually happens that drops everyone back into their traditional and primary behavior modes, the ones you wish hadn't been learned oh so long ago, and it's back to business as usual. It is important at this point to remember another Rubber Chicken.

 The longer any process, including engaging the staff, becomes ingrained in the way you function the more likely it is that under the stress of increasing or decreasing activity that process will remain a primary behavior mode.

In other words, figure out what engagement profile works for your group and practice, practice, practice until you can't collectively behave any other way.

Why bother with engagement anyway? A sale, at its core, is a contractual relationship. We agree that I provide you something that meets the set of specifications at which we previously arrived. In exchange you provide me something we have also previously agreed upon. Why can't it be the same way on the job? I provide you an agreed upon wage. In exchange, you provide a specified and agreed-upon service. Is it simple and straightforward, or simplistic and soulless?

Engagement produces psychic equity, a sense of ownership in the collective outcome of your endeavors. That equity can be passionate and productive. Productive individual behavior integrated into a team effort can create results greater than the sum of its parts. Everyone is on target; no one allows for any slack. There is a coordinated assault on business objectives.

Fully Engaged

The Yankees, the Celtics, and the 49ers of past eras were fully engaged. They were locked in. These became dynasty teams. What distinguished them was not their athleticism or even their discipline, although they obviously had their measure of these attributes. That which set them apart was their combined level of concentration and anticipation. As a unit, they were completely involved in their game. Everyone was fully engaged. Everyone on the 49er line knew their assignment and instantly knew when to pick up a missed block or switch off a defender. Receivers could sense when the quarterback was scrambling and knew when to break their routes and get open. The defensive backfield was seamless, sensing their relative positions on the field and compensating coverage. The Celtics were a team in constant motion, looking for the open man. Scoring was a collective triumph, not an individual achievement. It didn't matter who was on the court, the level of intensity never subsided. The Yankees took tremendous pride in their ability to play small ball, to position their teammates for the score. While much has been said about their offense, it was defense that won them many a game. And above all, there was a legacy to perpetuate.

Dynasty teams exhibit three characteristics beyond just successful stats. First, dynasty teams are in the zone more often than not. They see the ball and the dynamics of the game differently than their adversaries. Some call it being in the zone. Everything is moving slower at more comprehensible speeds for the dynasty team making their actions seem (to their opponents) incredibly accelerated and unstoppable.

Second, dynasty teams feel an obligation to the past and the pressure that their achievements are laying the groundwork for the future. They have a sense of their place in time and its associated responsibilities. It is what keeps them going during the grind of the season or when faced with setbacks. It's what helps them overcome and inevitably win.

Finally, dynasty teams support each other on and off the field. They get along. They appreciate each contribution and reinforce each presence on the team. True, there is a little chicken and egg sequencing in this aspect of the definition. Does winning promote positive relationships or do positive relationships promote winning? I would suggest the former is true in non-dynasty teams by virtue of the breakdowns that occur when these teams are not winning. Dynasty teams suck it up and keep moving forward. You don't hear about them trying to take each other's heads off when a game goes bad or the team hits a brief slump.

Every manager should want their sales delivery team to be considered dynasty material, fully engaged in perpetuating success during an extended period of time. And no manager wants this engagement to be accidental and subject to uncontrolled changes and possible evaporation. Building a dynasty, an ingrained way of successfully functioning, takes us back to the previous Rubber Chicken. It takes us back to practice, practice, and more practice.

In addition to the obvious monetary gains that come with sales success, there are a host of other beneficial reasons for the selling team to function as one. For the individual, engagement produces excitement and enthusiasm. It elevates the staff's level of performance and contribution. There is increased satisfaction derived from the job and the overall unit's accomplishments. And there is confidence acquired from having been successful and knowing it can be done again and again. For the company, engagement pays off in staff retention and a participative inclusive reputation that assists in recruiting continued bench strength. The company also benefits from a staff whose ongoing involvement and contribution to change allows the organization to smoothly and quickly shift gears into the future.

A while back, I mentioned collaboration between management and staff on shaping a sales reward program. Rewards, and most specifically compensation, carry the message of engagement. They lock the process up. They are the stated, tangible, elements that bind the sales staff and its management in a partnership. Each individual knows more than just what is expected of them and what the rewards will be. They know all the conditions of performance and reward because they helped shape them. They are mutually owned. The responsibility implications are significant.

Conditions That Influence

Before you can build a compensation "partnership" you have to build a conscious, genuine, ongoing climate of collaboration. Note the words "conscious, genuine, and ongoing." Remove those words and you are left with the bulk of what is typically the corporate training and development industry, the "go there and get it fixed" instrument of management. Collaboration is not something done to you or uncovered at a mountain retreat and brought back to the office. Collaboration and engagement, happens at work, it is part of work, and it is how you choose to be each day, every day. It is not easy. But even for commissioned sales staff, the personification of the lone hunter, it is easier than most think.

From my experience, I have observed that engagement is influenced, first, by management's awareness and understanding of several key points of organizational behavior, and, second, by their disposition toward sharing that understanding with staff. From that sharing comes a shaping and ownership of issues. And from that comes a collaborative approach to compensation design.

Engagement in the collaborative process is influenced by a collective understanding of your company's operating style in relation to its core behaviors. Specifically:

☆ How your company defines success.

☆ How your company's managers handle power.

☆ How the organization behaves when stressed.

☆ How much time and care your company takes in recruiting staff.

☆ How strong your delivery (management) system is at all levels.

☆ How much recognition goes on in your organization.

Being True to Your Operating Style—Context Revisited

There existed a manufacturing firm in the Southeast that for a time was the darling of organization development people. This company could do no wrong structurally, financially, and socially. Even their plant facility was a showstopper. They were studied, documented, and restudied. Everything they did had profound meaning. Everything they didn't do had profound meaning. And predictably, their practices were emulated across the country—emulated without much commensurate success.

The situation was an extreme example of what has been going on in business for ages: belief that another's success can be replicated by being its mirror and replicating those elements that made the other so notable. Is this the highest form of flattery? Not if you consider who is typically doing the flattering. When the insecure, the desperate, the shallow of vision and values, and the financially marginal choose to be "like you," it unavoidably diminishes the sheen on your practices. As those practices, originally attributed to your organization, are screwed up by others, some of that dysfunction can find its way back to your reputation. Ultimately someone has a revelation: Maybe what works for one company might not work for another. This moment of prescience is always short-lived. Another blinding flash of success is revealed in scholarly writings, and off the startled lemmings run.

There was more to the story of the Southern manufacturing firm. Before the limelight of discovery, they had started their existence quietly enough. They were a start up, formed from scratch, with an operating style all their own from day one. They had no competing history or players from a previous regime. They had no ingrained political rituals to overcome. Everyone who came on board was told to leave their baggage at the door. If you snuck some other competing culture across the threshold you found yourself being escorted to the exit. Their practices made sense to them and for them. Through time, as they acquired other businesses and increased staff across the country, they found some of their practices in need of revision and compromise. Although they held true to their fundamental values, their operating style eventually became indistinguishable from many other companies in their industry. But by that time the flatterers had already moved on, revamping their own operations to parallel the style de jour.

Each organization has a unique context of behaviors and priorities within which they do what they do. Superimposing someone else's way of doing things without reconciling to your contextual framework is a wasted exercise.

Go to the Core—How You Reflect What Is Important to You

Context is the terrain within which your company operates. Just as jungle gear won't do you much good in the mountains and mountaineering equipment is worthless in the desert, your operational effectiveness is impaired if what you do and how you do it is out of contextual alignment.

In part, the terrain is influenced by your sales chain (the type of product/ service offered, the structures needed to sell and support selling, and the type of staff skills and experience best suited to close, service, and perpetuate sales). In greater part, the terrain is a creation of your core behaviors, dictated by what is of value to you, how you measure success, and how true you are to those behaviors as the journey unfolds. It is this greater part that differentiates you from your competitors.

Forget the words, the peppy and concise phrases posted in the reception area. Go past the nicely framed mission statements sprinkled throughout the building. Don't take the time to think about these human resource marketing materials. To assess your actions and how they reflect your priorities, to inventory your condition, find a quiet space to ask yourself some pointed questions.

Questions of Climate

☆ What do you really think of your company's vision, direction, and purpose for being?

☆ What is your definition of success beyond making money and providing a meaningful return to your investors?

☆ Do you care what the general public, not just customers or industry insiders, think of your company?

☆ When you are at a party and your company is brought up, what do you hope to hear?

> ▶ "I understand you folks have invested heavily in the community through training and employment programs, and you make it a priority to purchase from local suppliers."

> ▶ "I hear you have great service as well as a great product. Seems you really care about what you produce and about customer satisfaction."

> ▶ "They say your company is a great place to work. Everybody says you treat people fairly and with respect. You hire people with the purpose of keeping them, not running them hard and then laying them off. Everyone seems to benefit from your success. It's a "we" atmosphere. You take personal development seriously."

▸ "You guys are never complacent, always experimenting and pushing into new frontiers. And not just product development, but in the way you do business. Planning and strategizing seem as important as operating and delivering. You never seem surprised at the changing economy."

▸ "Give me a call. I would be interested in exploring how we might be able to use your product/service."

Whatever it is that you care about, whatever it is that you feel are the overriding purposes for your company's existence, how do you personally transmit those feelings on a daily basis to others? There is no formulaic answer to this question. It requires introspective time. It requires going back over your calendar and remembering your actions, particularly those under stress. It requires closing your eyes and remembering. It may even require talking to confidants to see if their assessment reconciles with yours. And unless you are totally invisible to mankind, they will have an opinion. Every leader's actions acknowledge something, reinforce something, and value something. And every leader's actions are observed, evaluated, and often replicated.

With the answer in hand, go back to the reception area. Check the posters on the walls. Do you walk the walk and talk the talk? Do you reinforce the messages in those posted value statements? If not, don't just reflexively decide to follow the printed page. Evaluate their legitimacy in the context of what you want the company to value. Consciously decide whether you should change or the material should be changed to reflect what is actually going on?

Acknowledging your company's overall core behaviors and keeping them aligned with your vision and objectives are critical. It is not a question of which behaviors, in an absolute sense, are better than others. It is a question of appropriateness and consistency. Appropriateness is a product of reconciling behaviors against vision and company direction. Consistency of alignment equates to exhibiting discipline and discipline is learned through practice. Being consistent translates to practicing discipline. The most well-intentioned manager loses to the beast in the room if he or she can't exhibit discipline in their behavior with staff. People can tolerate almost any climate for a defined period of time, as long as there is predictability and consistency of behavior. Managers who consciously use inconsistencies of behavior to keep their organization on "its toes" are committing corporate capital crimes.

Questions of Style

As the embodiment of your company's core behaviors, it is important to know how you behave, and how you are perceived to behave, in the company arena. Gathering the answer to that question is not in the least bit easy. Self-evaluation requires an objectivity few of us have. Personal assessment can only be offset by a critical review of examples that reinforce your opinion.

Asking valued confidents and trusted insiders for information can produce very telling results. Do you regularly, candidly, and even informally solicit feedback? The level of candor will be proportionate to the comfort and trust level your subordinates or colleagues may feel when expressing themselves to you. Vague and unhelpful information may be a sign that you and they are not as in sync as you might have thought. A variety of perceptions on the same issue may lead you to believe that you act differently with different people, which in turn leads to the question of why. Some executives resort to anonymous questionnaires or third-party data gatherers. Some companies take their "climate" temperature on a regular basis and include questions designed to assess executive behavior. My counsel is always aligned with Sophocles; don't go nuts. Keep your inquiry in perspective. In the pursuit of balance, there are behaviors worth defining and evaluating for their congruency to your stated values—but there are only a few.

Besides ensuring that your actions reinforce the values you want resident in your organization, you'll need to examine how you and your company:

1. Define Success

Even in quantitative measures of financial achievement there are distinctions between how companyies view success. Some use absolute terms to express success goals; revenues of $200M, earnings of $25M. Others use incremental terms; 10 percent sales growth year on year, increased market penetration by 5 percent.

But beyond the numbers what are the other measures of success your organization uses and what does it say about the company? Do you look at innovation? What about retention of desired staff? Do you evaluate your contribution to, or presence in, the community? Is there a sense of achievement when staff continues to develop professionally and in societal sense?

Do you stick your collective necks out? Do you advance goals and directions that are challenging? Do you take as much responsibility when they are not achieved as when they are met or exceeded? Is that responsibility tangible and balanced? Are rewards and penalties commensurate with the results?

2. Wield Power and Influence

How do you influence your direct reports, others? Do you perceive yourself to be collaborative, parental, omnipotent, or collegial? Is that perception shared by others? Does your position of influence provide you with a great opportunity for insight into situations or does the pressure of being in charge blind you to options? What is your proactive score? How often do you anticipate situations and respond in a way that satisfies you and those around you?

Do you sense that people are surprised by your reaction to situations or does it seem that they can anticipate what your response is going to be? Consider how you feel when you are surprised by others and how you feel when your expectations are not met, when there seems to be no apparent congruity of action and reaction. Most importantly, how does your surprise or disappointment manifest itself? Would a third party consider that manifestation constructive or destructive, for you or others?

Does the company allow for constructive confrontation? Do you open up or shut down opportunities for differing points of view before decisions are made? Is challenging a superior's point of view considered insubordination, a violation of an unwritten rule, or acceptable, even expected, behavior?

Is there a striving for consensus decision-making or a need for collective buy in when decisions are made? Regardless of the degree of collaboration leading up to the decision, once made does the organization acknowledge the role of the decision-maker, accept the decision, and move forward? Are some decisions never fully accepted, resulting in passive or even counterproductive acting out?

3. Respond to Stress

Are you seen as a different person when under stress? Does that different person behave outside the stated values of the company? When stressed, how confident are you that you deal with people issues in your area constant? Is there a pattern to any perceived differences: location or level of staff?

Does stress exhilarate or debilitate you and your staff? What are the signs that tell you that your staff is in a stressful mode? How many of these signs intentionally emanate from your interactions with them, how many are unintentional?

How do you define counterproductive stress? How do you re-establish your company's equilibrium?

4. Recruit Staff

This is an incredibly critical area. Breakdowns in productivity, failure to unify the staff under a common banner and in the engagement process, begin with poor hiring.

Is there a process you consistently follow that includes reconciling the organization's culture with each candidate's value system when recruiting staff?

How carefully is the prospective job opportunity defined by its required competencies, experience, and attributes? Has a range of values been pre-determined that are predicated on how candidates will match to these requirements? How easily do the prospective job and its potential value fit into the existing organizational structure? How does the job's estimated value and impact affect peers and others in the company? How does the organization front-end any perceptions of inequity or lack of parity?

When going to market are you maximizing the use of your gatekeepers (internal or external recruiters)? Do you know who the gatekeepers are screening out and why?

Do you utilize multiple interviews and interviewers when evaluating a prospective applicant? Are multiple processes used for all jobs or only a few jobs? Do those who interview go beyond the resumé and probe the candidate's compatible attributes and values?

Do you anticipate the impact of the new employee and their pay on existing staff? Are adjustments made for existing staff to ensure that no one already on staff is adversely affected through vertical or horizontal compression or by marketplace pressures that provide disproportionately higher starting compensation boundaries for newer staff? Does anyone discuss with each affected current employee the career and development implications, or lack thereof, this new position has on existing staff?

Are all the messages that should be out there, out there? Are the new and the existing staff made ready for each other? Have all distractions been dealt with so that everyone can get on with the business of doing business?

5. Strengthen Management

As has been mentioned, line management and supervision have been described as the bologna in the sandwich. They are squeezed between the expectations of staff and senior management. They are the ingredient without which the sandwich lacks flavor and substance. Their ability to get things done through others and keep their management current as to the status of actions and conditions is directly proportional to the company's operating success. They bind the engagement process and hold it firm. They reinforce the values of the company on a real time, front line basis.

How do you accurately assess line management's impact on communicating, clarifying, and supporting your value messages to the sales delivery team? How do you support and enhance their ability to communicate?

Do you know if the individuals in these positions are seen by staff as having a positive influence in binding the organization together in its overarching purpose and direction? What actions do you proactively and regularly take to ensure their productive influence is aligned with the values and objective of the organization?

How tangible is your commitment to the success of this cadre? How are you meeting the developmental needs of the line management staff? How do you know if your perception of their learning needs is similar to theirs? What is the depth of the well from which supervisors and line managers are drawn? Are these ranks filled from internal applicants being prepared for this responsibility or are the positions predominantly recruited elsewhere? Are you satisfied with the pluses and reconciled to the minuses derived from integrating new management sourced from the outside to your way of operating?

6. Recognize and Celebrate

We have talked about recognition in Chapters 2 and 4. Looking within your own organization, how much recognition goes on regularly? What gets recognized? Is that recognition aligned with your stated values and goals? Does recognition make a difference in your workplace? If it does, how is it manifested? Better productivity or retention? If it doesn't make a difference is it the result of poor implementation or the climate of the culture? Do you know how the recipients and the audience actually feel about the recognition being given? Is it perceived to be both meaningful and genuine?

Has the Engagement Table Been Set?

The previous pages have been developed to help leadership focus on how aligned they and their organizations are to the stated values and direction of the company. That degree of alignment will indicate if the company is ready to engage around issues of vision and mission.

There is a "to do" implied in each of the previously listed questions. Management and staff can't successfully move into collaboration and engagement if elements of mutual respect, problem-solving participation, and a fundamental knowledge of the staff and their priorities go unaddressed. A demonstrated and working sensitivity toward people and the dynamics surrounding the workplace has to exist before any measure of collaboration and engagement can be achieved. You and your staff have to be at a point of self-awareness with regard to your mutual value system to permit productive engagement to take place. It isn't accomplished by memo. It isn't done through formal training programs. You are only ready to move on when the issues are assessed and resolution, in the form of face-to-face interaction, has begun.

Trust and Dialogue

Without trust and dialogue you cannot have engagement. Something contrived and hollow will take its place. Trust and dialogue have to be inherent in the way an organization functions if it is to not only succeed, but grow in depth, character, and ability. It is at the core of all that is good in a communal enterprise.

Trust is a dynamic that is built through time, often tenuous in its establishment and easily diminished by a poorly chosen action, comment, or unconscious omission. Trust has its own Rubber Chicken.

 Trust is the currency of collaboration and as with money it is hard to acquire and keep, but easily spent.

Trust is built from mutual respect, reliance, and a confidence that everyone's behavior benefits the group as a whole. Everyone acknowledges the common agenda and acts in concert with that design. Anyone who violates the trust compact, or is perceived to be gaming around the agreed upon covenant, not only destroys the engagement process, but puts themselves in jeopardy of ceasing to function effectively within the sales team. Trust is that important to a healthy team. It is that powerful.

Management, because of its position of influence, has the obligation of establishing and reinforcing a climate of trust through word and deed. Those words and deeds should be directed toward the creation of dialogue.

Another Rubber Chicken:

 Dialogue has to exist for trust to exist.

Collaborative confidence is acquired through collaborative communication. Dialogue transcends functional content. It is a form of social interaction. You can't really establish trust with someone unless you have had the opportunity of interacting with them and obtaining a sense of their values, their priorities, their ideas. Even if the dialogue stays within the boundaries of work, it can establish a basis for trust. Dialogue is not monologue. It is not the art of directing or instructing. Dialogue is the mutual discussion of agendas assuring all parties that they are being heard and that there is recognition for contributions made, that closure has been achieved.

It is pretty apparent that a productive engagement is anything but a superficial process. Sales managers have to be comfortable enough with their engagement role and collaborative skills to establish and maintain an environment conducive to constructive openness. They are charged with ensuring that the staff feels everyone's participation is crucial to the success of the overall business strategy. In pursuit of that participation the sales manager has to educate staff on issues affecting the company, and highlight the skills needed for future challenges. The underlying message being sent is that no one is left to fend for themselves, no area for improvement will go unaddressed, and no one will be made vulnerable by changing dynamics.

Sales managers generate excitement and reinforce success through celebration. They shepherd actions, making sure that energy is expended on results aligned with pre-established business objectives. Effective sales managers provide a strong sense of group satisfaction when any of its members achieve.

Senior management needs to have the right people with the proper orientation and development skills in these collaborative generating jobs. It is the first "to do" in building a dynasty sales team.

Collaboration Is Fine, but Designing Compensation?

First, the caveats; I am not advocating that the sales staff sit around a table and decide how much they are going to get paid. I am not advocating that a vote be taken on issues of goals and result expectations with the majority vote becoming the rule of the day. I am advocating that compensation is too important to have its structures developed in isolation without collaboration.

Money, with no meaningful context surrounding it, doesn't engage people. It holds their attention for a period of time, which generally correlates with the amount of money being realized. It might make staff follow directions, but is does not necessarily engage them. Money also sets continued expectations on the part of the recipient: in the size of an increase or in the total offered. Offer a great deal of pay based on whatever rationale you choose and the expectation for future generosity, regardless of logic or circumstance, has been established. The byproducts of failing to meet that expectation the next time around are reflected in motivation, productivity, possibly resentment, and distraction. For these reasons I don't subscribe to the "squeaky wheel" or "Santa Claus" philosophies of pay; compensation shouldn't be generated by virtue of complaints or extended as an act of benevolence. Compensation is earned.

Virtues of Compensation Collaboration

Compensation, beyond its obvious purchasing impact, has tremendous symbolic value. Regardless of the absolute amount of remuneration, its symbolism lies in its relative worth to the individual as reconciled against some fairly subjective criteria.

☆ Is the compensation perceived as fair when compared to others in the company?

☆ Is it fair when compared to the marketplace?

☆ Does the amount of compensation reconcile, in the individual's mind, with the worth of the function to the organization?

☆ What meaning is given to the amount relative to the company's stated worth of the individual?

These are comparative assessments often clouded with partial information or a skewed sense of self. Consider this scenario:

> They sat across the table from each other. The manager talked about the year past, the tough hurdles, the thin margins, and the achievements of his staff member. The long preamble ended with a sheet of paper sliding across the table top. A Personnel Action Form with the individual's increase amount. The employee looked at the paper and then questioningly at his manager. "That's it?"
>
> The manager slowly picked up a pencil and snapped it in two with his right hand. His face was red. The veins in his neck pulsed. "Yeah, that's it."

A little relationship repair would be in order. It is not uncommon for a manager to go ballistic, silently or otherwise, when a staff member is under-whelmed by what was considered by the management team to be a generous increase in remuneration. Is it just greed that motors the employee down the wrong road, or have they been oblivious of the economic conditions and fiscal realities facing the company? And if oblivious, whose role is it to steer them back on course?

An individual receives a relatively small compensation bump, but given that it is far more than the norm, the special implications of an award that stretches the budgetary band can build organization loyalty and reinforce self-worth. Being one of the few to receive a large slice of a small pie can be more energizing than receiving the same large slice as everyone else.

In a collaborative, engaged environment management has an advantage when awarding compensation. They can better anticipate the reactions of their staff and market changes. In such an environment the chance of creating slap dash reward structures is mitigated by the deliberations and involvement of multiple participants. Compensation has a better chance of meeting its intended goals:

☆ Reinforcing the alignment between organization, direction, company values, and expected results.

☆ Cementing the relationship between rewards and achievement.

☆ Translating business objectives into actions that have personal meaning and value.

Beyond just determining a competitive amount of pay, these goals articulate the primary messages behind sound reward programs. Sales compensation is too significant to be developed in isolation, not to be developed without collaboration. The results that pay messages can stimulate are too important not to be linked with more lasting, and more contextually meaningful forms of reward.

Who Gets to Collaborate?

As the caveats mentioned, not everyone gets to play, and those who do will play by the organizational process, not the democratic one. When selecting staff input, your first instinct is to include your very best performers. Fight that instinct; at least a little bit. They can be helpful. But if you have to choose between the great and the good, choose the good. The great will most likely be great regardless of the compensation structure. Their nature is to outclass their peers. Their contribution, feedback, and point of view represent a somewhat stilted and not necessarily representative sample of your sales population.

The collaborative effort is looking for a balance between what should be and what can be. The good performers better reflect normative reality. As such, they are in a better position to respond to structural issues in a practical and experiential manner. By good, I am referring to those performers who you would rate in the 70th to 90th percentile of your sales staff—better than the median, but not your top 10 percentile contributors. For every sales representative collaborating from the top tier, there should be at least three in this next grouping.

There is a rush, a feeling of enfranchisement, when one is included in any design effort. If you anticipate that exclusion from a representative sample of your solid sales performers is going to alienate those in the top 10 percent (those you had not planned to include) you have two options: (1) include them and keep peace in the job family, or (2) explain the benefits of a more representative sample and the complexities of the group process that are created when making your larger population a sample. Assure those "excluded but worthy" that they will be kept apprised of any program changes as they develop, and then let maturity run its course.

Maturity and demonstrated past psychic equity should figure prominently in your sample selection of participative sales staff. You want contributors who have shown by previous actions that they care about the overall success of the company, and that they can keep things in perspective. You want to avoid enthusiasm to the point of impassioned inflexibility or zealousness to the exclusion of balance. You want to favor egos that do not require self-aggrandizement. Flexibility, perspective, and moderation are desired attributes that may fly in the face of many sales personality profiles.

Engagement can be especially challenging with commission sales staff, particularly if your collaboration themes are team based. Most commission sales personnel wish only to be free of any company involvement that does not directly affect a sale or, more specifically, their income. Selling is their singular measure of success, closing a deal their primary source of satisfaction. They are inclined to see company meetings as a distraction, unless, of course, they are paid well for their time away from selling.

This raises an important and legitimate question, "Why get these people engaged in design at all? Why not just let them keep sailing?" The answer lies in their fundamental sales orientation.

Fundamental Sales Orientation

They were being paid the equivalent of a day's sales commission to sit in the room. It was the third time this year management was changing the plan. They looked knowingly at each other. "Who did they think they were fooling?" Management passed out the plan while extolling its virtues. "If this was so great how come the last two were also so great when they were introduced? They play their game and we play ours. They give us the plan document and we nod passively. Then it's everybody meet at Sam's Grill and first figure out how they're trying to screw us. Then we figure out how we can screw them."

Not real? Some form of literary exaggeration? Not in the slightest. This was extracted directly from a meeting in the financial district of San Francisco. Is it extreme? Sure. Is it telling in many ways beyond compensation about the negative relationship between sales staff and sales management? Oh, yes. But it is a situation that is unfortunately not that uncommon.

Commission sellers are typically aligned with their books and not the company. They are after the biggest bang for their efforts, often without regard for the company consequences. How many times have we seen commission folk pour over a new plan looking for the best way to maximize income with the least amount of energy expended? How often do they treat change with suspicion, looking for the weakness in a plan so that it can be exploited? Why not front-end the issues of orientation and suspicion by including these sellers in the basics of their plan?

There are companies that wholesale the term "sales" in their job titles. Everyone who breathes on a sale gets the appellate. This, in and of itself, is not a bad thing. This is particularly true in cultures of inclusion, where the concept of team action is valued and continually reinforced. And some of these support players may even warrant inclusion in plan designs provided, and this is a big provision, they are crucial to the selling effort. Those who install and service the product or respond to the customer's billing, logistics and operational challenges further your company's image of quality and care. They maintain the reputation you want with your customers and in your industry. Obviously that has value. Obviously they should be remunerated and rewarded for the results they produce. If these support personnel are charged with cross-selling or renewing services the revenue generating portion of their roles may be compensated from the same funding pool as the sales representatives and as such they may participate in the design of an appropriate team component of the overall sales reward plan.

The one group that this design initiative should exclude is, for lack of a better term, ticket takers. These are the functions that do not actually sell, but rather ring up sales in transaction environments that are predominantly self-service. These cashiers are not to be confused with retail sellers who are charged with selling up, encouraging the buyer to select from a higher or sometimes different price point, or cross-selling multiple products in the same sale.

True retail sales clerks exhibit universal selling characteristics and behaviors. They match needs with product, they probe for other products or services that might be helpful, they inform and educate the buyer, and they establish a relationship that promotes renewed business. The product line and the price will always have some influence on the sale, but effective sales staffs make a difference and influence repeat business.

Ticket takers may assist customers by answering basic questions or directing them to inventory, and they are required to perform their duties efficiently and courteously. But they are not selling. They are part of the quality and care image of the company. There is no variable at-risk consequence or upside potential associated with these functions. It's binomial; cashiers can only do it either according to the standards of your company or not. Customers find ticket takers efficient and courteous or they don't. If a cashier is unbelievably efficient it won't influence the sales figures. It won't create a renewed need to buy from the store. True, indifference and sloth may drive the customer away, but that is the product of poor standards of performance and not poor selling.

Selling below target, which occasionally happens to any sales specialist, does not equate in individual consequence to a ticket taker's poor customer service. Poor customer service can get you terminated. A poor sales result may be offset by increased sales in another period. As a sales specialist you could do everything correctly and still not meet sales goals for a host of externally controlled reasons. Your earnings will drop temporarily, but the battle continues.

Once you have met the company's desired expectations, there is little more that a ticket taker can do to increase the customer service performance bar. The customer will return with attentive and friendly service. Excessively attentive or overly friendly service may not increase the upside of the return business; it may, in fact, reduce its likelihood.

Whatever indirect impact ticket takers have on revenue generation can be remunerated through base pay and a mix of other compensation components other than commissions or incentives. Some organizational cultures include these functions in company-wide or overall store-based bonus programs. Even if substantively symbolic, this bonus opportunity can help focus behavior and regenerate a collective approach to the overall mission. But it is a bonus program and not an individually based, performance measured, incentive plan. Mixing the two messages in the same pay package only creates confusion, unnecessary complexity, and an artificially based pay mechanism—three conditions no one should want designed into any of their compensation programs.

How Do You Collaborate?

Before addressing the question, here's a most important Rubber Chicken preamble.

 If compensation design is the only meaningful aspect of corporate life in which a company attempts to engage its sales staff in collaborate behavior, the battle is lost before it is joined.

This process has to be an extension of other engagements with the staff. There are a host of reasons why successful compensation engagement is predicated on this assertion.

The engagement process is a reflection of your operating style. If there is trust and dialogue there have already been forms of engagement, formal and informal, occurring. If people are suddenly engaged in a collaborative mission for the first time, particularly one perceived to have great significance, the mission will take a backseat to confusion, disorientation, suspicions, and generally counterproductive thoughts.

Successful engagement requires practice in the skills and behaviors used in the process. Some behaviors are culture driven: the degree of candor exhibited, sensitivity toward others, and interpersonal conduct (for example, interrupting or personalizing reactions). All this has to be tested, validated, and exercised through safe, low-impact engagements. The participants need experience to trust that what is said to be acceptable conduct really is. Time also allows the building of learned skills necessary for productive collaboration; constructive questioning, active listening, time management, concise communication, and group decision-making approaches.

Increased exposure to the collaborative process improves the outcome. The skills and behaviors associated with collaboration are validated and fine tuned through their continued use. Results manifest themselves more efficiently. Conclusions are faster. Focus is sharper and to the point. In an optimal setting, experience and the complexity of issues to be dealt with increase at parallel rates so that key issues, such as compensation design, are dealt with by experienced teams.

The more collaboration occurring across organizational lines and on a variety of agendas, the lower the drama any one engagement produces. Continued activity puts the impact of each engagement in context.

Collaboration Boundaries

Collaboration requires certain parameters and resource limitations be reviewed at the outset of the process so that there are no misunderstandings and counterproductive fallout once the group begins working together. From experience, the top four that keep groups from falling off the organizational cliff appear to be:

A clear understanding of what the group is expected to determine and produce. And an equally clear understanding of what the group will not be addressing. Decision-making responsibility, in most organizations, rests with management. The group needs to appreciate what they can realistically contribute toward those decisions. The group needs a specific, measurable, and achievable agenda.

What are the roles the group is to assume? Will they be charged with creative design development, consultative input, editorial review, or all of these? If they are stakeholders in the final design outcomes, will they be charged with providing credible clarification and/or endorsement to their peers when the new plan is marketed to the rest of the sales force?

What information can management provide the group on the relative weight that market place, internal priorities and management will have in establishing compensation direction and design? These perceptions will have to be tested and validated if the collaborating team is to develop a sales compensation program that is aligned with both the objectives and the values of the company.

What ground rules apply to the group process? In most cases, these will be consistent with the collaborative processes that have occurred previously in the organization. Past practices should delineate and provide guidance in determining productive flows of inquiry, when and how individuals outside the group may be called upon, the role of the facilitator or chair of the group, and specific commitments group members need to make in terms of time and energy expended.

Pre-collaboration Checklist

The group needs some basic questions answered before it can fashion meaningful compensation recommendations. As you read through these questions consider not only the value they add to scoping a credible design, but the powerful statement they make to the recipients. They are being engaged, enfranchised in the organization's expectations. They are being brought into the information loop. Management is giving the group what it needs to size the situation. Management is sharing with the group both vital data and leadership's answers to key questions that are mulled over on a regular basis.

- ☑ What are the economics of the business? Specifically, the costs and margins associated with varying services or products?
- ☑ What aggregate support expenses (advertising, marketing, staff support) are anticipated during the next few years?
- ☑ What are the profitability expectations of the shareholders/investors during the next few years?
- ☑ Strategically, what products or services are going to drive the business in the next few years?

☑ Strategically, what markets is the company concentrating on in the next few years?

☑ Are there other economic considerations to be assessed that would impact any risk-reward sales or resource commitment scenarios?

☑ What are the best practices currently being used elsewhere? This would include practices relative to selling and compensation structures. How timely and comprehensive is the information? Are the information sources interested or disinterested third parties?

☑ What are the ethics the company wishes to promote within its sales delivery team? How flexible/creative is the company willing to be in designing methods to reinforce those ethics? What would the company's reaction be if these ethics were not adhered to?

☑ In management's view, what is right and what is wrong with the current sales results and their impact on future strategies? If they perceive problems with the current results, are those problems compensation related? What history or interactions that have nothing to do with compensation plans and practices continue to hinder optimum performance?

What Do You Collaborate on?

The compensation issues that can engage a collaborative group will vary, as the answers to the previously listed questions do, by organization in variety, depth, and intensity. But the shopping list that follows reflects the major themes with which most groups will be wrestling.

☆ Is management's point of view of what is wrong and right with regard to the current sales situation, the company environment, and actions associated with strategic initiatives consistent with the observations and opinions of the sales staff?

☆ If there are gaps, are they significant enough that they need to be dealt with prior to the group moving forward?

☆ With the company's strategic direction in mind, what should the organization's specific pay emphasis be regarding new business from new sources, new business from existing sources, and continuing business from existing sources?

☆ Should any compensation distinctions be made as to how the business is obtained (cold calling, referrals, colleague or management generated), whether the business comes from targeted territories or markets, whether accounts are actively managed by sales staff or not?

☆ Should distinctions be made in compensating for selling up, cross-selling, packaged sales, or contests associated with clearances or item emphasis?

☆ How should training, territory distribution, and management support impact performance, and in turn compensation design?

☆ What compensation mix (fixed salary, variable, perquisites, and non-cash rewards) will best attract the selling skills the company will require? What compensation mix will stimulate improved performance? What compensation mix best reflects the values of the company?

☆ What windfall issues or other business conditions will impact management and staff's perceived fairness of pay?

☆ Within the area of variable pay (commissions, incentives, or bonuses), what are appropriate levels of upside and downside risks and rewards as expressed by performance results, and as expressed as a percentage of the position's overall compensation?

☆ Should variable pay (commissions not withstanding) compensate for each dollar of revenue generated, or should a baseline of revenue performance be compensated (and funded) through base salary?

☆ How should threshold performance be defined with regard to variable pay? How close is threshold to target performance? Are there increments of competency between threshold and target that require related and discrete compensation emphasis? Should these increments be rewarded in a straight line relationship to performance or through the use of accelerators that generate greater, and disproportional, gains for specific result achievements?

☆ How should the organization value residuals?

☆ Should any compensation be awarded for contractual agreements where revenue has yet to be booked? Should any compensation be recovered if contractual agreements are broken, even after revenue has been generated?

☆ Should there be any compensation distinctions made for new staff and/or for transferring of accounts and/or territories?

☆ Is there value added in developing variable compensation approaches for all or specific members of the sales delivery team who actively and directly impact on new revenues from existing accounts? If so, what should be the impact of this component as a percent of their overall compensation?

☆ What, if any, administrative issues (for example, practices designed to prevent behaviors that benefit the individual at the expense of the company, arbitration procedures when disagreements arise, and how medical and personal leaves impact compensation) would the group want to emphasize that are predicated on past behaviors, experiences, and organization values?

The Forgotten Step

Program Epiphany, where group think discovers the long-lost solution, often leads to rushed activity and false satisfaction. Deadlines that seemed to creep along forever suddenly loom over everyone and produce frenetic last sprint behavior. Many a design has been fashioned and then sunk without the support of an all important step: modeling. Modeling strengthens the viability of the engagement process by demonstrating the impact the recommendations will have when measured against "what if" scenarios. Modeling should be a part of the team's proofing procedure and included in the presentation of recommendations.

Plan design suggestions arrived at by the group should be super-imposed upon reasonable performance scenarios. Suggestions should be measured against best- and worst-case situations. Bands of probability with related cost and performance implications should be presented. Modeling must be complete, compelling, and support the basic thesis.

The team has to build in the time to work out the modeling, discuss the findings, and reflect on their implications before arriving at their final conclusions. If modeling falls victim to the last minute rule, where deliberate plodding is replaced by last minute haste and speed, the whole plan design is in fatal jeopardy. Therefore, the team's project plan must include time for both modeling and the consequences related to its outcomes. The numbers may tell the team that further study needs to be done before findings can be presented to the wider audience. It's better the team realizes what needs to be done than having management send the team back to the conference room because of incomplete work.

Perspective

Flexibility and adjustment have to be the bywords of any engagement team. Pride of ownership and its attended stubbornness can doom the group. If there is any overriding attribute that seems to be indicative of upwardly mobile individuals it is that of maintaining perspective. It influences how one looks at a situation, how one interacts with others, and how one chooses which road to take.

Being asked to collaborate and become engaged in any strategic planning activity can be heady stuff. Losing one's head, and usually mouth, when extolling the "only" right course of action will hardly ever get one invited back to the table. Participants who demonstrate perspective are able influencers, who see all points of view and can negotiate common ground. Those who have provided past perspective are often called upon in the heat of group clamor to help make sense of it all. With perspective comes respect and significant influence. With respect and influence one can achieve results far beyond singular action.

Engaging the Wider Audience

The group's work is not complete until it has clearly presented its recommendations to senior management in as compelling a manner as is appropriate for the operating style of the company. Probable management questions have to be anticipated and addressed. Next step implications need to be definitively mapped out. The merits of each conclusion, and any of its potential down-side elements, have to be valued, put in perspective, and articulated effectively. It is a waste of time, energy, and credibility if a recommendation is rejected not for its substance, but because it was presented poorly. Intra-organizational change teams engaged in compensation design would be best served if they thought of themselves as outside consultants trying to present a program to a skeptical client. An orientation of this sort lends itself to various stages of preparation. The next chapter will spend more time detailing the dynamics of presenting executives with compensation proposals. For now, one theme is worth emphasizing.

The presentation itself with all its substance, modeling, and linkages to the business direction and values of the company should be clean, crisp, and stimulating, with an emphasis on stimulating. The best presentations are the ones where senior management offers a collective, "Ah-ha." When they not only "get it" but "it" carries them to another level of awareness and prompts animated discussion and resolution, the presentation is a success.

If there are communication gurus within the organization who can help package the presentation, the team should use them. If success requires resources from the outside, the team should consider the expense well worth it, provided it meets the presentation objective without being a distraction or going overboard.

Stand Alone Documentation

The engagement is not finalized until both the process and the conclusions associated with the project have been documented. We're not talking note scraps thrown into a binder. Not indecipherable scribbles wrinkled and filed. Documentation requires a linear package of information that could be brought out two years in the future and whose contents would easily explain to someone not associated with the original engagement team what took place, and when and why actions were taken. It is a stand-alone package that will prevent reinventing the wheel at some future time and, equally important, ground the reader in the precepts that influenced the recommendations made; are as much the legacy of the collaborative effort as it is the recommendations that were adopted as a result of the engagement process.

Putting All the Pieces Together

Engaging the sales delivery team in the collaborative design of their compensation is achievable if the engagement process is already part of the company's fabric and if it is a genuine reflection of the organization's values and beliefs. Engagement and collaboration cannot meaningfully exist without an operating style that treasures trust, dialogue, and an open exchange of ideas. The quality of the engagement is not an accident. Collaboration has to be managed. Successful engagements are orchestrated through a careful selection of participants, ensuring there is clarity of mission and its boundaries, providing the time and resources required to do it right, and demonstrating ongoing support and encouragement by management.

If the engagement process has limited history in your organization it will add to the collaborative challenge. It may be well to carefully choose other issues with which to develop the team's talent for this type of activity before setting compensation out as the agenda. On issues of design generation, loyalty, psychic equity, and ultimately job performance, there can be no greater stimulant than allowing the sales staff to influence the structure that governs their future earnings potential.

Sales staff engaged in compensation design brings a thoroughly unique perspective to the process. Compensation design is about marrying strategy with action. It has far-reaching implications on productivity, individual satisfaction, retention and recruitment, skill development, and profitability. Building compensation structures involves a degree of mechanics, and of measures, numbers, and stages. For the structure to be durable and effective it has to be built around a framework focused on the future. The sales staff on the team is not only engaged in design consultation, helping management select the appropriate framework; they are also going to be living within its walls. That is their unique orientation. That should be the perspective from which they communicate to the wider audience. Compensation and human resource specialists will be involved in helping to refine the design and add their own expertise. So too will specialists in finance, operations, marketing, and IT. But the value of the engagement is always heightened by the perspective of those who will reside under the canopy being constructed. The sales force must never abdicate that role.

7 Cultivate an Inter-Functional Community:
Putting the Company First

I once worked with a fellow who had a bromide for every occasion. It wasn't unusual to hear about, "Too many cooks spoiling the broth." My rejoinder in keeping with all his hackneyed phrases was always, "It ain't necessarily so." And it isn't. Designing an effective sales compensation plan is an orchestration (not an omission) of ingredients. A good restaurant has a hotline of well-coordinated cooks working their stations, with each complimenting the final product. Even the broth can benefit from multiple inputs provided two factors are present: (1) everyone knows how their contribution effects the combined result, and (2) someone is ultimately in charge.

Jed, our ever-present CEO, wanted input from his direct reports on what they envisioned a new sales compensation program would look like. He put the question to his team at their weekly update meeting. "When you get a chance come by and tell me what you think." Their reaction to his question was telling.

Information Technology was first in the door—with a warning. "I don't care what is agreed upon as long as you don't go letting this whole exercise get too complicated. Right now, we've got a good handle on sales revenue by territory. Beyond that, measuring and reporting on anything is going to take an upgrade to our systems, increased staff, and increased costs. Give the sale's guys more time off (everybody wants more time off) or throw them a party when we hit revenue targets." As he turned to leave, he added, "I'm not sure our current platform can handle any changes. Not to mention the added pressure on my staff. Please, just leave our systems well alone."

Marketing dropped off a binder detailing the value of rewarding for increases in specific products and for growth in territory. The binder was a work of art. Products and rewards were displayed on a grid that ran the length of a legal sized sheet. Each product, of which there were 10, had at least 14 increments of growth with corresponding rewards. The territory penetration section was no less detailed. The last growth indices had formulas that exponentially grew incentives into infinity.

Human resources and sales almost knocked each other over trying to get through the CEO's door. "What was Jed thinking when he asked for everyone's take on sales rewards? This is clearly the purview of sales, with HR support. What do the other areas know about rewarding sales people?" The head of sales was already focusing his core team on the issue. They were becoming engaged in the process. Now he was going to have to explain and deal with this outside interference? Was the CEO dissatisfied with his leadership in the area? Was there a hidden message in disenfranchising him?

"I just wanted to know what the rest of the group was thinking. It's no big deal, really." Skeptical ears didn't respond well to Jed's attempt to calm the waters.

The CFO had e-mailed Jed a table of information. One side listed the objectives that the management group arrived at as a result of their recent strategic planning meetings. The other side listed those objectives translated into a priority of sales deliverables. Each deliverable had a revenue and profitability value that she had extrapolated from existing data with corresponding incremental cuts that could go to funding a sales comp plan.

Jed's head of operation stopped him in the hall. "You asked about our views on a new sales compensation plan? What new plan? Why change? Are we fixing an unbroken wheel?" Jed shook his head and waived off any further discussion for the moment.

The Unlucky 13

So, what happens to the believers of inclusion and synergy when what should have been sautéed halibut with ratatouille comes out of the kitchen looking more like fish chowder?

There are 13 factors that contribute to group madness, where intent and outcome look nowhere akin. These factors, while extremely relevant, are not exclusive to sales design. Any one of them can send a collective course of action into the tank with the additional tragedy of creating a company history that will probably preclude use of the group process in future initiatives.

1. There is a lack of clarity of purpose.

The impetus behind any change is not clearly understood. The mission of the group is equally vague.

Jed needed more than a casual statement in his staff meeting to both set the stage and provide perspective. At the very least no one should have left the room without a clear understanding of what he wanted, why he wanted it, and what he intended to do with the information. Was it going to be food for thought, the beginning of a formal initiative, or the ground rules for a project? Was the management team to dedicate time and energy researching their ideas? Was it just a precursor to group think or something that had to be carefully postulated?

2. There are unaddressed vested points of view.

Concerns by certain participants that their "important" points will be overlooked drive them to behaviors that are not necessarily in the best interests of the overall direction of change or the mission of the group.

Jed wouldn't have any trouble figuring out vested interests—everyone had them. They ranged from don't do anything that causes my area more work to territorial prerogatives. It's good that the CEO knows where his team is coming from. It's potentially bad news if their predispositions will be carried forward in any design activity involving them or their staffs.

3. Alignment issues remain unresolved.

Something in the change process or design is in conflict with the direction, goals, operating style, or priorities of others within the organization. And more importantly, no one wants to look for and surface the gaps or misalignment.

It is interesting to note that only Jed's CFO went back to the strategic planning results and formed her response to his question around those outcomes. At best there was inattention to the alignment of priorities, direction, or operating style between the management members.

4. Everyone is not on the same page at all times.

This is a red flag to other dysfunctional behaviors. There could be a lack of clarity or leadership. There could be a misunderstanding of the objectives. For whatever reason, people walk away from particular points in the process confused as to where things are going or why so much time (or not enough) is being spent on tangential (or critical) issues.

As mentioned previously, Jed's intention (and, by default, his leadership) could have been clearer, yet no one pushed back for clarity of purpose. Only the heads of sales and human resources acted collectively.

5. The perceived need for change is in dispute.

Not everyone on the team believes that the changes being proposed are required. There is commitment lacking. The fundamental reason for undertaking a design rework is being questioned by some of those charged with bringing about or supporting the alteration. It is irrelevant whether the resistance is due to history, cynicism, or substance, the project is susceptible to derailment. Counterproductive activities geared toward defeating commitment could be subtle, overt, or even lethargically subconscious.

The head of operations, for whatever purpose, challenged the basic change assumption. The head of IT, for very clear purposes, didn't directly challenge the need; instead they only challenged activities that would bring about the change. It remains to be seen whether these biases will extend beyond Jed's initial inquiry and permeate the design team.

6. Company and personal history muddle the agenda.

Issues of personal competency, territory, power, or expertise get in the way of moving forward productively. Defeatism, fatalism, and a bunch of other "isms" replace focused drive and energy. "We tried that once before and it didn't work." "Whatever changes we try never stick. Why waste our time just to be disappointed in the end?" "Good gravy! You want Walt's opinion?"

Of all the curses that can plague group process, an imbalance of influence within the team is the most daunting. If power can corrupt, it will most certainly do so within the confines of the group. If team members are intimidated or distracted by the behaviors of their cohorts, then a more fundamental problem than sales compensation design needs to be dealt with. The team should be balanced, representative, and competent. It should not be the domain of any one member.

Jed hasn't taken his design process beyond an informal question to his direct reports, so it is premature to speculate on what will or will not get in the way of the design effort. He will still have to keep in mind the concerns of his heads of HR and sales. And he can't lose sight of the messages planted in the responses of his other staff. Some responses were elaborate in method and detail while others may forecast future passive aggressive, or just plain aggressive, conduct.

7. **A lack of process or plan design undermines task completion and time management.**

An all-too-common pitfall in task achievement is rushing to produce change without mapping out what has to be done, and who gets involved. A lack of deliberate steps may overlook the need to promote good will, understanding, and cooperation from critically impacted areas before the actual project stages get under way.

If planning is too rigidly maintained without flexing for unforeseen changes, the group will be in trouble. If plans are written and rewritten hours before implementation, the group will be in trouble. If planning is seen as a necessary evil to be dispensed with as quickly as possible and then placed on a shelf so that the "real" work can be done, the group will be in deep trouble.

We will talk about plan management in Jed's environment a little later in this chapter.

8. **Chaos becomes king.**

A wise man once said, holding a Rubber Chicken in his hand,

 Action without vision is chaos.

Without a clear and focused vision, issues get out of balance. Meetings become debate sessions. Too much time is spent on the wrong things. Performance indices are too precise or too general. Other project problems manifest themselves in the counterproductive interactions of the group. If being on a different page is a dysfunctional red flag, then chaos exhibited by the group is a red flashing light at the scene of the accident.

Jed has an opportunity to front-end any chaos by the type of group and charter put together at the beginning of the design effort. We will explore more on that later.

9. **There is a lack of company discipline.**

A reasonable definition of distress encompasses being required to produce too much in too short a time frame with limited resources, and having decisions that affect your outcomes being made outside of your control. A Rubber Chicken:

 Management should exist to minimize distress and maximize conditions for energized behavior.

If company leadership establishes unrealistic parameters or avoids resolving damaged conditions, the design project will begin to crack.

For Jed, the tests are yet to come.

10. **The project team *isn't.***

The team talent mix is wrong. This isn't to say that key stakeholders are not represented, but they may be represented in name only. If there was a contest, and first place was an exemption from any cross organizational team projects, second place was participation on such a team, and third place was the team leadership role, imagine the direction that talent and commitment would take in order to win. It may not be as overt as a contest, but the messages often sent when a project is in the offing are just as clear. If players are competing to get off a project team, there is obviously something wrong.

Jed and his management group are going to have to work at being a more engaged team if he expects productive team behavior from the rest of the company.

11. **There is a lack of meaningful recognition for all team players.**

Recognition goes beyond the Lucite paperweight with the company logo, the zippy project code name, and date of completion frozen inside. Recognition involves rewards for the commitment of time and energy expended that are given by the team members' bosses and *their* bosses. Recognition involves genuine, expressive acts that make team inclusion something to strive for. Recognition involves creativity and sizzle that reflects the results achieved and is significant to the recipient.

One of Jed's personal goals is to change his organization into a team culture, where initiative, mutual support, and participation are considered both worthwhile and critical. This project will be a milestone test of that desire.

12. It's not my fault.

The phrase that should produce capital punishment in any organization is, "I saw it coming, but there was nothing I could do." Whether we see the definition of team as all encompassing as society, or as finite as a work task force, team membership means being accountable for your actions and the actions of the team. Serious project work translates to serious consequences when agreed upon deliverables are not met. Serious project work means stepping up and supporting the team.

Another of Jed's goals is to build a company of accountability, in which everyone steps up and acknowledges their obligations and responsibilities. If accountability exists in the organization, if accountability is demonstrated by those who would be part of the design team, the project will be off to a great start.

13. Project teams break down when members are unclear about their specific role responsibilities.

Certain team members are asked to participate because of their consultative skills—their ability to keep the group constructively moving on point. Others provide expertise sparked with creativity that allows them to see every problem as a challenge with workable solutions. Groups require editorial skills that can synthesize information and produce clear communication outcomes. At the source of every changed agenda is information. Some enter the group skilled at research, analysis, and data management, and some members provide multiple skills for the group. Those members need to know why they are part of the team and what is expected of them.

For Jed this will be the culmination of all his efforts moving the compensation design to fruition. Will he be able to get his management group to volunteer those staff with the skill sets needed to form a successful team?

Starting the Design Project Off on the Right Foot

As Jed's next management meeting began, the CEO asked his group to put their pens down and *really* listen for a second.

"I screwed up last week. I was too cavalier when I asked for your views on what our sales compensation plan should look like. That's not really what I had intended. Phil, in sales, is already forming a nucleus within his group to provide input, reaction, and perspective—but this is bigger than just sales.

What we reward sellers for, and how we reward them has implications across the whole company. That's why I want all elements of the company vested and involved in this effort. That's why I want an inter-departmental team working with Phil's group. I don't want you and me figuring out what the plan should look like. I want us sitting back and letting this more-hands-on group figure out our company's options and present them to us. What I should have said last week was, how do we put this group together and what marching orders shall we give it?"

The next two hours were spent outlining the management team's result expectations, the design group's charter, what boundaries it would function under, whose skills and personalities from the company's talent pool would be the best fit for project membership, who would manage both the design process and the team, how the group would be rewarded and recognized, and finally what management's responsibility was to be in both emphasizing the importance of the project and reinforcing that emphasis throughout the life of the team.

It was decided that each senior manager would meet with the potential team members in their units and outline the project objectives, its importance, and their personal endorsement of both the effort and the selected candidate. Depending on the amount of time required of the individual at various design stages, intermittent coverage of their regular responsibilities would be provided. But each team member would be serving two masters: their unit and the design team. No one was being entirely freed of their role in their department. There was one exception: The team leader would have no other responsibility than bringing the design to fruition. The design team leader met with the CEO to go over the planning process in some detail and to receive assurances from the very top of the organization that as leader of the team this was not their last job with the company, but rather the continuation of an upwardly leading trajectory into the company's future.

All accepted the challenge. They met as a group for the first time at the CEO's kickoff luncheon. It should be noted that formal lunch meetings at this company were considered a big deal with heavy cultural implications. In addition to senior management's presence, the luncheon was also attended by the division and regional sales managers. They, too, had been briefed on the design team's charter and timetable. They too would have a role in the design and final outcome. This was to be both a critical and transparent endeavor. No surprises, with everyone working toward the same goal. Jed was very clear that this was not only an important project by virtue of the subject it was tackling, but it would be a test of how well the company could function as a mutually supportive team. With that, an excited and motivated group prepared to set about designing a total sales reward structure.

Whose Plan Is It Anyway?

There is an 800-pound gorilla that circles the conference room at the start of any design project. Its hairy presence can influence the quality of the group's harmony and commitment. The gorilla is ownership. Who owns the plan design? The dominant claims usually come from sales, finance, and human resources.

The selling team feels it has obvious ownership, having to live and die by the plan. Finance contends that the bottom-line numbers which steer the plan also provide its legitimacy and the development and recording of those numbers, both projected and their actual impact, are within its purview. The compensation discipline is usually housed in human resources, who are quick to point out their expertise in issues of best practices, behavior, and performance. Human resources' self-image is that of the keeper of the company's ethics and the maintainer of balance between employee and shareholder interests. Through its professed concern for the common good, uman resources transcends all areas of the company and feels qualified to own a plan whose prongs will inevitably touch multiple areas.

In truth, the company owns the plan from start to finish. The company funds the plan and the people who shape and execute its provisions, but there is a more fundamental reason for company ownership. The company, through all its collective parts, supports both the design and implementation of a sales plan. Company ownership is an inclusive mindset. It is predicated on the premise that the company is not merely a set of offices in the headquarters facility. Ownership is pervasive. Everyone who touches or contributes, everyone who benefits from its provisions, has equity in the plan's design and outcome. And that should be everyone whose livelihood is funded, directly or indirectly, by the revenue generated by sales.

Design Management

While ownership of the plan and its success is pervasive, management of the plan design is *not*. Design management is the responsibility of the sales group. They have to implement its provisions. They have to energize behavior to produce the desired results. They know the internal and external audiences driving the plan's components, and they make them realistic and workable. This is why the design group works closely with engaged and proficient sales staff members who will be shadowing and commenting on the design product. This is why projects of this nature are usually headed by someone from within the sales family; it is in their blueprints to execute.

Design management is a tall order. It is a tricky art form, guiding the plan design to its fruition. It takes both skill and perspective to be able to lead a group with a wide variety of talents and points of view. The leader has to recognize and respond to all perspectives including that of management, other departments, the design team, the sales engagement team, and line sales management and staff. Agendas have to be navigated and kept on point. Everyone has to be involved, if not substantively then emotionally. Contributions from all quarters have to be evaluated and actions taken to ensure quality standards are maintained. Conflicts will inevitably have to be reconciled.

Design leadership encourages full participation of the project members, actively promoting constructive commitment by all the participants. The project has to continue to flow on time, on budget, and on target. The project leader is accountable for the plan's alignment with the overarching priorities of the company. As mentioned previously, during the design phase project leadership becomes a full-time endeavor. The member of sales management typically chosen to be the process leader is often assisted by a third party who acts as an experienced guide in the journey.

Sequence of Events

A design team's approach is going to vary somewhat depending on historical and situational variables, but there is a basic template that is replicated by successful project groups. Senior management should expect to see the 15 points that follow identified as the dominant part of their design team's operating process. Some of these points, such as status presentations and editing/refining steps, repeat themselves at predetermined critical junctions in the design cycle.

1. Clarify roles and responsibilities.
2. Identify design goals.
3. Surface all considerations by each discipline within the organization.

4. Address, don't avoid, those issues that could affect the design plan—reach agreement on issue strategies.

5. Produce an outline of team activities.

6. Gather information from required resources.

7. Present updated findings and/or conclusions that influence design recommendations to executive management; identify how these results will affect the design stage timetables previously reviewed.

8. Craft the plan design.

9. Present the preliminary plan design to executive management.

10. Edit and refine plan design based on executive review and discussions.

11. Model the reward program design.

12. Develop a communication approach and related procedures that targets all those impacted by the plan.

13. Present a developed reward program design and communication plan to executive management.

14. Finalize plans and process timetables.

15. Begin communication roll out.

Points Worthy of Emphasis

While the previous list is relatively self-explanatory, there are themes intertwined in these steps that are worthy of review and discussion.

Team Health

The best teams are those who grasp the underlying meaning of what it is to be part of a real team. Equally important, they never forget that significance, regardless of day-to-day distractions, as they collectively respond to the challenges facing them. Unfortunately, project teams in many organizations are often teams in name only. These so-called project teams are best characterized as gangs. And gangs are about power, both internal and external. The concept of team breaks down immediately when these groups are configured as gangs.

Consider the following cases in point: Every department selects an energetic third-level manager to be part of "the team." The CFO decides this is too important an undertaking to send anyone but himself. End of team, beginning of gang. Marketing and human resource team members have each been separately told, subtly or otherwise, that their personal futures, as well as the future of their respective departments, depend on how well executive management views their individual contribution to the overall success of the plan design. They have been specifically chosen to be members because they have demonstrated before that they are capable of setting their banner above that of the group. End of team, beginning of gang.

In the first example, no matter how fair-minded and participatory the CFO may think he is, or how well intentioned the gesture of support may seem, a power statement has been made that both subordinates, the sales role in the leadership process and distracts the motivations and openness of the team. The CFO isn't "just one of the guys." His access and its implied influence, his knowledge of the broader picture, what he says or doesn't say are all going to add tremendous directional weight to group decisions and outcomes. Even the most casually mannered and unassuming general cannot sit among field grade officers and expect them to ignore the stars on his uniform.

The second example is much harder to remedy than the presence of a well-intentioned heavy weight. The counterproductive marching orders that have been given speak to damaged perceptions of relative worth, and the desire to achieve secular needs with little regard for overall company priorities. In such a climate, it is problematic that a productive team would be able to thrive. Were it just one self-serving member, the team might be able to circumvent, discipline, or tolerate their behavior. But with multiple self-interests at play, it becomes impossible for cohesion to take hold within the group. Teams within teams dilute both purpose and focus. The intervention of dictatorial power is usually the only alternative to weed out the bad and protect the good. By that time it is too late, the team no longer exists.

Both examples reflect an obvious Rubber Chicken, but one worthy of articulating:

 Healthy teams are derived from healthy organizations.

If the organization can't climb out of the gang mentality, choosing the right players for a sales design team is the least of its challenges.

The Critical Two—Maturity and Chemistry

The company has a history of valuing collectively focused behavior. It is sensitive in creating level, balanced groups to participate in designing a sales plan. It has an abundance of staff eligible for team membership. What does it do when faced with one spot and two equally talented candidates? The answer is to look away from the resumes and look toward the two most critical considerations for team success: chemistry and maturity.

Working chemistry should not be confused with a mutual admiration society. Just because everyone admires everyone else doesn't mean they can work together effectively. Chemistry equates to comfort. The comfort that comes from respecting each other's competency and demonstrated past behavior. The comfort that comes from knowing team members will collectively support each other in an open and accepting environment. It doesn't imply agreement on all issues—at least not without some rigorous debate. It does signify mutual commitment of the overriding purpose of the team and its resolve in producing, as a team, the best outcome possible.

Maturity and indifference are sometimes confused. Maturity isn't assessed by grey hair, or the vacant stare and pre-snooze head bob that are mistakenly confused with introspection and unarticulated wisdom. Maturity is not about the quiet demeanor that is one sigh away from the state of comatose. Mature employees can be passionate about their work, about ideas, about the company. They can be active and full of life. But there is a perspective that surrounds that energy. There is an ability to see a wider screen, to appreciate all the pieces that comprise a situation. There is an ability to differentiate the long view from the short term issue, and there is the capacity to integrate those perspectives into constructive and complimentary actions. Mature players don't just look the part, they are the part. Mature individuals have a track record that reflects an even keel when it comes to reacting to success and disappointment. They express that demeanor everyday in everything they do.

Mature individuals understand and accept the dynamics of inclusion and exclusion. The military of my experience had two ways of determining access to privileged information: clearance and need to know. Clearance ratings labeled Top Secret with Code-Word Clearance were based on a set of criteria that ensured the rating holder would respect and hold the privacy of information they were accorded. Need to know related to the relevancy of specific data access at a specific point in time. There are times when no matter how valuable the person may be to the company and no matter how key their project, it would be inappropriate for them to be exposed to certain information. They just don't have a need to know at that point in time. Maturity is not tested just on how people manage their access to data, but on how they conduct themselves around the absence of privileged information that might be known to others but not to them. It is something executive management can observe on a daily basis.

Team Roles

Accepting the role of a design team member requires the individual to cross a bridge and enter into a land governed by rules of engagement whose emphasis may be slightly different than those of past journeys taken within one's own department. As members of the design team a new allegiance is formed, not just to the project goals, but to the team itself. For a time, it may seem like a schizoid existence, working back and forth between the relative comforts of a known department setting and then shifting to the uncharted waters swirling at the fringe of organizational convention. In this initially disorienting climate, team members naturally look for grounding points of reference that will help them navigate effectively.

As the sequence of events is developed and reviewed it should become clear to the team who is going to be doing what in the process. But there exist role responsibilities that go beyond the specific tasks being doled out, and both transcend and shape daily project activities.

☆ It is the design-team leader's role to assign leadership positions for any sub-group activities either anticipated or created as a result of the ongoing planning process.

☆ It is the design-team member's role to accept assignment decisions, whether given directly to them or others, whether desired or not, and move forward constructively.

☆ It is the design-team leader's obligation to make certain that all members clearly and continually understand the parameters of the project and, in turn, what can or cannot be done within the context of the plan design effort.

☆ It is the role of each team participant to surface any and all unforeseen issues as they become apparent, so that a timely determination can be made as to their expedient disposition.

☆ It is the responsibility of the team to hold themselves accountable to both the project map and each other.

These interdependent roles cannot be implied or discovered through revelation. They must be recognized and understood at the outset if the group is going to set itself right and navigate its course effectively.

Coming to the Table

There is a communication premise that suggests most people are unable to really listen until they have first said what they have to say. The mind must be cleared before new information can enter. The premise has some value when approaching design team interaction—particularly the first group encounters.

We have all known people who are too busy formulating their next response to hear what is being said in the moment. Task force participants come to the table with a host of expectations and anticipated agendas. Until each of those issues are addressed and put where they belong inside or outside the group's list of issues, the team will find itself either dragging through its inventory of to-dos or sailing past points that should have been examined more carefully. Bottom line: Collaboration is not going to happen until expectations are addressed.

Although potentially uncomfortable and time-consuming, the team leader has to get every member to verbalize their questions and concerns. It is the classic spigot analogy. Keeping one's initial point of view hidden not only stifles listening, but it builds pressure within the holder. As the group moves in directions that are not aligned with the member's hidden preferences, the participant finds it harder to focus and more difficult to perform collaboratively. The spigot is closed as the water pressure continues to build and push forward. Eventually the pressure is too great to be contained. The resulting explosion may come from anywhere along the pipeline and have little to do with what was driving the team member nuts to begin with. The resulting anger, confusion, and mistrust on everyone hit by the spray will be hard to reverse. Communication, verbal or nonverbal, is irreversible and irrevocable. Once it has been done or said, "Never mind" isn't going to change anything.

For issues to be addressed, they have to be known. As obvious as that solution may appear on paper, many teams go out of their way to avoid the obvious.

 It is the responsibility of the group to get all its baggage out on the table before any design activity begins, and it is the role of the leader to ensure every outstanding item is addressed, regardless of the discomfort it may initially generate.

It is not uncommon, at the outset of the collective task, for some team members to make it a point of identifying all the constraints they see might lie ahead. This is done for a variety of reasons. The team leader needs to be aware of the motivations underlying the commentary. Some vocal members, who are great content sources or skilled practitioners of an art needed within the group, have been dipped in the waters of cynicism a little too long. They may be mistaking substantive dangers with fleeting shadows. If their commitment and perspective cannot be reestablished, they may best serve the team effort in measured and controlled ways—and from a distance.

Other team members, out of innocent intention, just want to be sure everyone knows where they stand on any and all issues prior to even examining those topics. They are not just grabbing air space with these alerts. They are setting up the conditions for discussion and signaling the team that certain topics can't be glossed over. Still others may have specific questions relative to the design parameters or the group's ability to push the envelope. This is all good. The more the members know of each other's dispositions beforehand, the better.

Everyone coming to the table has expertise, real or imagined, in something. A few may even have the need to set boundaries within which they feel their knowledge is unquestionable. This can set up some dangerous and stilted dynamics within the team if left unattended. All too often their department of origin will predispose them to narrow the focus of that perceived expertise. Solid design teams are created blending a combination of needed content and skills. Those needs drive the composition of the team and may preclude all departments being represented in the mix. That said, most teams will have at least one representative from the following disciplines.

Human resources may express concerns as to the plan's impact relative to cultural reinforcement, retention, recruitment, reducing legal liability, the current talent pool, career progression, or integration of the sales reward structure with other forms of compensation and with other job functions. Often human resource professionals are well versed in best reward practices. Human resources typically serve as a clearing house for third party compensation surveys. Some see themselves as negotiators and consensus builders, brokers of views, and mediators of agendas.

Finance navigates beyond revenue. They move through the company's entire economic map. As such, their vision is influenced by earnings, cash flow, costs, and performance ratios. They appreciate economies of scale, and how much can be spent to achieve meaningful gain. Finance people need quantitative justifications when transiating upside implications. Finance is about differentiating hard and soft dollars, counting booking's over commitments, and recovering expenses (compensation in this case) when contracts sour. Finance translates inventory figures into implications regarding product turnover and sales performance. They translate receivable activity into the quality of customer service and overall operations. Finance sweats the details.

One can never be sure what Information Technology is focusing on at any given moment. It is rare that the IT individual sitting at the table does not feel overworked and underappreciated. There are always one or two gigantic initiatives in progress which produces a reluctance to change anything, lest the initiative or its parts are adversely affected. The cause that brings the team together will have an effect on IT. IT, in most organizations, is about tracking and processing. Sales performance is all about tracking, and the manifestation of rewarding is all about processing.

The best IT participants are those who bring their problem-solving skills to the group—those who are engaged in more than the implementation of systems and measures. The best will help focus activity, watch out for black holes in the enhancement approach, identify overriding issues, and share their project management skills. The best see information as the key to everything and everyone, and possess a unique set of skills that allows them to find the information, call it up in user friendly fashion, and build data flows that maintain its credibility.

Operations take several forms in an organization, encompassing everything from manufacturing, to logistics, to customer service. Their sensitivity usually centers on not overselling the product or service. The area is a huge problem-solving juggernaut. As such there can be a disposition to see the glass half empty. Compensation design change is only one more manifestation of the changes they are being charged with bringing into working reality. Concepts can be studied, customers profiled, markets targeted. None of it becomes real until the product is produced, delivered, installed, and serviced. A great reward structure that focuses sales performance, that may shift product or service emphasis, that may have implications on volume activity, is fine for the company—fine, provided everyone appreciates that operations is the neck in the funnel that all this change is being poured into.

If any one member will be distracted entering the project, it will most likely be the representative from operations. Day-to-day crisis will try to follow him into the room. Yet, if anyone has practical experience in the effects of change on the customer and the inner workings of the company, and, by implication, the realistic steps needed to make change seamless, it will probably be the operations member.

There is a disposition in some marketing managers that revenue is derived by determining client/customer needs, fashioning a unique product to meet those needs, and creatively targeting information that creates a demand for that uniqueness. To them product differentiation is a result of brand awareness. In the marketer's mind, a sale is the confluence of image, need, and location. In essence, they feel that a good marketing department ensures the product sells itself. With a mindset buried in the demographics of the company's target audience and absorbed in the creation of informational materials, there may be little room to accurately appreciate the role of the sales staff. Yet with an accurate appraisal of the sales role, the marketing member could be one of the most versatile players on the team. Marketing requires a skill set well suited for project work encompassing research, analytical, creative, and communicative abilities. The individual representing marketing can act as a bridge between many of the other disciplines represented on the team.

All functional disciplines add value to the whole design process—provided they are balanced and integrated into the common vision. The leader, as well as those who selected the team members, has to make clear to the members that they are part of the team not just because they know the workings of their areas of expertise. In addition to knowledge, the members bring skills and attributes to the group. Everyone on the team has the ability to effectively probe and question, to reason independently, to analyze, to create. Everyone on the team has communication skills and the capability to support the common goal. Everyone on the team has perspective and the capacity not to forget that. Some may have more. Some may have less. All come equipped in good measure. No one falls below the baseline of the needed quantity.

It is critical to the project's momentum to provide everyone on the team the opportunity to share their current points of view at the very outset, allow management through the project leader to respond to those points of view, and furnish the participants a clear frame of reference from which to proceed. Once this dialogue has taken place, stuff has to start happening. The design team engine has been turned on.

Keeping Universal Issues in Mind

It is important to point out within the context of developing a collaborative design team that some tasks have established frames of reference (we will explore this in greater detail in Chapter 8). Although specifics as to approach, content, and emphasis will vary from company to company, the team does not have to handicap itself by working in a vacuum.

Effective sales plans, regardless of industry or targeted positions, have a variety of common best practice design elements. These elements fall under the basic headings of "keep it simple" and "keep it focused." A well designed plan:

☆ provides upside potential within a prudent economic framework.

☆ ensures that desired behaviors/results are within the control of the participant.

☆ considers team implications for inclusion or exclusion in plan design.

☆ aligns desired results with the appropriate type of variable pay program (commission, incentive, or bonus).

☆ creates ramping bonus opportunity (accelerators) or multiple rewards carefully and only when significant performance achievement can be obtained.

☆ pre-establishes windfall provisions.

☆ consolidates various unfocused activities in the sales stream.

☆ establishes the desired sales emphasis, and rewards discriminately for new product/services being rolled out, remixed products/services, and/or sales from established sources of revenue.

☆ accounts for staffing changes during the sales cycle.

☆ creates enough flexibility in the plan to adjust for annual changes in emphasis.

☆ sends a strong and clear message as to what needs to be accomplished.

For every best practice there is its opposite (the worst practice). One worthy of note is abusive plan changes. Investing in a collaborative design team should have at least a three-sales-cycle investment return. Barring some unforeseen and cataclysmic turn in the marketplace, the foundation and elements of the sales reward programs should be left to their own devices for that period of time. It is business necessity to change the annual cycle goals to reflect the realities of your business. It is more than reasonable to refocus at the end of a business cycle the value of energy to be expended on already established plan elements. But don't change the fundamental elements of the program unless the fundamental elements of your business change. Why?

I once was asked to redesign a commercial banking sales plan. As always, I asked to interview with several key managers and staff before agreeing to the engagement. The bank felt pressured by time constraints and production expectations, so a joint meeting was to be held in an ornate conference room; the kind where chairs that look like small sofas are impossible to comfortably sit in, and once seated your chin clears the highly polished table by a few inches. It didn't take a detective to uncover the tension in the room. Three sales representatives, selected among the best in the bank, had managed to move their chairs against the back wall and away from the table. Three sales managers were glaring across the table at their division manager.

Nobody was talking. Eventually I asked my typical opening question, "Why change?"

Everybody was talking. The division manager started by explaining how the industry was in flux and that previous plan designs weren't addressing these changing needs. Sales management felt that the current plans were operationally impossible to manage. Sales staff courageously pointed out that every time the staff exceeded its goals the plans changed. They felt that something repressive and sinister was afoot.

"How often was every time?" I asked. Eight times in the last three years— this would be the third time in this sales cycle. It is not impossible, but it is really hard, to create eight lousy plans in three years. Eventually, experience takes hold and you start to get it right. Management wanted to change the plan again; staff did not. The fight was over whether to keep or change the plan.

They were fighting the wrong battle. The enemy was a fragmented process. All their past plans were devoid of any alignment with the vision and objectives of the commercial banking area. All their past plans were mechanical adjustments of designs replicated from competitors. All their plans paid out based on arithmetic formulas that didn't take into account half the costs associated with generating the revenue. In most cases, they were overcompensating for the actual return they realized from the sale.

They were so angry, or frustrated, or entrenched that it took hours for them to finally appreciate their collective situation. Once they realized their true predicament, progress toward a common goal could begin.

I point this out because no design team should ever enter their task with the feeling that their efforts will be revisited in the short term. No executive group should commission a plan design with the expectation of frequent and frenetic change. Not only will frequent redesign generate a form of chaos, its origins will be suspect as well. Such change will bring about a natural inclination of the staff to wonder if management is capable of planning, particularly if at every turn in the business road a new compensation program has to be launched to meet some unforeseen challenge.

When one questions management's ability to plan, one questions a fundamental reason for management. A cascading set of distractions begins to evolve that undermines productivity and any confidence in the quality of subsequent decisions being made.

Then there are those executives who love to "stir things up." Change for change's sake is not what plan design teams are about. Shaking up the organization just to see it quiver, and using compensation as a tool in that effort, will get you nothing but dysfunctional turnover.

While every plan should be revised periodically, a sales compensation plan should be designed carefully enough to be viable for those three sales cycles and fashioned well enough so that any subsequent redesign builds upon the solidly laid foundation of the previous planning. That is the legacy of the sales design team.

Intergroup Collaboration

As mentioned previously (in Chapter 6), the sales force is not wandering in the dark while the design process is going forward. This group, through designated role models, should be functioning as one of the design group's principle research and editorial resources. The design team should be soliciting the engaged sales staff to ensure that they:

- ☆ understand what specific results the plan is intended to produce, how those results translate into compensation and/or other rewards, and how the plan is to be administered.

- ☆ perceive the plan to be straightforward and fair.

- ☆ feel an ownership in the plan's elements.

- ☆ are challenged by the goals of the plan.

- ☆ are able to articulate how the plan is aligned with the company's vision, priorities, and objectives.

The credibility of the design team in the eyes of the sale's staff will be reflected in how responsive and candid the team is to the questions, comments, and suggestions of their engaged representatives. Regularly scheduled interaction with this group has to build into the plan.

Presentations

There is a Rubber Chicken rule of thumb:

 Regarding management presentations do not overwhelm.

The design team needs to concede that it will never have the time needed to adequately express all the nuances and shadings entailed in the project. So put away the deck of 65 slides. Be the audience. Maximize their time. Anticipate their questions and their perspective and move in that direction. Be assured that, if there is continued interest, the team will be encouraged to expand on its presentation. If it is appropriate the team may choose to informally brief specific management members at points prior to any presentation, or submit preparatory materials before the presentation. If it helps the management staff, do it. If it clutters their offices or is an inappropriate use of their time or advocacy, avoid it at all costs.

Gather What is Needed Not What is Merely Available or Desired

Leaders don't let the team run amok when gathering information. Stay on point and on schedule. Determine at the outset the criteria that make information critical to the project. If a query doesn't reconcile itself to the standards set, move on. More groups lose their way in the forest of information than necessary, either because they follow a trail too deeply into the trees or become distracted by potentially enticing flora and fauna.

Each team member has an obligation to translate their data so a general understanding can be established between disciplines. The collective team has to be clear on the meaning and implications of all economic, market, competency based, sales, logistical, production, merchandising, and measurement information used in crafting a new compensation design.

When Crafting

At the very least the following discussions should be going on when putting together the plan design:

☆ Human resources and sales should be leading discussions about staff competency gaps between what skills and attributes are needed, what exists, and what resolution strategies should be considered to close the gaps.

☆ Finance, sales, and operations should be leading discussions about organizational productivity needs and how the overall economics of the business will affect the design.

☆ Marketing and sales should be leading discussions about realistic sales estimates and market penetration of various customer segmentations.

☆ The team leader should be focusing discussions on measurements of success within the control of the sales staff.

☆ Human resources, sales, marketing, and finance should be leading discussions about staffing size related to the new design and result expectations.

Once this initial crafting stage is completed the sales engagement team should be brought into the process again for their reaction to the direction being carved out.

Between Conception and Inception

The steps between crafting and finalizing the plan will test the resolve of the group. In the face of steadily growing pressure, the members will have to:

☆ subordinate pride of authorship.

☆ carefully consider how change is presented to senior management.

☆ maintain the core elements they feel are critical to the plan.

☆ ensure that all issues have been dealt with thoroughly.

☆ test all conceivable situations against the plan elements.

☆ react to the unforeseen.

☆ repeatedly step back and regain perspective.

The team leader should assess the interaction strength of the group before proceeding into this phase of planning. The pressures the group will now confront will only exacerbate whatever outstanding issues of style or substance remain unresolved. It is best to reach an understanding between members. This is their time for unity of purpose. Irreversible action is at hand. All issues that need to be reconciled before the team proceeds further should be addressed and concluded now, before the group collectively crosses the threshold and enters the final arena.

Communication

For at least the last 30 years, companies have been reviewing survey results which assess the perceptions of their staff relative to the actual worth of the compensation programs that affect them. In one case, a company's overall compensation program was mid-range when leveled against its comparator group of companies. However, the staff's perception of the value of the compensation program placed the company in the 90th percentile of the same comparator group. The staff, regardless of objective dollar-to-dollar comparisons, had a more positive perception of their program as compared to employees of other companies whose programs were actually more generous and/or focused on their staff's demographics. Most employee perceptions align themselves with the employees of those other companies. Staff populations tend to under-appreciate the value of their compensation.

The over-appreciation in the previous example was directly correlated with the amount of resources dedicated to communicating the particulars of the company's program. It should be pointed out that there was no deceptive information presented to the staff. The strategy was to explain, as clearly as possible, the elements of the plan, the economics behind the design decisions, and how the program realistically impacted that particular workforce. Obviously, the merits of the program were talked up. But nothing was masked or hidden with the exception of any emphasis on specific marketplace comparisons. Nothing was blown out of proportion.

The positive perceptual result, as reflected in the surveys taken, reinforces the power of careful communication. By careful, I am referring to planned, targeted, and well-prepared communication strategies. Communication of sales compensation programs often seems to be an afterthought on the part of management. After expending considerable energy on design, the plan is disseminated in the most haphazard of ways, and often at the last minute.

Companies confuse effective communication with slick, colorful fold-out print materials. Perhaps there is a video from the CEO or head of sales. I have seen sterile plan documents fresh from the legal department constitute a communication roll out. There is almost a dismissive feeling of getting the information out quickly, away from management and into the hands of the staff, so that the process is somehow officially over and everyone can get back to work. It is as if the plan is peripheral to the day-to-day business of selling. Nothing could be more wrong. The plan IS the essence of the day-to-day business of selling.

Sales Managers—Pivotal Dialogue Point
  Rubber Chicken:

 Communication of a new sales compensation plan is not, repeat not, a monologue.

Monologues cannot test whether the clarity of the plan's purpose is aligned with the clarity of the program elements. Monologues cannot test the target audience's understanding of that alignment. Monologues cannot test the credibility of the program in the eyes of the sales staff. Brochures, videos, leaflets, written Q&A sheets, and formal documents are monologue devices. They have preparatory value before and reinforcing value after the dialogue. But they don't take the place of dialogue.

Dialogue begins with your delivery system, the line sales managers. The design team has to take the importance of these line managers into account when crafting this phase of the process. The credibility sales managers have with the staff and their understanding of the changes being initiated can bring about a disposition of acceptance and involvement on the part of the sales crew. Sales managers need to be as well versed in the plan elements as are the plan creators. Nothing should be communicated outside the management circle until this group is briefed, debriefed, and ready.

It should be the objective of sales management to have discussions with everyone who is a participant of the compensation plan. In most cases this is a combination of group meetings and individual follow ups by the moderator or the line sales manager.

One population, the rainmakers, should be singled out for special consideration. The top producers in the firm may need much more individualized attention to ensure that their perspective on any changes is factually grounded. The top tier of your sales force should be attended to by as relevant a member of management as possible prior to any subsequent group meetings. Two messages are being communicated: change is about to happen and this high performing group is considered special enough to be accorded singular treatment. The last message can be a powerful gesture with loyalty and retention implications.

Show Time

As in all actions within the company, choose communication approaches and materials that are in keeping with the culture and style of the organization. Make the communication experience real, not distracting.

I knew of a senior manager who would present change, pause for a brief moment, and as he headed briskly out of the conference room announce, in one breath, "Are there any questions, well if not thank you for coming." His footsteps could be heard down the hall as his voice still lingered in the room. It's not the most participative of proceedings. Allow for the pressing questions and comments to be surfaced for discussion. Let the blood and guts issues spill out. It is going to happen anyway. Let the revealing forum be one that involves management.

Once the initial materials have been disseminated and the individual and group meeting held, allow for some absorption time before going back to the sales staff for their additional comments or questions.

As important as it is to have a complete communication sequence take place (from explanation through understanding to ownership), there comes a point where the cycle ceases and everyone moves forward. The sales staff has to know the length of time set aside as a reasonable period devoted to the roll out. After that, it's show time.

A last communication step, which symbolically finalizes the roll out period, is the distribution of the Summary Plan Document. The document lays out the purpose of the plan, its elements, participant eligibility, administrative process and caveats, problem resolution steps, and examples of how varying degrees of performance are rewarded under the plan provisions. It may seem unnecessary, but it is strongly advised that each participant acknowledges, in writing, receipt of the plan document. It not only reinforces the importance of the plan, but secures an understanding between both staff and the company that may alleviate any possible confusion as to plan management in the months ahead.

Conclusion

When forming the sales plan design team, don't avoid inclusion, manage it. Get everyone on the same page and make them stay there. Select a representative, mature, and mutually respectful team that can function harmoniously as peers. Each member must feel accountable to the team and its goals. Ensure the team surfaces and addresses any and all participant issues and concerns before beginning the design process. Define the sales compensation design goals, keeping in mind that validation of those goals will be a product of the sales staff's ability to own and understand the plan elements. Review the team's sequence of process steps and help them stay on track. Encourage team discipline. Use the individual talents of the team to their fullest. Eradicated surprises by having the team test and model the design. Have the team think of the audience when preparing presentations. Help them stay positive. Help them stay focused. Help them stay balanced. Watch them succeed.

8
Strive for Simplicity:
Streamlining Your Design Strategy

It is not atypical to be engaged by a client who hopes that, somewhere in your consultant's bag of tricks, there lays a silver bullet, a quick solution that will remedy the ills of the past. You enter the investigatory stages of each assignment prepared for anything. There is almost always a surprise or an untold "issue" or "situation" that throws the project off its axis. Once in a while, you get involved with a company that raises the bizarre bar.

You know plan focus has been lost when the sales staff hires, using their own funds, an individual to audit their monthly commissions. You know plan focus has been lost when the sales staff hires, using their own funds, another advisor who counsels each sales representative on which combination of services sold will return the greatest overall commission. And you definitely know plan focus has been lost when these conditions have gone on for several years.

The only person in the company who understood the mechanics of the commission plan was its designer: a young fellow marginally out of puberty with a questionable social life, who was fascinated by the power of the personal computer and the intricacies of smashing logarithms against exponential functions. Oh, the graphs and charts he could produce. He also had a nifty way of formatting information so that a manager could punch a revenue number onto a corner of a spreadsheet and watch it produce a payout figure in another corner of the same sheet. To them, it was magic. It was a plan that was also grossly overpaying the sales staff for services rendered and also paying them for the wrong results. There were transactions closed where, through the complexities of the design, compensation unintentionally exceeded the income produced from the sale.

Sales management just stared at their screens mesmerized both by the plan's complexity and its colorful displays. Excel formulas and linking cells appeared to be other world concepts. Eventually, reality caught up with this multi-state service organization when a new COO asked his sales management to explain, without outside third-party help, how the plan worked. Putting a number in here and watching it produce a number over there was not a satisfactory answer. When the COO asked a few of his so-called rainmakers to explain the plan, they couldn't. Instead, they encouraged him to contact either the auditor or the adviser they had on retainer. The COO said he had a better idea. He contacted me.

Arguably this is an extreme case of complexity and all its ills run amok. It is the only one of its kind that I have run across in my 30 years of doing this type of work. But it illustrates the fact that when such conditions exist complexity can often mask both the message and the focus of the sales effort with significant economic repercussions. The computer geek and his program were merely symptomatic of a much larger and fundamental problem, one that required more than a silver bullet to remedy.

As an after point to the previous situation, many of the sales representatives were not really selling, but taking orders. Their influence on sales was marginal and the value awarded that influence was disproportionate to its effect.

So, What's Wrong With Complexity?

Let's assume that the sales staff is really selling and not just processing orders and that management is really coaching staff and analyzing activity. What's wrong with being intricate in slicing and dicing results? How can precision of design in the pursuit of analytical clarity be a bad thing? After all, a lot of other aspects of business are intricate and complex. Why not compensation designs?

Here is the Rubber Chicken answer:

If they are to have the desired impact, sales compensation has to be a series of clearly focused and coordinated messages that are aligned to the goals and values of the company.

At its essence, sales compensation is more than an arithmetic exercise.

The first message is quantifiable. Every sales member needs an unambiguous definition of what is to be accomplished. In a situation where there are multiple results to achieve, their relative weight must be explained. There needs to be an unobstructed line of sight between sales results and the economics of the company. The more factors, the more twists and turns, the more variations on a subject, the greater the chance that line of sight will be broken.

The second message is motivational. Effective sales reps are engaged sales reps. They not only understand the economic message, they buy into it. They are able to measure their own success against the plan on a daily basis. There is a sense of psychic equity that comes from both their achievement and the gains of the entire sales group. To them sales success translates into company success. Beyond the monetary, there is pride in the reputation the sales group establishes in the industry and the community. Success feels real and pervasive. Feeling real generates enthusiasm and a continued sense of urgency.

Effective sales design sends *a third message: sustained action.* The plan moves the staff to immediately engage and to stay engaged. There is always another hill to climb. Complacency has no place in the sales compensation. There may be rest stops, but the journey has no end because the vision of the company has no end. The horizon has yet to be reached.

Complexity Is Rarely Accidental

There can be an equally compelling argument made against extreme simplicity as against extreme complexity. There is nothing wrong with complexity IF the staff doesn't perceive the road from result to reward as overly complex. We are not talking about achieving this realization through hypnosis or sleight of hand. Complexity is relative. That relativity is predicated on the type of industry and selling as well as the history of the sales group. What may seem like gibberish to an outsider may be seen as clear and well-structured within the sales team. If the plan design allows for all messages to be effectively conveyed, complexity is neutralized.

In most cases, this may be easier said than done. Why? Before there are plans, there have to be planners.

Sales performance goals are an aligned subset of larger business objectives developed for the company in a variety of ways by various business planning sources. These business objectives are usually inviolate. There may be some flexibility as to their segmentation and assignment, but the targets are visible markers that the company is driving to achieve. In too many companies, longer-term planning and commensurate annual objectives have become an imprecise management discipline. On the surface performance goals appear to be established from sound marketing intelligence, dialogues up and down the organizational ladder, and scrupulous financial analysis. Unfortunately, too many of these goals are actually established based on top-down expected returns developed with little regard for the realities of the market, the strength of the staff, or the conditions of the company. Success is not always measured by the viability of the goals, but rather by the art form in selling those goals to the ultimate approval source. Ownership is given compelling financial forecasts, regardless of objective reality.

The genesis of this overall lack of care in forecasting is rooted in a variety of related conditions that can foreshadow the quality of a sales compensation program. Companies have always been challenged by a degree of intellectual laziness, but in the last decade the virus seems to have proliferated. Add to that the pressure for short term results; a tendency not to compete, but rather buyout competition; and a constant fear of being seen as "wrong" in the eyes of shareholders, analysts, or the public and the possibility of sound long term planning appears daunting. In that context, poor performance planners are prone to take credit for what appears to be the result of successful planning in one year, and blame the vagaries of the marketplace for aberrant results-to-forecast in the next year. They perceive a far greater risk in trying to plan effectively and take responsibility for outcomes, than in using stretched logic attempting to convince their audiences why marginal results were really beyond anyone's control. In many of today's so-called risk/reward environments, when it comes to management compensation for planning, risk has an inverse relationship to reward.

Even assuming that legitimate performance-goal processes are in place, imprecise performance goal-setting can occur at the beginning of a new product or service's life cycle. And "guestimating" is okay, at first. It is not atypical in the start-up phase to plan based on aggregate goals. As knowledge of the product's acceptance evolves, specifically designed goals will replace the more all encompassing and less focused variety. If target goals and actual results deviate by more than 10 percent after the first three planning cycles, and are not the result of an act of God, don't abandon goal setting, get yourself better goal setters.

The Design Umbrella

Effective sales reward plans, regardless of industry or targeted positions, have common best practice design elements that fall under the basic headings of keep it simple and keep it focused. Before examining these elements in some detail, reflect on the following umbrella statements. These statements are Rubber Chickens that form the fabric of any good sales compensation plan.

1. Salespeople are an investment to be developed, listened to, collaborated with and shown genuine attention and concern.

Rapport with the sales staff, achieving mutual trust and respect, transcends any design flaw and allows for flexibility and modification after the fact. Rapport permits everyone to move away from interpersonal distractions and focus on the critical needs of the company and the staff.

2. Design time should reflect the design's strategic impact on the company.

Compensation planning is a natural extension of the organization's strategic and financial planning. It is one of the primary mechanisms used in realizing the business' objectives. Compensation design is not something that can be put together a week before implementing next year's goals. It is not an afterthought. It is a reflection of how important the sales effort and its staff are to the success of the company's direction.

3. Compensation plans never replace management's decision-making responsibility to the sales staff.

All too often compensation programs are designed, whether intentional or accidental, to short circuit the judgment process and cement that process to an inflexible set of formulas, conditions, and time frames. Good salespeople do not want to function under capricious leadership, nor do they wish to be left to the devices of an indifferent payout schedule with provisions that do not allow for consideration and adjustment to unique circumstances.

Design philosophy is rooted in the belief that everyone touching the plan must understand what expected results the program is reinforcing, how and when it compensates for those results, and why those results are critical to the future of the company.

4. A well-designed plan is not just a pay vehicle. It is a powerful validation of the message. It cannot be abused or treated indifferently without abusing and neutralizing the message.

Design Elements

A productive design pattern:

☆ pays for the **Act of Selling.**

☆ adheres to the **Rules of 10**.

☆ selects the most aligned **Message Drivers**.

☆ defines the **Sales Event**.

☆ measures for **Focus and Change**.

☆ models for the **Unforeseen**.

☆ communicates, communicates, and then **communicates**.

Pay a Salesperson to Sell

There is a reflex assumption in some organizations that if you sell a product or service, you automatically have salespeople doing the selling. That assumption can lead to costly and unnecessary compensation structures and pay programs that never really change or encourage the preferred behavior. In these situations, behavior will not change or improve because reality and the reward program are not connected. The Rubber Chicken in sales compensation is fundamental.

Salespeople are paid to persuade.

Consider this scenario:

He sits there staring into space. Ask him a question and his gaze shifts slowly in your direction. But the blank stare remains. She walks down the aisle. You stop her with a question. "I'll have to check on that," she replies. Then, as if frozen in time, she remains motionless. "Were you going to check on that?" you ask. "Oh, yeah," she mumbles, vanishing down a corridor never to return. These are not salespeople. They are not persuading you to do anything—except perhaps leave the store screaming.

He shows up all smiles and bon ami. The small talk and jokes finally subside as he extracts his order pad. It's time for your regular renewal. A goat could wander into your office with an order pad strapped to its back and you would place the order. You are buying the product for reasons other than persuasion. Perhaps the accompanying service is outstanding. Perhaps the pricing is very competitive. Perhaps it is just a great product. But it is not because of the fellow with the order pad.

Shift the scenes a bit.

He approaches you as you make your way to his counter. He not only answers your questions but recommends other products, perhaps a set of products that better suit your needs. She, formally of the disappearing act, does the same while guiding you through the aisles and ensuring you are satisfied with the product selection.

He shows up with a new line of products and extols the virtues of those that best fit your business. He is empowered to make deals, to discount for volume or length of contract. He will follow up to make sure installation is done according to your specifications and will direct the installers in any modifications that are needed.

In these cases selling is taking place. Persuasion is taking place. In the first examples, at best, direction giving and order taking is occurring. In the second example, cross-selling, selling up, and negotiating are occurring.

Salespeople are not ticket takers, they are not suppliers, and they are not inventory control specialists (particularly with resellers). These functions should be paid differently. They may be part of a selling position's job description for a host of business reasons, but remuneration for these tasks falls under a pay heading with very limited risk and reward potential: base salary. Keep sales compensation focused on sales. Keep it pure.

How Much Is Too Much—Capping Compensation

The three bears had it easy. The porridge was supposed to be just right. Nobody wants cold mush and no one can eat from a blistering hot bowl. When establishing the cost structure to support sales performance, when does one know if sales remuneration is too little, too much, or just right? As mentioned in a previous chapter, if you ask the right questions the marketplace will tell you what competitive total sales pay is at target for jobs of similar scope and challenge. It will also tell you the 25th and 75th percentiles of pay. That helps. It is still the company's task to determine how much of total pay opportunity will be dedicated to at-risk behavior and how much will be institutionalized in base salary.

Some organizations cap the sales staff's upside opportunity. Others continue to slice a piece of revenue, sometimes at a diminishing rate, for sales well beyond targeted performance. The argument for capped opportunity has typically been centered on shareholder value. At some point, the argument goes, money dedicated to exemplary sales performance has to stop and be diverted back into the company, either to benefit it's investors directly through dividends, or to benefit the owners in the longer run through corporate investment. The feeling is that once sales compensation is banging against the 90th percentile of marketplace pay, regardless of individual performance, it is time to stop.

There is another rationale to divining whether to cap or uncap sales pay. Answer the question of client loyalty. If the client's relationship is with the uniqueness or desirability of the brand and/or the product or service, cap the compensation. If the nature of the sale binds the client to the company and makes it extremely difficult to break that relationship without the customer suffering extended aggravation or financial loss, cap the compensation. This is not to say that selling is not taking place. There may still be acts of persuasion and negotiation occurring in the selection of pricing and product. But the primary motivation surrounding the client's business relates to the selling company and not the sales person.

However, if the sales person is the difference between the client buying from the company or moving her business across the street, consider uncapping the opportunity. If the sales person can take his book of business wherever he goes, and sell from that book in a comparator company, typically unenforceable but ever present non-compete clauses notwithstanding, uncap the opportunity. In these situations the sales person controls the sale and is the primary point of loyalty for the customer. Both the client and the salesperson have a more independent orientation away from— not toward the selling company. Business with that kind of vulnerability has a price.

The 10 Rubber Chickens of Sales Design

1. Value the sales event and pay that value once.

   Sounds obvious, but it is often ignored. For example, the value of the sale is reflected in the commission. It is reflected again in the quarterly bonus for aggregate sales achievement. And it is recognized a third time in the annual incentive for selling to new clients, or existing clients, or whatever. It would be reasonable, in this example of redundancy, to divide the value of the sale among these three measurement forms, but often the company pays competitively for the first result criteria and then continues to add pay for that same result several times over.

2. Separate behavior and result in how you compensate.

   Variable pay compensates for results, for meeting the measures. Base compensation provides a vehicle to remunerate for expected behaviors: following a code of conduct, performing ethically, attending sales meetings, contributing to the common good, and in some cases for baseline results. The more qualitatively the criteria used in assessing variable pay is, the bigger the administrative and assessment headaches and the more distracted the sales staff. Bonuses, incentives, and/or commissions should be funded from the incremental gain of the sale. Sound variable pay links that gain (result) to the individual's results and opportunity.

3. Don't fluff up variable criteria.

   Playing well with others should be a fundamental requirement for employment and not something that finds its way into the variable reward stream. It is unfortunate and not uncommon to see the "nice" factor surface as a modifier or mitigating reason for rewarding someone through at risk pay. Variable compensation should have an upside and downside potential. If a representative's sales are marginal he will receive less remuneration, recognition, and rewards than a salesperson who achieved target performance. If there are no sales forthcoming over a designated period of time, there may well be no job for the individual. These are the realities of the performance continuum. Where logical reasoning takes a spin is in the assumption that playing well has a continuum—it doesn't. You either play well or you don't. If you don't you should be out. That's an expectation of the job. Except for human resource types, does anyone want to get into the art form of defining and valuing playing well versus playing not so well versus playing really well or playing really, really well? Nonsense! And that goes for any other fundamental behavior requirement.

4.   Design sales programs to maximize focus.

Don't equivocate by introducing unexpected contests or promotions that make up for poor management planning. If launching a new product or service requires some promotional focus, all is well and good. It is a planned event and built into the program. Appreciate that most sales folks hate to have their focus shifted away from their big deliverables to clear inventory at a discounted rate. Contests can often result in the staff working as hard, or harder, yet earning less per unit for the associated aggravation.

5. Related to the above,

  Don't create a program that sends an unintended message to the staff.

Two classic failures in design are establishing rewards for selling one product to the unexpected detriment of another, or guaranteeing income from easy business to the detriment of all other opportunities. Human nature pushes salespeople to evaluate the territory before them and look for the paths of least resistance for the value derived. If you put up the road sign that says, "This way to comfortable gain for minimum effort" guess where people will go? Note the term "comfortable." Everyone has a sense of what is comfortable. Sure, they may not break the bank with sales form renewals, for example, but it is more than enough to get by. So they'll get by, and new business will slump. All commissions being equal, a sales representative is going to go where the most money can be made. And if the message has leveled all sales into one category of value, you will have to take your chances that the sales you want are the sales you will get. But if you pump up the rewards for selling a particular product inordinately, don't be surprised if actions shift in that direction and away from other important products.

6. Establish a complete template, or sales compensation map, before implementing a plan.

Think through windfall provisions, territory transfers, business generated from internal referrals or business leads, and payment for residuals. (These issues will be covered later in the chapter.) The point of emphasis here is to ensure that all the issues are surfaced, decided upon, and communicated clearly at the outset of a program.

7. Design for challenge, not impossibility.

Sales compensation for all participants should be the result of responding to achievable and controllable measures. Don't create hurdles so high that you risk aversion on the part of the staff. Even the most hardened commission sales personnel value some stability in their income stream. Reasonably set risk boundaries with commensurate (and reasonable) loss/reward opportunities, generates better overall performance. It has been my experience that high risk and rewards for achieving high deliverables, with equally dramatic potential downside risks and rewards, generally drive away talent or develops a monster breed of salesperson whose counterproductive behavior is a bigger headache than the achievements they realize. Don't create universal indices that apply to all sales staff when differentiating territories or clients. That inflexibility creates immediately evident barriers to achievement. Have the measures reflect careful planning that reconciles specific sales challenges with the reality of the specific sales climate.

8. Design for balance and flexibility.

Emphasize message and intent over mechanical perfection. Rigid structures will topple the best intended plans. Effective sales design anticipates. Don't finalize your plans until you are satisfied that the vast majority of conditions that could affect its design have been modeled and the outcomes factored into your conclusions. And when you have modeled the hell out of your plan, stop and allow time to bring into focus that which you didn't initially foresee. Anticipate the unanticipated by permitting common sense to intervene when things become muddled. Fall back to your original intent and see if your ad hoc decisions anchor well to those principles and objectives. Don't allow pre-fabricated designs to dictate actions regardless of circumstances.

9. Don't discount the power of base salary when designing your overall sales compensation.

With the exception of the fully commissioned sales function, which typically builds into its formulas a virtually guaranteed "base" amount for results from which sales goals effectively begin to payout, most sales staff have anywhere from 20 percent to 70 percent of their total cash compensation derived from base salaries.

☆ What is the utility of base pay? It provides a margin of secured income for the salesperson. The amount of compensation dedicated to base pay is productive when it is substantial enough to alleviate the salesperson's day-to-day survival anxiety, but not so substantial as to diminish the sales drive.

☆ What should a company expect in return for base pay? Base pay reinforces the organization through compensating for behavioral integrity, professional conduct, sales generated that cover the cost of base compensation, a modicum of team awareness and support, and remuneration for special mentoring and/or lead services rendered.

☆ The key point is to guard against the expectation of providing high base salary levels merely as a condition of employment. Use base compensation aggressively and consciously to differentiate those expectations you have of your staff other than selling beyond threshold goals.

10. Note the behaviors of your sales staff before you make changes, make them aware of your sensitivity, and let their reality help guide those changes.

Or put another way, remember the quad. A story is told that an Ivy League college was preparing to pave the paths that joined the buildings surrounding a large square of greenery in a newly constructed part of the campus. The initial design called for angles and intersections of spatial symmetry. Someone pointed out, based on the proliferation of brown ruts in other parts of the college, the futility of following any geometric pattern. Students generally ignored the developed paths and trampled across the grass in paths of their own making. So it was decided to wait and observe the students as they selected their avenues across the new quad. Eventually concrete was poured along those self-selected paths. The result was healthy lawns, a unique pattern of efficient pathways, and an enfranchisement of the students who responded by taking exceptional care of their new surroundings.

Selecting the Message Driver—Commission, Incentive, Bonus, and Contest Pay Programs

Using the wrong compensation vehicle not only overcomplicates the selling and reward process, it derails it.

Commission

If selling is transaction based with appreciable volume and quick turn time from initiating contact to close, paying by commission is the preferable choice. Whether you use a full commission plan that includes a recoverable draw, or base and commission, there is an expectation of a certain level of sales volume that will sustain the salesperson and cost justify any salary or operating expense associated with the position. After that threshold is met, it is up to the individual to meet goals that not only reward for results, but provide income beyond subsistence. The big failures in commission programs seem to occur when the targets are poorly placed or the individual is not really selling, but taking orders. We have talked about order-takers before. Targets placed impossibly high deflate any motivation to achieve. Targets placed too low create a false sense of accomplishment and eventually turn into entitlements. In both cases, productivity is far from maximized.

Incentives

Incentive pay is highly individualized. Specific goals, sometimes divided into result steps, lead to remuneration during an extended period of time. It is not atypical to have incentive measures that have a quarterly, semi-annual, or annual window. Relationship selling, either for the time it takes to build the relationship before a sale is closed, or the expectation of continued business, is typically paid through incentives. Incentive criteria are easily muddied. Criteria established for the uniqueness of the position can turn into personalized criteria adjusted to the individual and not the expectations of the position. Qualitative factors, which really belong in base pay, can also creep in.

Whereas a commission salesperson may rely on at least 70 percent of their income to be derived, at target, from variable pay, an incentive-based individual may realize 40 percent of their overall income from variable compensation. Virtually everything about commission selling and incentive selling is different. Because of that, the individuals who gravitate toward those kinds of selling challenges are different. Their fundamental selling profiles, the way they are managed, and their reward expectations are different. And the lesson implied is not to hire a full commission oriented salesperson to sell business with result windows greater than a month. It'll drive you, the customers, and the salesperson crazy. The reverse is equally true. Incentive-based relationship sellers will find it extremely difficult to move fast enough and be thick skinned enough to achieve commission-oriented goals. Consider the behavioral differences almost a law of nature.

Contests

Contests can jazz up a sales staff, particularly commissioned sales staff where results can be quickly achieved. Effective contests send a short-term, but critical, sales message. They can be used to clear inventory, boost the sale of a new product, increase the attention paid to a sagging line, or generate action around packaged offerings to the customer. The danger in contest pay is its ability to dilute and shift the focus of the sales staff away from the fundamental sales goals that they are charged with producing. There is also the potential of being redundant in both message and pay opportunity.

Companies charge the sales staff with selling X, Y, and Z. Through time the company becomes frustrated with the lack of movement in category X and institutes a contest to focus energy in that direction. If a contest results in increased sales of X, should that be considered successful behavior or should the company question both its sales management skills and its fundamental sales compensation program? Is the contest being used to correct problems in coaching or compensation structure? In addition to avoiding the trap of having contests become the quick fix cure all, companies need to be careful that the contest message is clear to the sales force, and that the extra expense associated with the results of a successful campaign, cost justify the return.

Bonus

Bonus pay finds its home in situations that reward for collective and aggregate results. Usually they are based on a net measure. When paid, bonus rewards are typically at the end of a financially significant milestone such as the close of business for the year. Bonus awards create a circuitous reward line extending from the sale through a catacomb of vague individual expectations to an outcome that is often difficult to substantiate in the mind of the participant. If the reward outcome is positive, few recipients bother to figure out how it was derived. If there is regularity in the bonus award, it can turn into an entitlement. If there is a downturn that shrinks or nullifies the anticipated bonus, only then do the wheels of inquiry begin to grind.

Bonuses are a form of feel good money. It reinforces the illusion that everyone on the team is being compensated for their contribution to the incremental gain that funds a bonus. There is a notion in some compensation camps that team pay is a positive. It is the belief that one vision, one focus, one unified effort, and one overall result leads to one collective payout. The musketeers would be proud. We as a society embrace the idea of team. Team is a good word. Be a team player. Team builds character. Teams are action oriented. Teams subordinate the individual agenda and come together to achieve the bigger picture. What could possibly be wrong with extending those images into the pay arena? Just about everything.

Feel good pay never works for the same reason that team effort is an oversimplification of a complex organizational process. The reception's cheery and helpful manner may set the service tone. The installers and customer service representatives may reinforce the quality of the company and its products. Logistics may speak to dependability and responsiveness. The facilities manager may keep the work site presentable, assisting in productivity and impacting the client's perceptions of the business. Each of these functions performs a valuable organizational role. Each function should be compensated competitively based on internal and external considerations. Some of these functions may be eligible for incentives focused on specific goals, which have a potential upside and downside risk. Some of these goals may even realize cost savings. But, with the infrequent exception of customer service and installation personnel securing renewed business, none of these functions has a direct line of sight between themselves and generating revenue.

Paying people for what they do, using base and focused variable compensation, and not for the symbolic illusion of what their contribution implies, is a much clearer and more meaningful message. Better that the secretary tells his colleagues in other companies that he can receive a reward greater than his base salary by achieving specific expense reductions without decrementing customer service or efficiency, than to tell them he gets a bonus if the company achieves a certain profit level. Better the secretary takes pride in accomplishing something within his control than accept a symbolic and paternalistic award for an abstract connection to his job. Yes, it takes more management energy to create meaningful incentive goals. Yes, it takes more coaching and assessment time to help the individual achieve his or her goals. But it also cements a meaningful relationship between management and staff that has retention and productivity benefits that far outweigh profit sharing bonuses.

Although bonuses send an egalitarian message that sales are up and we all get rewarded, and they reinforce the theme that everyone is important to the fundamental purpose of the company, bonuses are an expensive, diluted, and sometimes confusing method of compensation. Bonus pay creates a broken connection and a failed opportunity to reinforce desired results specific to the function. "Feel good" pay can also be "feel lousy" pay when there is a failure to connect individual outcomes with meaningful rewards.

Team Compensation

Selling teams do exist and in a variety of forms. Daily, prospective clients meet with salespeople (charged with developing the relationship and negotiating the agreement) who are accompanied to the client site by technical specialists (who will speak to specific content issues and operations

218

folks responsible for installation or customer service). Sometimes there are two sales specialists: a lead generator and a relationship builder. And then there is the ever-present hand of management that may be needed to add heft to the final pitch. If the occasions are frequent enough, and if the presence of these functionaries are seen as tipping the point of influence in favor of the sale, then rewards for that direct intervention are cost-justified and appropriate to the level of impact the team member played in securing the business.

Some companies do not accept this philosophy, believing that a technical expert is paid to provide that expertise to the potential customer as part of their job. As such, their base compensation reflects that value. Other companies decrement base salary and build a greater total cash compensation opportunity by including incentives for the tech specialists who do participate in sales presentations. And still other companies will pay beyond the competitive values of the tech job for what is seen as a unique individual presentation skill beyond the norm of the job.

None of these variable forms of pay should be structured as an abstract bonus. Rather the remuneration for sales support should be an incentive derived from part of the incremental gain of the sale. In most companies, these forms of reward are structured and documented specific to the function being compensated. Just as the sales staff has their own variable pay plan, so does the technical specialist or operations function. Although the plans interrelate they are kept discrete to reinforce the nature of the message. That message is that everyone on the team plays a role in consummating the sale, but not everyone is a salesperson.

Sales compensation rewards for sales and for the influence associated with selling. The revenue and margin dollars derived from those results have a straight line relationship with sales pay. If a team is part of the influence process, be it a new sale or a renewal, or cross-selling another product or service, team pay is appropriate. For the rest of the general staff, management should be guided by the concept that the best way to compensate staff is to directly reward for focused results, and the further away from focus and result pay becomes, the more misdirected the performance message.

Defining the Event

To reinforce the performance message, the best practice has always been to pay variable rewards as close to the actual event that generated the reward as possible. With the exception of inherent reporting and payroll challenges, the concept is reasonably simple to implement. Confusion can surface in two instances: sales cycles longer than 12 months and paying residuals.

Long-term relationship selling places an emphasis on base salary as a percent of total cash compensation, and splits the variable reward process among interim weighted steps leading to the actual sale. The steps are seen as goals with pre-established timing and result expectations particular to the type of sale and industry. Generally, milestones such as formal presentations to key client decision-makers, securing letters of intention, subsequent demonstrations, and related detailed operational inquiries receive some increment of compensation with the greatest amount of reward reserved for the signing of the contract. Each step needs to produce a measurable result in a timely fashion, and each reward should provide an impetus to move to the next and final step. There is an art form in designing a longer-term incentive program that generates a sense of urgency for results on the part of the sales professional without creating a sense of undo anxiety.

Residual compensation recognizes value derived over time based upon the continued influence of the seller. Too often just the value derived part of the equation is given attention. The two elements should be sized together with influence being the governing factor. A salesperson's variable compensation should be paid commensurate with his or her influence on the client. Residual compensation that is paid when there is no follow up responsibility on the part of the sales representative is generous and misdirected.

Some companies reward sales staff on an ongoing basis parallel to the revenue that continues to be booked. There is a certain linear logic to this approach, but it assumes conditions not necessarily evident. The sales transaction itself has compensation value and the salesperson is paid for the influence brought to that agreement. If that influence is continued beyond the signing of the contract, the result of that influence should be compensated if it leads to renewed and continuing business.

Continuing to pay sales compensation for revenue generated during the length of an extended contract assumes that the full value of the sales person's influence was not paid at the time of the agreement. If that is the case (from an economic standpoint), continued pay, while not focused on reinforcing any specific behavior or new result, is at least cost effective.

But if competitive variable remuneration has already been realized and new awards are predicated on the additional revenue realized from the agreement, the company is paying a premium for selling services already rendered and discounting the weight that market conditions, customer service, and routine play in continuing to generate monies for the company. The selling function in this latter scenario has left the picture after the first year and its ghostly presence need not be rewarded so far after the event.

Either situation does not imply that the salesperson does not need to remain in contact with the customer. Base salary should accommodate any sales/client interaction until another selling opportunity is realized. Generating business from established sources is typically easier than conquering new business and the degree of rewards for the salesperson should be factored into the next agreement reached.

For those companies that do wish to continue residual pay as a means of motivating staff to stay in touch with clients or stimulate the sale of long-term agreements, be aware that another term for residual can be "annuity." With enough residual income streaming in, a salesperson can retire in place. Why continue to sell aggressively when an economic cushion exists? If residuals are utilized the amount paid should have a steep decline commensurate with the distance from the selling event and have a fractionalized relationship to the continuing revenue realized. The salesperson has met their obligation. Rewarding them for activities of others who are employed to continue servicing the client is unnecessary.

Measuring for Focus and Change

Measurement is where the rubber hits the road. The best sales plan ever conceived, with its creative pay structures and delineated objectives, is just a pile of concepts without aligned measurements intended to bring about and assess degrees of change.

Measure What

Measurement creation requires the mindset of an investment analyst or shareholder. What quantifiable measures would you look when determining where to place your assets? These same criteria become priority indices when establishing sales compensation measures. A good investor looks beyond short-term returns and ratios. A good investor assesses the longer-term strengths of the organization, its ability to deliver on its commitments to its owners, customers and staff, its growth opportunities, its niche, and its management and sales talent. Sales compensation measures must be aligned with all these considerations. The art form lies in creating indices that reflect measures of achievement an investor would be looking for without diluting the focus of the sales staff.

In the previous context, only those key sales results which impact an organization's purpose for being should be measured. If the results do not reflect current and future desired revenue, margin growth, sales mix, and/or market penetration, one should question devoting much time to their assessment.

Not every performance measure requires a connection to variable pay. There are ancillary measures of behavior and company orientation that can be adequately reflected and valued in base salaries. When it comes to compensation for selling, the operative word is "pruning." Leaving a few roses on the bush to focus upon will increase the sales staff's awareness of each bloom's position and value. In addition to increasing focus, comparing measures to only those that are critical to the organization's paramount goals ensures reduced tracking and administrative costs and their related complications. Priority goals speak to a company's value climate and to a management with vision and direction, the kind of purposeful and aligned environment that draws and retains desirable sales talent.

Every measure is a message. Establishing the desired message by consciously emphasizing, through rewards as well as other recognition vehicles, related sales measures gives meaning to a sales plan. Is the company emphasizing the sale of new products and services, a specific mix of products/services? Is market penetration accompanied by emphasis or selling to established sources of revenue? Does the reward structure reflect that emphasis?

Break away from historically based measures if their value is just that—historic. Companies shouldn't measure just because they can. Measurement must be based on need. If the systems are currently not available to accommodate an assessment of that need, their establishment should be made a crisis priority. It is better to initially and perhaps somewhat imprecisely assess performance of key indices and evolve that assessment to measures in which the company is more confident, than to focus on information that is report ready, but off focus.

The financial types, and sometimes their counterbalance in employee relations, will grow queasy at the suggestion of measuring without precision. Trust is the element that banishes the nightmares that temporary ambiguity can create. If there is a mutual trust between staff and management, it is amazing what obstacles to precision can be overcome. The big message actually turns into the big message. People stop sweating every detail and start concentrating on meeting the super ordinate challenge. The focus is on improvement, on getting the data to where it needs to be while continuing to drive business. The window is temporary (it must be), but it is open and fresh air is passing through.

As stated previously, measure as soon after the event as possible if for no other reason than to provide early warning signals when core sales may be slumping or market directions are changing. In addition to providing the business with a picture of critical results in time frames which allow for effective reactions, timely measures provide a source of frequent reinforcement.

Another restatement: don't confuse effort with result. Don't measure generating 30 phone calls or a dozen onsite visits; measure what they are intended to produce. Measure and compensate for the value of the action, not the action itself.

Anchoring Measurements

There are three established markers in the continuum of sales performance that exist without much dispute. They are not arbitrary, but predicated on sound quantitative criteria. They manifest themselves differently if the sales results are rewarded through bonus, incentive, or commission. These markers are called Threshold, Target, and Beyond Target.

Threshold performance is the minimum incremental performance gain considered acceptable by the company. If sales meet Threshold, costs are covered. From that point to Target sales performance, a modest return is realized and the salesperson shares, to some degree, in that return. For commission staff, the sharing is typically a specified slice of that return as it is accumulated. For sales compensated by bonus or incentive, the reward can be linear from Threshold to Target or can have more elaborations and permutations depending on the degree of perceived difficulty in achieving Threshold to Target results.

Because base salary for commission staff is a nonexistent or very small portion of total cash compensation, covered costs are achieved quickly.

But there still exists a sales generating baseline that represents what a typical salesperson should achieve in the job to be considered an acceptable contributor. Failure to cross the threshold line, regardless of covered costs, can result in someone else assuming the sales role.

Target performance achievement should be seen as challenging but attainable. Reaching target levels equates to meeting the company's financial and business expectations for the cycle. It is at that point that investors smile. Mission accomplished; returns are healthy. Although the target goal is definitely quantifiable, the element of reward for those results has some qualitative features related to it. In some organizations, the definition of Target is more challenging than in others. If the challenge is a stretch, 100 percent of market pay will not be enough for Target results that are perceived to be far beyond the industry norm. In these situations target cash compensation (that is, all elements of pay from variable to base salary), may be greater than target pay in the market. And the lever for increasing pay value will be the variable component. It is the company's qualitative judgment of the result expectations to be achieved, relative to comparators, which will determine whether a one for one relationship between target performance and target pay exists or whether target pay will exceed that relationship.

Somewhere beyond Target performance is a mountain peak. It is at that summit that exceptional performance is achieved and remunerated. Investors don't just smile at the results, they become giddy, almost frighteningly so. Occupying that promontory is an every 3- or 5-year event.

Blowing the socks off Target performance year after year should raise questions about the goal-setting process. There are volatile markets to be sure, but their dramatic upswings are typically accompanied by equally dramatic downsides. There are also companies that significantly outpace their competitors on an annually consistent basis. Organizations with that unique track record are either very rare or monopolistic in every feature but label. Although virtually all pay structures have upside ladders that reach for the stars, climbing that ladder beyond 115 percent of Target performance should be infrequent enough to meet the 3-to-5 year window.

Individual exceptional performance can exist in any overall performance environment, but it too is a rarefied occurrence. In the distribution of individual performance, exceptional achievement should be the purview of about 5 percent of the sales force.

Anchors Aligned With Rewards

Although it defies logic, it is unfortunately not that uncommon, particularly in incentive and bonus plans, to have overall company performance assessed at Target while an inordinate number of sales staff is rewarded at exceptional levels without any corresponding offset realized by poor performers. The message that the company did well (Target) while its staff did great (exceptional) just doesn't reflect aligned goal setting.

This misalignment of performance and reward generally leads to a mantra that should undergo some phrasing revision. This happens when the line manager stands before authority and proclaims, "Sure we pay well. We can't attract the talent we need without providing exceptional pay." Someday, somewhere a sales manager is going shock senior management by saying, "We can't produce exceptional results without exceptional talent. And we can't attract exceptional talent unless we ensure that they will receive exceptional pay for exceptional results. So we are going to knock off the practice of paying premium pay for target results and only pay at premium for premium results."

Accepting Accountability for the Reward Structure

Equally annoying is bemoaning the marketplace. "The market made me do it. I didn't want to pay as much as we did, but I had to." If a company can't creatively control its compensation mix, maintain parity and equity of pay with its current staff, and provide a productive environment for personal and organizational growth, it is managing with half an engine.

Good salespeople (those who want to gain from their efforts, and not just by "gaming" the system) look at total opportunity. If someone is looking for safe compensation, such as a high guarantee or a high base, one has to wonder whether they are truly built for selling or whether the job is truly a sales position. Ticket takers worry about their base or want guarantees. Good salespeople in good selling environments look at their total opportunity, as realized by their commission or incentives, and then just go for it.

For reasons best fathomed by sociologists (and perhaps psychologists), creators of incentive and bonus structures have always felt a need to emulate commission pay. As previously stated, incentives and bonus opportunities are not commissions, but that false perception has manifested itself in complex pay ladders supported by multi-variant criteria. Linear ramps, straight line or sloped curves, one-on-one ratio between performance and pay, as well as more complicated formulaic payout schemes dot the compensation landscape. It has become an administrator's wonderland. What better way to ensure job preservation than to hold the passwords into the kingdom of slicing and dicing. Yet once the sales performer is able to comprehend the intricacies before them, will 20-minute differentials in performance and payout really influence behavior? Will it really motivate a sales representative to increase sales by .06 percent? The clouds on top of the mountain peak are thick and gray with the fog of dilution and minutia. The ascent is definitely perilous.

And where is all the money coming from to support these grand incentives and bonus designs, particularly at their higher payout levels? Commission funding is relatively straightforward: a slice of the margin dollar or a slice of the revenue generated. As long as the company is still viable at the end of the day, the commission salesperson walks away with that which has been earned. Even in an overall stagnant business climate, a good commission sales person can be rewarded handsomely for their singular results.

There is far less of a straight-line relationship between funding and incentive and/or bonus compensation. To be sure, they are interrelated, but not bound as strongly as in commission pay. Funding for incentives and bonuses is accrued based upon aggregate achievements over an extended period of time. The incremental gain above and below target may not stimulate the one for one pattern found in commission sales. The definition of Target encompasses a great deal more than just the revenue from the sale. Achieving 120 percent of performance target may only realize 110 percent of incentive target payout. Although this may reflect well forecasted economically based incentive criteria, in some environments the criteria is more amorphous, making any relationship between margin dollars and pay that much more tangential.

Bottom line: if you create a complex incentive matrix or payout structure that rewards handsomely for sales achievements, but omits key economic indices that affect the cost structure of your business, the money to pay for the sales segment of performance may not be there. There will be no one in the basement manning the printing press and cranking out new funds. You may be forced to choose between the lesser of two evils: decrementing everyone's opportunity or providing a healthy incentive to your bigger fish, while reminding the rest of the staff that they swim in a smaller pond.

On Being an Air Farmer

Measures and their rewards need to reflect results based on energy expended. By default establishing measures also allows for the discounting of those results that require a disproportional lack of energy in their achievement. Most notable in his category are windfall gains, and results from high volume sales. A number of origins to the term "windfall" have been put forward. I particularly like the one being attributed to the concept of wind causing the fruit to fall from the tree. Not only does it speak to another piece of sales jargon (that of low hanging fruit—a euphemism for sales easily obtained), but to the passive nature associated with waiting for forces beyond your control to determine your sustenance. And windfall sales are just that, "other" initiated business with the saleperson left to process the order and not appreciably influence its close.

High volume sales are slightly different. In these situations, the salesperson has expended energy and closed the sale. But the degree of sales influence utilized is disproportionate to the volume being generated by the deal. High volume sales illuminate the basic relationship between the act of selling and the result of selling. Rather than windfall sales, where the salesperson has done little if anything to generate the sale, in a high volume transaction, the salesperson has used influence and skill to fashion a buy. The successful use of those talents has value. Should that value reflect the sales event or the manifest result of that sale? Logically, it is a bit of both.

The upside potential is funded by the financial impact of the sale. The question becomes to what degree that value should continue to be rewarded. How much is too much? Are geometrically staggering rewards really indicative of the value of the sale? Should there be a ceiling or a flattening slope to reflect both reward and company good sense? Should the sale person who secures 10 good sales be compensated less than the one who secures only one larger transaction?

Windfall sales and those from high volume deals deserve rewards. Without some form of recognition, opportunities could be lost and ill will could be formed. But reward should be measured relative to the skill required to secure other sales and the value those other sales realize. In many organizations, high volume sales have predefined parameters and are compensated through a different payout structure. Windfall sales, also having predefined criteria, are often discounted from the existing payout structure or remunerated with a flat amount.

As might be suspected there is no precise right or wrong answer. The culture of the company has a lot to do with determining the "how much is too much" question. Most sane salespeople are going to impulsively opt for the more generous alternative, and find some form of virtuous rationale to justify that desire. Most organizations are going to try and maximize their sales costs by not over compensating unless over achievement comes into play. Both parties should be mature enough to appreciate that the immediate glow brought about from compensating "too well" will soon be replaced by the chilly realization that short-term avarice may result in longer-term hardship as needed funds are now unavailable for the continued health of the pay program. Sophocles would rise from the grave and proclaim the more prudent path; something for everyone, just not too much.

Territorial Symmetry Is to Measurement as Gold Is to Tuna

If there is a golden rule I subscribe to in measurement, it revolves around measuring and setting goals based on the individual's unique territory and/or selling challenges. Objective building based on the specifics of the environment reinforces clarity of mission and aligns goal setting with super-ordinate company goals. It also addresses equal opportunities for achievement. I have seen the ass-backward approach (universal goals applied with equal force to all sales segments of the company) produce only confusion, malice, and age lines. By not taking each environment into account, sales performance measurements and behaviors can degenerate into mediocrity.

A national sales manager wants balance. There is something Zen about balance. Symmetry is good. Harmony is good. Yogurt is probably also good. He spends his time trying to form the perfect sales territory for each of his staff. Perfect in the sense that potential sales generated are equal. In order to do this, he splits natural industry markets and geography, creates shared territories, and overlaps potential clients. Everyone can produce the same amount of desired margin dollars. Some territories are larger than others, some perceived as easier than others, but based on the sales manager's experience everything will be equal in the end. Everyone will generate the same target revenues. It will all work out.

It doesn't. One territory undergoes a massive growth spurt while another shrinks in opportunity. One is easily penetrated; the other has historically never been as easy to gain a foothold. Projected activity is off, producing grumbling clients who feel under serviced by the salesperson with the enormous calling area.

It is back to the drawing board. Sales segmentation that benefits everyone equally is too hard, too imprecise. The sales manager tries another idea and everyone benefits from the collective outcome. How does the salesperson perform when compared to the average sales of the unit? The largest incentive or slice of the bonus goes to the best producer as compared to the average. End of the first year; sales suck. The threshold bar has been barely crossed. The best producer is really the "best of the worst." The low average provides this best producer with a large slice of the variable pie and mediocre performers with an average incentive slice. A thought strikes the group: *If they can keep the bar low next year, everyone benefits to some degree.*

But, next year, sales go through the roof. Frobish has done better than ever, but he will receive a low incentive because now instead of being the "best of the worst" he has become the "worst of the best." Expectations have long since been exceeded, but Frobish is below the average and will be rewarded accordingly. Frobish is looking for work elsewhere. He has proven he can sell. Why should he continue to put up with this wholesale form of recognition?

None of the above is fiction. It has happened. It continues to happen. What's the alternative? Set measures where an individual competes against himself, competes against his environment and its challenges. Have the measures, and in turn the salesperson, tuned to the specific selling situation.

Consider two selling environments: One is an emerging market for the product with lots of opportunity with low hanging fruit as well as potential strategic long-term business; the other environment is saturated and there is opportunity for renewed business and possibly the introduction of other products, but the area is extremely competitive and the company has held a significant portion of the market. A 2-percent growth in sales in the second environment would be Herculean. A 2-percent growth in the first environment would get the sales person fired.

This is a simplified example of the kind of measurement challenges that should be going on in a sales manager's mind during goal setting periods.

To maintain market share in one area may produce a similar sales compensation value as increasing market share in another. In this way, the salesperson in the saturated market doesn't throw up his hands in defeat and the salesperson in the emerging market doesn't salivate over the wealth of prospects. Both will be compensated competitively and effectively for the changes they bring about. Only those changes will reflect the challenges they face and not an abstract "one size fits all" marker.

In addition to sizing the challenges correctly, the sales manager's role is to staff both areas with the most suitable sales personnel. It is in staffing that individual situations come into play. It is in staffing where relationship building versus transactional selling is balanced. It is in staffing where experience and skill is applicable. It is in staffing that the selling message, the measurement goals, and the talent are aligned.

It Could Be a 4- or 40-Foot Fall

Jed's company has developed and aligned its sales goals, its measures, and its staff deployment. They are ready for the coming sales year. They are ready for takeoff and counting. But someone in mission control has her hand on the red button. The countdown is stopped. Modeling hasn't taken place. Just as you wouldn't fly a jet without testing it, compensation plans need to be modeled to ensure they will meet expectations in all kinds of weather. Modeling is the most common victim of a company's rush to meet implementation deadlines.

Here's a Rubber Chicken:

 The best prevention to implementing a bad compensation plan is modeling.

Test the hell out of the plan. See how it performs in a variety of situations. Fine tune and debug its elements. Model the plan against expectations and then model away from expectations. Show how the plan would payout were it implemented in the last performance cycle against previous sales results. Go back as far as need be to demonstrate to yourself and your sales staff why the new plan is viable. If modeling produces intentionally different results than the current plan, that is fine. It is probably why a new plan has been developed in the first place.

The goal of modeling is not to replicate the past with a new design. The goal is to anticipate any problems and demonstrate that the new design will do what it is anticipated to do. If that anticipation, for example, is to drive down sales compensation dramatically as sales are increased, and modeling demonstrates that those conditions will be met under a variety of circumstances, you have designed well.

Your plan may still go up in flames and send your staff looking for work across the street. Designing a structure to operate may be validated by the modeling effort, but it doesn't mean that the basic design is sound. The previous plan example may be crafted well, but will paying less for more sales work? Modeling doesn't correct philosophical errors; it works only on the operational aspects of design. Modeling won't unscrew concepts. It will only verify that they can withstand the ride into space.

Communicate, Communicate, and Then Communicate Some More

For clarity and for a sense of emotional or psychic equity, send strong, focused, and frequent communications about the design and intent of the sales compensation plan.

A large national consulting firm published an annual index that measured aspects of total compensation, company to company. It also measured the perceptions of the employees relative to those compensation elements. One organization consistently scored high among its staff as being perceived as the best compensation program in its industry. The index also showed that this company was in actuality not the best in its industry, but rather very much in the middle of the pack. The difference between perception and reality was the amount of energy and resources the company expended communicating its compensation package to employees. The company with the best elements failed to capitalize on the benefits it was providing for its staff because it felt that the plan spoke for itself. There was no concerted effort to market their program internally; a program that carried a significant cost to the company. In this situation, negative perception did not meet positive reality.

Communication does not mean using sleight of hand or deception. Communication establishes an arena for dialogue around the plan issues. Communication is information presented by credible sources that are open to reasonable interaction. Communication is tailored to the target audience so it is easily understood and accepted for what it is, a genuine attempt at ensuring that all parties effected understand what is being changed and why.

But the art of communicating encompasses more than just information presented credibly. Information has to grab the attention of the audience. It has to fight to hold on to the viewer or listener. And then it has to leave a lingering, positive impression.

Because every environment is different, communication should be tailored accordingly. But there is a set of common outcomes regardless of organization. At the end of the day there must be and understanding of:

☆ the specific results the plan is intended to produce.

☆ how those results translate into compensation and/or other rewards.

☆ how the plan is to be administered.

☆ how the plan is aligned with the company's vision, priorities, and objectives.

The parallel objectives of communication are harder to measure. They encompass the verbal and nonverbal cues that reinforce staff perceptions:

☆ do the participants find the plan to be straightforward and fair?

☆ do they take ownership in the plan's elements?

☆ are they challenged by the goals of the plan?

Staff responses to open-ended questions help verify whether the intent of the plan is being met. Volunteered commentary by the staff will help establish their feeling of commitment to the plan.

It is a statement of reality that, if open dialogue, mutual respect, and trust do not exist in an organization, employee perceptions will remain a mystery. If those elements are in play, one needs to do nothing more than allow the forum that already exists for other elements of company dialogue to remain open.

If your sales staff can answer the "how" statements bulleted previously you have met the first test of communication effectiveness. If your sales staff comments favorably on the plan's intent, structure, and opportunities, all the work preceding your presentations has been well worth it.

Design Isn't Easy, but It Doesn't Have to Be Complicated

Although complexity is relative to each specific environment, there are generally agreed upon boundaries that can be established to keep compensation design focused and on message. Design isn't easy, but it can be made less complicated by following a few planned steps.

- ☆ Align the plan to visible performance markers that reflect priority business goals.

- ☆ Develop plans in a climate of trust and dialogue that will allow for flexibility of implementation and adaptation to change.

- ☆ Pay commissions and incentives for the results brought about through influence.

- ☆ Don't double pay for the same result.

- ☆ Don't pay variable compensation for behavior rather than result.

- ☆ Don't complicate the message or create counter-productive behavior with too many submessages.

- ☆ Treat base salaries as an active component of total compensation.

- ☆ Choose the right variable option for the type of selling you need.

- ☆ Model and test the design for the unexpected.

- ☆ Dedicate time and resources in communicating the plan's provisions to the sales staff.

Above all, keep stepping back to the high ground to take in the progress of the road you are charting through the forest. And watch out for those long hanging branches.

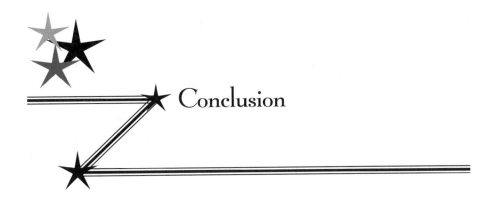

Conclusion

There have always been three ways to read a book such as this. The first, and personally preferable, is to read it cover to cover. Somewhere on some page lies a rough nugget of thought that will resonate for a specific reader who happens upon it. That thought will become their Rubber Chicken and give the journey meaning. Enough readers find their own thought nuggets among the pages and the book will have been worth writing.

The second approach followed me from graduate school. When reviewing materials in the social sciences you became adept at reading the first and last paragraph and subsequent topic sentences of each chapter. This is equivalent to chewing a meal without swallowing: you get a sense of what the dinner is all about but with none of its depth and very little of its enjoyment. Not a very appetizing approach. And you won't make any friends in the kitchen, either. But at least if offers the scanner an opportunity to delve into a chapter, should the overview prove interesting.

The last, and most expedient option, is to read the concluding chapter in the hope that all the key points will be highlighted and restated. You are checking out the menu so you at least know what the restaurant serves. Maybe someday you'll stop in and partake, but not now. There is too much else going on. Besides, reading is a drag; all those words in sentences no less, not even sound bites. And there are no pictures or video streams. If a book is to be read make it a "tell all" or at least a murder mystery.

If you have read through the book, and made it this far, hopefully you swallowed at least a couple of times.

If you have just opened the book and this is probably as much as you will read, be careful. Choose to display the cover and you run the risk of someone entering your office and bringing up its subject matter. If that happens, here's a tip: Nod sagely and say, half smiling, "How about those Rubber Chickens?" If the other person starts going off on the content, do what you usually do. Fake it. If you both stare at each other in silence, with no clue as to what a Rubber chicken is, you are having a mirror experience. Start talking about travel, sports, furniture, anything.

Sales and Sales Compensation

Selling is about enthusiasm and a sense of urgency. Sales compensation is about bringing the enthusiasm generated from an exciting vision and direction, from having significant control over your performance destiny, and combining those elements with a compelling reward structure that recognizes meaningful achievement. Sales compensation is about reinforcing that sense of business urgency, by establishing goals and measures that are focused and critical, that are challenging, and that require constant energy to be sustained.

This book has emphasized several Rubber Chickens; those items that transcend and linger. They are consolidated in the section that follows. If one were to categorize them, they would group around five themes:

1. Aligning all facets of a company's expectations, style, and structure allows for integration of action and commonality of purpose. Alignment governs the viability of the reward system.

2. Compensation is a series of unique, clear, and coordinated quantitative and qualitative messages.

3. Don't discount your sales staff, your sales managers, or key support functions when planning and designing a sales reward program.

4. Dialogue and inclusion, based on mutual trust and respect, transcends any initial plan flaws, or at the very least smoothes out the wrinkles created by explaining needed revisions.

5. People are not stupid. Over the long haul, you can't fool any of the people all of the time.

It is the premise of this book that before ideas can be translated into action, seven steps need to be taken. Each of these steps represents a complimentary action. If these actions aren't addressed within the framework of how your company operates, the best sales compensation plan design doesn't have a chance and those exciting ideas first formulated will never reach fruition.

1. Align your company's vision and purpose with sales compensation.

The fabric of who you are, how you operate, and what you value is already out there. It is a question of examining all of these facets for alignment, correcting any inconsistencies, and stating, for clarity and understanding, how your vision, purpose, and style will help you get where you are going. Alignment promotes corporate sanity; knowing what behaviors the organization values and shuns.

Successful companies seem incredibly focused on their purposes. Every action they take is consistent with achieving their goals and measuring against their purpose. These companies are disciplined and committed. They invest in their people, enforce a balanced perspective, foster communication, and develop and hire great managers.

Alignment puts compensation into perspective. Yes, total compensation has to be competitive. But compensation design is less about determining what the money should amount to, and more about segmenting and reinforcing the message behind the money.

2. With the help of external data, form your own opinion about what is appropriate sales pay.

A company cannot position its own compensation components intelligently or competitively until it knows the tendencies in the marketplace. Find out how total compensation is divided among annual cash components, longer-term pay, health and retirement-related benefits, non-cash recognition and reward programs, and perquisites.

At the very least, be skeptical of why and how compensation data is presented, who put it together, and the motives behind the sources. Assess the pay rate distribution between the 25th and 75th percentile values of the data you examine. Look for the missing pieces as well as what is obvious and visible. Gather intelligence on the companies you collect data about.

Examine their vertical and horizontal pay structures, their pay emphasis, whether they cap compensation, or have windfall provisions or safety nets. Is their variable pay a result of generating "dollar one" revenue or based on threshold and target goals? What kind of an emphasis does non-cash compensation play in the overall package sales staff receives? Weigh information on the same target from multiple sources for triangulation: surveys, recruiter intelligence, individuals you know and trust in the industry, and ex-employees of comparator companies.

More importantly, know your own frame of reference; what behaviors your company values, how you perceive individual and collective results, and how and why you differentiate job impact. What pre-established parameters, if any, do you place on rewards? How do you currently use your various pay components? How do you perceive and act on issues of pay parity and equity?

Align your decisions not to the market, but to your own business strategies, operating style, and internally grounded belief system. Use your market data, don't let it use you. Make your decisions conscious and active, not a reflex of what others are doing.

3. Acknowledge what compensation can realistically achieve and what it can't.

Compensation programs can help differentiate pay based on competitive necessity, such as a living wage or benefits from rewards for achieving results related to the economic gain of the company.

Each compensation component addresses a unique purpose and utilizes unique reward methods for achieving that purpose.

☆ Base salary offers security and predictability of income. It reinforces the development of skills, attributes, and standards of behavior. Base wages can also reward for baseline, fundamental, and bottom-line results.

☆ Benefits offer both security and a representation of the company's commitment to the demographic needs of its population be it in healthcare, retirement, or social presence in the community.

Because of their fixed cost, these two components (marginal relation to generating income, and tendency to be seen as entitlements) should form the least significant portion of sales compensation value whenever practically possible. Entitlements blur vision, dilute effort, and disengage staff from the goals that are to be achieved.

Sales compensation is never about entitlements. It's about risk and reward, about value derived from results.

☆ Short-term variable pay offers motivation and job satisfaction, and focuses on results. This form of pay encourages a feeling of equity, of sharing in the economic growth of the company through the incremental gains realized in achieving sales priorities. This form of pay is based not on effort, on persuasive actions, or on the influence that brings about sales, but on results.

☆ Longer-term variable pay offers capital accumulation and rewards for performance commensurate with the company's increased value through time.

Avoid using variable pay for functions that do not influence the economies of the company; reserve its use for when not paying variably will have a significant impact on results to be generated.

If a company is going to use variable rewards as a form of feel-good bonuses that strive for inclusion and psychic equity, but are too superficial and disconnected to meaningfully influence any behaviors, make them symbolic. Channel whatever additional funds might have been paid in bonus into building the business.

☆ Non-cash compensation provides for extra ordinary recognition and motivation in concert with the values of the participants. It is a component whose impact on retention, motivation, and loyalty is appreciably greater than the cost it incurs.

No two components should pay full value for the same achievement. If marketed effectively, each compensation component can bind the individual and the company in a common set of purposes that focus on both achievement and personal job satisfaction.

4. Maximize your line sales manager function.

The conduit for all sales performance and subsequent rewards resides in the sales manager corps. They add credibility and clarity to corporate intentions. They connect their teams to the goals and direction of the company, creating mutual ownership and a common vision.

Recruit and develop these managers carefully. Look for individuals who show enthusiasm and a sense of urgency when analyzing, planning, and executing their own sales goals, who desire to be actively engaged in the overall planning process. Retain managers who hire individuals with strength and independence and managers who would rather guide than direct. Develop managers who enjoy developing others, not paternalistically, but inclusively. Seek those who generate ideas and can express them well.

Equip these managers with the information they need to be able to articulate the company's context with their own staff. Be sure they are clear as to your expectations and work at maintaining their trusts.

Allow them to mentor, to educate, to stay in tune with their staff's needs and respond to those needs, and to manage rumor. Provide them the resources to plan, prioritize, and assess the business condition in their area to recruit and to prepare for future staffing needs. Pay them to act, to be full time managers.

Support them by busting barriers that present obstacles to their productivity and by developing their own careers through strengthening whatever skills and experiences you mutually feel the need to develop.

5. Engage your sales delivery team.

Collaboratively shaping a meaningful reward system is a powerful expression of the confidence and trust you have in your sales team's maturity and perspective. Engagement produces a sense of ownership. It's emotional equity that can generate passion and productivity that exceeds the sum of its participant parts. Any process that is this powerful has to be introduced carefully. No organization should start the collaborative process with compensation as its initial agenda. Orient the group to collaboration around less volatile subjects so they can build confidence and expertise before wrestling with major aspects of the organization's operation and culture.

Select mature staff for collaboration who will represent your very good performers. These are individuals who have demonstrated perspective, flexibility, and moderation in how they approach situations. These are also individuals who appreciate that their input is one of many sources leading to management decisions.

Equip them with an understanding of the strategies and economics of the business, an appreciation of the best practices used elsewhere, and management's point of view and emphasis. Then, charge them with reconciling management's views with their perception of the current situation. Have this group surface ideas as to specific distinctions and/or emphases in pay, as well as suggest responses to the operational issues of territory distribution, training, windfall concerns, levels of upside and downside risk and rewards, residual pay, definitions of threshold performance, and arbitration procedures. Make this an editorial function for all interdepartmental activity directed at program design. Task the group with modeling their thoughts and looking for pluses and minuses when applied to historically based or projected situations.

Engagement is the result of an ongoing climate of collaboration. It is part of the way a company works together, day in and day out. It is not something pulled off the shelf for one specific topic or undertaking. Engagement has to be part of and fit your operating style, the context within which you do everything. It is a reflection of what the company cares about, and why it exists beyond making money.

6. Utilize and balance company-wide participation in your sales design.

There are many areas in the company involved in developing data, supporting implementation, providing status checks, and helping sales to succeed. Draw these elements into the process. Again, use the power of inclusion to create a sense of mutual equity and assistance in fashioning the vehicles that reward for sales results. Ensure their participation compliments the overall mission and that all participants are in agreement as to what has to be done and why. Reach an understanding at the outset as to role responsibilities, that ownership of any plan design belongs to the company, and that sales is accountable for the plan's design and charged with its implementation and management.

Project teams of this nature succeed in part because of participant selection and in part because of project management. Participant selection should be predicated on balancing the representation of the various areas of the company. Participation should be seen as a positive reflection of management's confidence in the individuals' expertise and sense of company. As such, involvement in any design team should result in meaningful and tangible recognition.

Managing a cross-organizational project team requires a host of skills from launching a plan framework with timetables and deliverables to establishing design principles, managing group interactions and focus, and continually drawing out the talents and content knowledge of the group.

The manifestation of any project team is the presentations its makes to its sponsors, typically senior management. There is both substance and technique in these productions. The substance relates to modeling and debugging content before declaration, and from being prepared in depth to respond to any question. Even though the group may have 40 hours of information stored and ready for use, the most successful presentations work form the premise of selective communication with the audience's point of view in mind. By not overwhelming senior management with detail, and sticking to the key points and letting the listeners probe and inquire, the message will not be lost.

7. Design sales compensation away from complexity.

Even accounting for the relative nature of complexity from one organization to another, adding elements and subdividing objectives and measures in an attempt to cover all bases often becomes a smokescreen for poor forecasting. Compelling financial forecasts usually obviate the need for complexity. Compelling forecasts take into account those factors that investors consider key when assessing a company: the company's immediate and longer term growth opportunities, its realized and potential capabilities, its track record with customers and owners, its niche, its management strength, and its sales talent.

As mentioned previously, rapport across and between management and staff focuses everyone on the critical imperatives when designing sales compensation and subordinates the pickier issues. Developing, listening to, collaborating with, and showing genuine interest in your sales staff will transcend any minor design flaws that may initially surface.

To avoid complexities pitfalls, stay with the fundamentals of good sales compensation design:

☆ Establish a clean line of sight between results and the economics of the company.

☆ Design the plan for immediate and sustained engagement.

☆ Ensure that the design will compliment and not take the place of management decision-making.

☆ Make sure the plan is such that anyone touching it can understand what results are expected and why. Make the plan the message.

☆ Pay people when they sell. Value the sales event once; whether you divide that value among various components or not.

☆ Don't discount the value of base salary; it is more than just the cost of doing business. Make it count for something. Let base salary compensate for critical behaviors and in some cases baseline sales results.

☆ Have sales staff competing against themselves and not each other, against goals that are relevant to their territory and market penetration.

☆ Fund the plan from the incremental gain those sales generate above baseline, above what it costs to pay fixed salaries.

☆ Maximize focus by keying only on those results that are paramount. Don't cloud the picture with a host of sales criteria and weights.

☆ Set challenging, doable goals that are within the scope of the function. Hold the sales representative accountable for what they plan to accomplish.

☆ Establish a complete and tested program before you implement. Consider all the elements to the plan and model them prior to going public.

☆ If you have to emphasize anything, make it the message and not the mechanics of the plan.

☆ Use the right vehicle for the right message and avoid feel good money.

☆ Finally, communicate the plan design clearly, frequently, and with a positive open disposition. Establish an arena for dialogue. Use culturally credible means to grab the attention of the audience and leave a positive impression.

About That Easel

Does the great idea at the strategy meeting that was first scribbled on an easel in a moment of epiphany really have long-term benefit to the company?

Does it fit the vision? Does it work in the context of who you are as an organization? Can it be translated into action and can that action be measured and rewarded?

This book's intent is about developing an approach that will help answer those questions, about making the efforts associated with sales reward design count, about stepping back from the mechanics and addressing those elements that can either screw up the best plan designs or ensure that they fulfill everyone's expectations. This book is about creating not only an all star sales team, but an all star sales environment.

Appendix:
Rubber Chickens

The Rubber Chickens mentioned in this book have been grouped into four sections, which are specific to:

1. Staff/Management Interaction.
2. Management.
3. Compensation and Rewards.
4. Plan Design.

Staff/Management Interaction

☆ Whenever you have a meeting, structure it to counter participants' tendencies to hear what they want to hear and see what they want to see. Structure the meeting to make sure they hear what is actually being said and see the reasoning behind it.

☆ Communication is irrevocable and irreversible.

☆ Interaction is based on more than just the immediate event. It is based on the history all parties bring with them to every encounter.

☆ People respond to inclusion.

☆ People are not stupid.

☆ People, consciously or sub-consciously, are always searching for the meaning of things.

☆ The longer a process, including engaging the staff, becomes ingrained in the way you function, the more likely it is that under the stress of increasing or decreasing activity that process will remain a primary behavior mode.

☆ Trust is the currency of collaboration and as with money it is hard to acquire and keep, but easily spent

☆ Dialogue has to exist for trust to exist.

☆ Everyone deserves respect until they have failed to continue to earn that respect.

☆ Everything is ultimately discoverable.

☆ It is a reality of business that if the staff distrusts management in one aspect of their work lives, there will be a compelling urge to distrust management in all aspects affecting their work lives.

Management

☆ Rarely do the swift engage the plodding.

☆ Rarely do good leaders hire weak subordinates.

☆ If your company's expectations and operating style are not aligned and consistently applied to the day-to-day workings of the organization, your compensation program, whatever it is, is going to go nowhere.

☆ Development, whether it is through formal training, mentoring, or the natural process of supervision, has to be an accepted and integrated part of the workplace and a daily role accountability of every supervisor.

☆ Sales managers have to trust executive management's intentions and agree with their ethics.

☆ Never surprise your manager.

☆ Management always functions under the scrutiny of multiple audiences.

☆ Safe behavior mires, and eventually kills, a company.

☆ Action without vision is chaos.

☆ Management should exist to minimize distress and maximize conditions for energized behavior.

☆ Healthy teams are derived from healthy organizations.

☆ Salespeople are an investment to be developed, listened to, collaborated with, and shown genuine attention and concern.

☆ Compensation plans never replace management's decision-making responsibility to the sales staff.

Compensation and Rewards

☆ The effect of pay, used as a pain killer, always wears off.

☆ Compensation isn't just action taken. It is a message.

☆ Compensation is always and only defined in the context of your organization.

☆ If a company chooses to use a variety of compensation approaches to value one outcome, it must never inflate the worth of that result by having the remuneration from each of those multiple approaches exceed a reasonable total value.

☆ Always size the value of a sale before determining compensation for that result. Value should reflect an acceptable net all of expenses (to include compensation).

☆ Pay at risk (commissions, incentives, bonus) should be predicated on the degree of persuasion required.

☆ Commission pay should only be used when there is an expectation of volume.

☆ Total sales compensation for a sale should encompass all parties rewarded for influencing that sale.

☆ Factor benefits and participation in any longer-term-pay program when valuing the total being paid.

☆ Utilize appropriate (demographically and culturally aligned) non-cash recognition events and programs whenever possible. Factor the "value" of these opportunities into the total compensation value being attributed to sales.

☆ If they are to have the desired impact, sales compensation has to be a series of clearly focused and coordinated messages that are aligned to the goals and values of the company. The first message is quantifiable. The second message is motivational. The third message is sustained action.

☆ Sales people are paid to persuade.

☆ Value the sales event and pay that value once.

☆ Separate behavior and result in how you compensate.

☆ Don't fluff up variable criteria.

Plan Design

☆ If compensation design is the only meaningful aspect of corporate life in which a company attempts to engage its sales staff in collaborate behavior, the battle is lost before it is joined.

☆ It is the responsibility of the group to get all its baggage out on the table before any design activity begins, and it is the role of the leader to ensure every outstanding item is addressed, regardless of the discomfort it may initially generate.

☆ Communication of a new sales compensation plan is not, repeat not, a monologue.

☆ Design time should reflect the design's strategic impact on the company.

☆ A well-designed plan is not just a pay vehicle. It is a powerful validation of the message. It cannot be abused or treated indifferently without abusing and neutralizing the message.

☆ Design sales programs to maximize focus.

☆ Don't create a program that sends an unintended message to the staff.

☆ Establish a complete template, or sales compensation map, before implementing a plan.

☆ Design for challenge, not impossibility.

☆ Design for balance and flexibility.

☆ Don't discount the power of base salary when designing your overall sales compensation.

☆ Note the behaviors of your sales staff before you make changes, make them aware of your sensitivity, and let their reality help guide those changes.

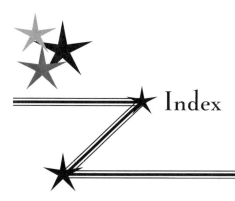

Index

E

economy, rise and fall of the, 7
ego, 65
    issues of, 118
elements,
    design, 208
    down-side, 171
employee perceived compensation value, 85
engagement,
    collaborative process and, 150
    psychic equity and, 147
    sales staff and, 163
    successful, 166
enthusiasm,
    creating team, 149
    leadership and, 118
entitlement ethics, 83
entitlement, importance of, 97
entry positions, sales, 66
environment, transferring to a sales, 130
environment, true sales, 123
equity, psychic, 111, 162
ethical recruiters, 131
ethics,
    entitlement, 83
    leadership, 118
    team, 24-25
events, sequence of, 184-185
excitement,
    creating team, 149
    generating, 159
expectations,
    company, 90
    controlling, 105
    false, 100-101
    marketing, 109-110
    staff, 9
expenses, reducing, 111
external compensation data, 85
external data, sales pay and, 237

F

facilitators, responsibilities of, 19-20
flexibility, 171
    designing for, 213
focus,
    compensation, 113
    measuring for, 221-226
focused vision, 43-53
framework, economic, 193

G

genuine reinforcement, 102
goal setting dialogues, 110-113
group madness, factors of, 177

H

habits, importance of, 65
health plans, 93
health, importance of team, 185-187
hierarchy, vertical, 81-82
hiring bonuses, 84
hiring, outside, 135

I

incentives, 139, 215
    sales goals and, 141-142
inception, conception and, 198
individual performance, 224
influence,
    point of, 100
    power and, 155
influential conditions, 149-150
information,
    distribution, 18
    preparatory, 18
insulation, issues of, 118
interaction,
    customer, 26
    face-to-face, 158
    management, 245-246
    staff, 245-246
intergroup collaboration, 196-198
intervention, sales, 146-147
interview dynamics, 131
issues,
    administrative, 170
    key sales, 32
    structural, 162
    universal, 193-196

J

job pool, 72-75

L

leader, responsibilities of a meeting, 17
leaders,
    qualities of good, 17
    successful, 18
    using strengths of, 8

About the Author

For the last 16 years, Dan Kleinman has been an independent consultant for a broad spectrum of regional, national, and international companies, providing performance and organizational planning, and reward-system design services that establish direct links between strategy, organizational cultural, and performance with an effective reward system. Although Kleinman specializes in supporting small to mid-sized organizations, his clients have included:

Apple	Levi Strauss & Co.
AT&T Wireless	Logistics
Bare Escentuals	McKesson
Blue Shield of California	Planters
Cisco	Sephora
Clif Bar	UCSF
Kaiser Permanente	VISA
Landor	DFS

Prior to consulting, he spent 20 years in the financial and telecommunication industries. He managed compensation and benefits departments for subsidiaries of Pacific Bell (now part of AT&T). As manager of Wells Fargo's compensation department, he designed the bank's initial company-wide variable-pay programs.

Dan managed Wells' Employment, Training, Executive Development, and Staff Analysis Group. While there, he was one of only two human resource executives to participate in the company's first major acquisition planning for Crocker Bank, the largest in banking at the time. He was chosen to help form one of the bank's major divisions and to manage its human resource department as the division grew from 600 to 5,000 employees.

His last corporate assignment was as vice president and manager of compensation, benefits, human resources information systems, and payroll for Charles Schwab during a time of significant growth, profitability, and change for the company.

Dan has actively participated in regional and national associations and has written articles for *Personnel Journal*. He still speaks on human resource, reward, and performance management subjects at such organizations as the Northern California Human Resource Society, the Bay Area Compensation Association, and at various industry conferences. In addition, he has taught compensation principles for the American Compensation Association (now called World at Work) and the American Banking Association's graduate school.

Two of his clients, independently of each other, mentioned his work to *INC*. One of the magazine's editors interviewed him and highlighted his sales design work in their September 1998 issue. After nine years, he still averages six e-mails a month from readers of that article.

In 2004, he was profiled, and his commentary on consulting was included in, *A New Brand of Expertise* (Butterworth & Heineman).

With more than 30 years of involvement in productivity plans and practices, both as a corporate and as an independent practitioner, he is the expert who can help companies return to the fundamental practice of coupling rewards with sustained productivity in order to develop, retain, and reward a super sales staff.